CULTIVATING PROFESSIONAL RESILIENCE IN DIRECT PRACTICE

CULTIVATING PROFESSIONAL RESILIENCE IN DIRECT PRACTICE

A GUIDE FOR HUMAN SERVICE PROFESSIONALS

Jason M. Newell

Columbia University Press
New York

Columbia University Press
Publishers Since 1893
New York Chichester, West Sussex
cup.columbia.edu

Library of Congress Cataloging-in-Publication Data
Names: Newell, Jason M., author.
Title: Cultivating professional resilience in direct practice :
    a guide for human service professionals / Jason M. Newell.
Description: New York : Columbia University Press, [2017] |
    Includes bibliographical references and index.
Identifiers: LCCN 2016055339 (print) | LCCN 2017014118 (ebook) |
    ISBN 9780231544900 (electronic) | ISBN 9780231176583 (cloth : alk. paper) |
    ISBN 9780231176590 (pbk.)
Subjects: LCSH: Social workers—Job stress. | Social service—Practice. |
    Burn out (Psychology)—Prevention.
Classification: LCC HV40.35 (ebook) | LCC HV40.35 N49 2017 (print) |
    DDC 361.301/9—dc23
LC record available at https://lccn.loc.gov/2016055339

Cover design: Jordan Wannemacher
Cover image: © Carmen Spitznagel / Trevillion Images

To my wife, Dora, and our daughter, Eliza, for all of your loving kindness, support, and laughter. Thank you for allowing me the time and the space to write this book. To all those who selflessly choose human service work as a way of life, I challenge you to actively pursue your own personal and professional well-being as you attend to the needs of others. This ongoing practice is essential to staying on the path to resilience.

CONTENTS

WORKSHEETS

PREFACE

The capacity for compassion and empathy seems to be at the core of our ability to do the work and at the core of our ability to be wounded by the work.

—CHARLES FIGLEY

THIS BOOK evolved over a decade of academic research, scholarship, and professional training. My interest in the well-being of social workers and other human service professionals began nearly two decades ago after the completion of my undergraduate degree. My first professional job was as a direct care provider for a state funded inpatient and outpatient mental health agency. I provided services for elementary-aged children diagnosed with comorbid psychological diagnoses and psychosocial conditions in a therapeutic day program. The program was designed to improve treatment outcomes for children with "problem-behaviors" over the summer break. This was my first direct exposure to the pervasive challenges of parental drug use, poverty, poor education, neglect, physical abuse, sexual abuse, mental illness, and innumerable psychosocial challenges all too common to the practice of social work. In the most unfortunate cases, I witnessed children affected by the compounding effects of these conditions as they occurred simultaneously. I quickly realized the impact of these behaviors on the emotional health and well-being of these very young children, most of them under the age of 10. Many of the children were historically, generationally, and currently involved with the child welfare system. Some had experienced removals from their biological homes due to the severity of their parental abuse and neglect. I still vividly recall my initial reactions of shock, disbelief, and sometimes horror. I remember thinking to myself "no wonder these kids are mentally ill" and "how in the world can I help them?" I felt compelled to choose a career path that would allow me to make a "real difference" in the lives of people, especially those affected by trauma in the form of child abuse and neglect.

Witnessing the conditions of these children could have easily turned me away from the profession of social work. Instead, their struggles and narratives fueled my spirit to embrace a career with meaning, purpose, and reward beyond financial gain.

As a professional social worker for almost 20 years, I have provided therapeutic and case management services for children in public child welfare, in a residential facility for psychiatric care, in a faith-based group home, in a nonprofit family counseling agency, and at the Veterans Administration with veterans and military families. Over the years, I have knowingly and willingly encountered countless stories of pain and human suffering, but I have remained resilient and committed to the spirit of the work. Too often well-trained, earnest, and dedicated social workers leave the profession because the organizational and emotional challenges of the work simply become overwhelming. More than in any other practice setting, social workers in public child welfare experience what they described as "burnout," which too often resulted in resignation as a form of personal and professional self-preservation. Sadly, this left many of our most vulnerable children abandoned by a caregiver once again. Until vacancies were filled, other social workers carried higher caseloads, which meant additional stress on already limited resources and diminished services due to the overwhelming demands of the high caseloads. It seemed like a never-ending cycle. Fifteen years later, I observe students in their field placements and sometimes find myself thinking, "things have changed, but not that much."

When I began my doctoral program, I knew I wanted to find a way to keep social workers resilient and thriving in the workforce. The overarching goal of my research is to preserve our human service workforce by cultivating resilience for all social workers through meaningful practice experiences with those who are poor, vulnerable, traumatized, or otherwise suffering in some way. Part of my commitment to the social work profession is to educate students and other professionals on the potentially deleterious effects of the emotionally challenging aspects of direct practice described in the literature by terms such as vicarious traumatization, secondary traumatic stress, compassion fatigue, and burnout. My theoretical and empirical work with these constructs and how to address them, both personally and professionally, are weaved into every fabric of this book.

Generationally, my professional career coincided with the global effects of the terrorist attacks on the World Trade Center and the official declaration of war shortly thereafter. Watching the effects of the September 11, 2001, terrorist attacks, and more recently the increase in school violence, terrorism, extreme racism, and other forms of mass interpersonal violence, it is clear that the emotional effects of trauma, grief, anger, suffering, and other forms of human emotion are indeed "transferable." Through my work I have learned that people have the ability to "bounce back," to overcome even the most traumatizing and horrific life experiences, a quality I have seen many times as children, families, soldiers, and communities recover from personal trauma, terrorism, natural disaster, and other forms of human suffering. I believe there is no greater professional reward than to be a part of someone's recovery process.

As a social worker, it is my great privilege to serve those who are experiencing personal distress and trauma and an even greater privilege to educate the professional social workers of the future. I feel it is my ethical obligation to students, their families, and to the clients they serve to provide a resource on what I call the "essential practice" of self-care. As a social work educator, I feel an even greater sense of ethical responsibility to provide a thorough and adequate education to neophyte social workers who self-select to do this work. I want to preserve the energy, drive, and spirit of humanity that I see in the classroom as my students enter their field placements and later our workforce.

I have reviewed countless textbooks on social work theory, practice, and field education. It is rare to find a book that includes any substantial content on the practice of self-care. On the uncommon occasion that self-care is included, it is often minimally discussed in the context of other "more important" information. Despite years of empirical evidence suggesting that the emotionally challenging aspects of social work practice contribute to professional burnout and compassion fatigue, there is no mention in the newly revised CSWE Educational Policy and Accreditation Standards for content on self-care to be included in social work curriculum, course content, or field education.

There is overwhelming agreement in the empirical literature that new social workers, particularly those going into child welfare or other areas of trauma-related care, are the most vulnerable to the indirect effects of the trauma work itself. This book provides a comprehensive treatment of the psychosocial effects of trauma-related care, professional burnout, and compassion fatigue through the holistic practice of self-care. I describe the ongoing practice of self-care as "the key to professional resilience." Using an ecological systems perspective, I propose a holistic framework for self-care as a comprehensive series of practice behaviors from the physical, interpersonal, organizational, familial, and spiritual domains of the psychosocial self. The practice of self-care involves regulating empathy resources, which must be maintained over time to cultivate and sustain personal and professional resilience. I use the word "cultivating" in the book title to refer to the great potential for personal growth that can occur through social work practice, training, and education. The practice of self-care must be cultivated across one's professional career to be effective.

My hope is that students will learn from this material and begin to develop their self-care practices before entering the workforce, so they may remain resilient and committed to the values, mission, and spirit of the social work profession.

Teaching students, fellow social workers, and other human service professionals to be professionally resilient is my life's work. I hope this book reflects my deep commitment to the education and professional development of social work practitioners, particularly those in trauma-related care, and to their personal and professional health and well-being.

ACKNOWLEDGMENTS

TAKING ON a project of this size has been a challenging yet invigorating phase of my professional development and of my scholarly work. This book would not have been possible without the support of many mentors across my professional career. For nearly two decades, I have cultivated their wise counsel to collectively inform my practice, research, and teaching abilities. I would like to thank the University of Montevallo, particularly Dean Mary Beth Armstrong of the College of Arts and Sciences, for supporting my research through internal and external funding opportunities, travel allocations, and sabbatical leave. Thanks to Ruth Truss, my mentor and now chair, for her sage advice, patience, wisdom, and support of my sabbatical to complete this work. More than you know, I have gleaned valuable insights from your diplomatic leadership style and your genuine nature. My sincere gratitude goes to Jeannie Duke and Meredith Tetloff, my loyal colleagues and companions in social work, for assuming my job duties without complaint to allow me the rare opportunity to write without distraction.

Thanks to my mentor and colleague Deb Nelson-Gardell for always believing in the value and meaning of my work to our profession and for her constant encouragement and mentorship of my professional career.

My sincere thanks to Will Hasenbein who supported our program as a graduate student worker for two years and made considerable contributions to this book by assisting with research, editing, and bibliographic entries, not to mention his daily contributions to the functioning of our program and to the faculty. Thanks to James L. Jackson Jr., the graduate counseling program coordinator at the University of Montevallo for his contributions to chapter 8.

Thank you to my parents, family, and friends who bring joy, laughter, and resilience to my life every day. Words simply cannot express how much gratitude I owe my wife Dora for her constant love and support, both personally and professionally. Thank you to our beautiful daughter Eliza for being the source of our joy and our resilience, for inspiring my creativity every morning, and for reminding me when I need to seek the balance and equanimity that is the subject of my research. Finally, thank you to Columbia University Press, Stephen Wesley, and to my editor Jennifer Perillo for taking time to review my initial book proposal and for her enthusiasm and support of this project. Working with your guidance has been my great pleasure.

CULTIVATING PROFESSIONAL RESILIENCE IN DIRECT PRACTICE

1

AN INTRODUCTION TO CULTIVATING PROFESSIONAL RESILIENCE IN DIRECT PRACTICE

I learned a long time ago that those who are the happiest are those who do the most for others.

—BOOKER T. WASHINGTON

CHAPTER GOALS AND OBJECTIVES

1. Describe social work and other human service professions as career paths equally rich with emotional challenges and with opportunities for professional growth and resilience.
2. Introduce the importance of personal and professional self-care as an essential component of daily practice with human service populations.
3. Identify the need in social work education for curriculum and course content on the utilization of professional self-care by social workers and other human service professionals to cultivate professional resilience.
4. Briefly introduce the terms *stress, empathy, resilience,* and *self-care* as the four core constructs essential to understanding the material in this book.
5. Conceptualize self-care from an ecological systems perspective as a holistic practice with components from various domains of the psychosocial self.
6. Provide an outline and a rationale for the presentation of the chapter content, materials, and book features so that they may be utilized efficaciously by students, faculty, and other interested professionals.

As future professionals, many students who self-select the pursuit of a professional social work education feel that human service work is more to them than a career path: it is the call to embrace a professional life of deep, meaningful, and rewarding service. Congruent with the mission, values, and humanitarian spirit of the social work profession (National Association of Social Workers [NASW], 2008), social work students willingly dedicate their college lives and future professional careers to providing services to those members of our society who are poor, vulnerable, underserved, underprivileged, or otherwise suffering in their human experience in some way. For some, the true face of social work practice is not revealed until the gateway to the profession is opened in field education. Many, even those who complete field education as part of their degree, subsequently enter into social work practice unaware of the potential impact of the chronic day-to-day exposure to clients and the emotional and often distressing narratives of their psychosocial problems. In her classic work on relationships, Perlman (1979) described the emotional impact of her practice experiences in this way:

> I found myself reluctant to detach myself from clients I had come to invest in, to like, sometimes to love, to be concerned about, to puzzle over, to be angry with, to be awed by. In short, I came to understand that it is hard to separate from persons whom you have joined in emotional experiences, even when at times they have not been wholly happy ones. (p. 5)

Nearly three decades of empirical research has demonstrated that the emotionally challenging aspects of direct practice in social work and other human service careers have potentially deleterious and sometimes consequential psychological effects on the providers themselves. This research bears particular relevance for students and neophyte social work professionals pursuing careers in child welfare, clinical social work, disaster mental health, military social work, or other forms of trauma-related care (Black, 2006; Cunningham, 2004; Gilin & Kaufman, 2015; Knight, 2010). It has been suggested by some that occupational stress conditions such as professional burnout, secondary traumatic stress, vicarious traumatization, and compassion fatigue may be underestimated "occupational hazards" for those providing social work services (Pryce, Shackelford, & Pryce, 2007). Occupational stress related to the emotional and organizational challenges of social work practice have confirmed that these conditions are a reality when working with vulnerable populations, particularly with those who have survived traumatic experiences (Figley, 1995; Pearlman & Saakvitne, 1995; Stamm, 1999).

THE PEDAGOGICAL NEED FOR PROFESSIONAL SELF-CARE

The wealth of evidence in the research literature on the emotional effects of human service work on direct practitioners clearly implies the need for a well-developed and comprehensive trauma-informed educational curriculum (Strand, Abramovitz, Layne, Robinson, & Way, 2014). Part of the academy's obligation to future social work professionals is to deliver course content inclusive of personal and professional practices related to self-care. It can be argued that the implementation of instructional efforts to cultivate the continued resilience and well-being of our social work and human service workforce is an ethical imperative in social work education (Newell & Nelson-Gardell, 2014). Yet there appears to be a gap between the integration and application of the evidence in the practice literature, suggesting the need for content on self-care as a component of trauma-informed education (Courtois, 2002; Jaynes, 2014; Knight, 2010).

The emotional and psychological risks associated with being in direct practice with vulnerable populations and the essential use of self-care strategies to address this important aspect of human service work has been an overlooked issue in social work education (Cunningham, 2004; Newell & MacNeil, 2010; Shackelford, 2006). The need for continued student education, training, and professional development at the undergraduate and graduate level is supported by the National Association of Social Workers (NASW, 2009), which suggests that social work education programs should recognize "their critically important roles in educating social work students about the practice of professional self-care by integrating such content into existing student standards, policies, foundation and advanced curriculums, field practicum, and assignments and projects" (p. 247).

Despite the evidence in the recent literature and the recommendations by the NASW, the most recent revision to the Educational Policy and Accreditation Standards (EPAS) produced by the Council on Social Work Education (CSWE, 2015) makes no direct mention of the importance of including material on the practice of self-care in social work educational curriculum or course content.

This book was developed to address this important gap in professional training by providing an empirically based yet pragmatic and user-friendly educational resource to social work students, faculty, and professionals. Some social work students graduate from their professional training programs with little knowledge or ability to appropriately utilize self-care as an ongoing and essential practice behavior (Shackelford, 2006). Further, many social work students may be exiting their programs and entering the workforce lacking the professional training to recognize or address the signs and symptoms of occupational stress–related conditions such as professional burnout and the indirect or vicarious effects of trauma-related care (Lerias & Byrne, 2003). In the hope of using education as prevention, a comprehensive review of the theoretical and empirical literature addressing clinical issues such as countertransference, vicarious traumatization, secondary traumatic stress, compassion fatigue, and professional burnout are presented. The risk factors and behaviors associated with these experiences in service providers are also examined.

It is more than reasonable to suggest that education on these conditions be infused into micro and macro social work curriculum and course content. Teaching students the practice of professional self-care requires little more than the interpersonal application of the theories, skills, and knowledge considered essential components of social work education. Basic practice skills such as problem-solving and task-centered approaches and strengths-based assessment can easily be applied when creating a useful, functional, and ongoing plan of professional self-care. Social work programs have the opportunity and the infrastructure to provide education as the first line preventive measure for the training of social workers who, by virtue of their inexperience in the field, are the most vulnerable to the effects of these conditions (Harr & Moore, 2011; Lerias & Byrne, 2003).

THE PRIMARY GOALS OF THIS BOOK

The overarching goals of this book and its contents are twofold. The first major goal is to provide students, faculty, field educators, and direct practitioners with a comprehensive work addressing the emotionally challenging aspects of being a career social worker, counselor, or human service professional. Although my perspective on this work and its contents comes from areas of social work practice, I also use the generalized term *human service professional* frequently throughout the book because the material is appropriate for any professional working with individuals, families, groups, communities, or organizations experiencing vulnerability or suffering in some way. Therefore, the material presented has utility and relevance for students and direct practitioners in social work, psychology, counseling, criminology, and other human service–related professions and agency settings.

Second, there is a central theme on direct practice, particularly the treatment of trauma-related disorders, and the practice of professional self-care as an essential component of daily practice and of the treatment relationship with clients. Each chapter includes material in the areas of direct practice, research, education, and professional development. This book is versatile as primary reading material, as a supplemental text, or as a resource for student professional development. The last 10 years of conducting research and providing professional education and training in this area has revealed that the existing literature includes many books that focus on one specific aspect of stress, trauma, or professional self-care but no comprehensive text. Moreover, much of the information available is predominantly anecdotal, paying little attention to the theoretical development, empirical evidence, or current trends in the professional discourse.

This book is intended to inform students, faculty, and professionals that this material may be infused into BSW and MSW curriculums to better prepare social work students to enter their future practice areas. The content can be used with courses at both the micro and macro levels of direct practice. The chapters follow a timeline that begins with the history of trauma-informed practice in human service professions and ends with pragmatic strategies for self-care for current and future professionals. Embedded within the chapters are exercises for professional development appropriate for a classroom setting or as part of agency training and professional development. A key aim is to provide a comprehensive resource with chapter offerings useful for beginning practitioners or classroom learners, for experienced professionals in the field, and for academics who wish to pursue research in the areas of trauma-informed practice and professional self-care.

THE CORE CONCEPTS

The chapters in this book are guided by the understanding of four basic core concepts: stress, empathy, resilience, and self-care. The term *stress* can be conceptualized both as environmental stimuli (stressors) and as the individual or collective behavioral responses to these stimuli. It is generally understood that chronic stress can be pervasive, having cumulative effects on human beings and all of their working systems. The sources of stress originate from various domains of the biopsychosocial self, including physical health, mental health, family well-being, and spirituality (Waller, 2001). Traumatic stress occurs when normative internal and external resources become overwhelmed and exhausted due to the intense physical or emotional challenges of the stressful situation. Examples of traumatic experiences include natural disasters, fire or explosion, serious automobile or other moving vehicle accidents, exposure to a toxic substance, child sexual and physical abuse, severe child neglect, domestic violence, physical or sexual assault, torture, rape, sex trafficking, life-threatening illness, bearing witness to severe human suffering, homicide, suicide, or sudden unexpected death or serious injury to a significant person or persons (American Psychiatric Association, 2013). Traumatic stress reactions are the consequential, complex, and problematic patterns of behavior that result from the impact of a traumatic incident or event involving either actual or perceived threat on the obvious victim or victims of that incident (American Psychiatric Association, 2013; Friedman, Keane, & Resick, 2007). Traumatic stress can occur either at the micro level, as in the case of surviving physical or sexual assault, or at the macro level, such as a community's response to a natural disaster, chronic forms of racism and discrimination, or an act of mass interpersonal violence.

The second core concept is *empathy*, a construct that has been studied from various perspectives and professional disciplines. Despite its frequent use in the common language of social work practitioners, the literature fails to reveal a universally accepted definition of the empathy construct. Empathy is often associated with, or assumed to be used in combination with, other professional skills, such as the ability to be compassionate, genuine, nurturing, and caring toward others. Therefore, a collective description of empathy includes the cognitive, emotional, and somatic reactions to human beings by providers as well as a developed clinical skill that is essential to the practitioner to meet the needs of clients and their families (Gerdes, Segal, Jackson, & Mullins, 2011). Practice with those who are vulnerable and suffering in some way requires service providers to be actively ready to use their own personal psychological resources in the form of empathy and compassion on a daily basis. The chronic use of empathy is a requirement unique among the helping professions, and without the proper methods of self-care, it can become depleted, leaving providers vulnerable to indirect effects of trauma, compassion fatigue, or professional burnout.

Like the concept of empathy, the term *resilience* has been examined from multiple perspectives, including neurobiology, cognitive and social psychology, and human development. Resilience is often understood to be the ability to "bounce back" or recover from a challenge in a meaningful and productive way. This book uses a multidimensional approach to both personal and professional resilience as an overall process of well-being consisting of intrapersonal, interpersonal, and social dimensions, rather than explaining it solely as a function of personality (Kent, Davis, & Reich, 2014). A recent paradigm shift, particularly in the area of trauma practice, has identified the positive and growth promoting aspects of human service work as fuel for sustaining professional resilience over time. This shift in research and practice literature has been conceptualized through the use of terms such *posttraumatic growth, vicarious resilience, self-compassion,* and *compassion satisfaction.*

The fourth core or essential concept is the ongoing commitment to utilize methods of personal and professional *self-care*. Professional self-care has been described as both a process and a defined set of practice skills and strategies to mitigate the emotionally challenging effects of providing services to individuals, families, groups, or entire communities (Skinner, 2015). NASW (2009) defines self-care as "a core essential component to social work practice that reflects a choice and commitment to become actively involved in maintaining ones effectiveness as a social worker in preventing and coping with the natural, yet unwanted, consequences of helping" (p. 246). The synthesis of the research literature on the various definitions and recommendations for professional self-care summarizes the practice as the utilization of skills and strategies by social workers and other human service professionals to maintain their own personal, familial, emotional, physical, and spiritual needs and to actively and consciously promote holistic well-being and professional resilience while attending to the complex emotional needs and demands of their clients (Cox & Sterner, 2013b; Lee & Miller, 2013; Pearlman & Saakvitne, 1995; Stamm, 1999).

AN ECOLOGICAL SYSTEMS PERSPECTIVE

One useful and comprehensive context from which to understand stress comes from the practice of social work and the manifestation of human behavior as it interfaces with the various systems in the social environment (Levers, 2012). This fundamental perspective in social work practice is grounded in the field of ecology, which suggests that human behavior evolves as a living organism across the life span based on a combination of biological factors and human experiences occurring within the social environment (Payne, 2014). This perspective also provides a useful approach for conceptualizing human resilience as a transactional process based on human relationships and experiences across various domains of the life course (Waller, 2001). Consistent with the broad context used to describe stress, empathy, and resilience, this book proposes a holistic approach to self-care using an ecological systems framework with activities across the biological, interpersonal, organizational, familial, peer-related, spiritual, and recreational aspects of the biopsychosocial self.

CHAPTER CONTENT AND ORGANIZATION

This book provides a resource for social work students and faculty on the prevention of occupational stress conditions due to the emotional and organizational challenges of human service work. The current literature base is missing a dedicated book in this topical area with broad utility for students training in professional service programs. To effectively cover all the material, a pragmatic and linear approach is used for presenting chapter content. The book is divided into two distinct sections. The first section addresses the conceptual, theoretical, and empirical work in the areas of stress, trauma (in both direct and indirect forms), professional burnout, and self-care. The second section focuses on the application of self-care practices to cultivate personal and professional well-being.

SECTION 1: THEORY, CONCEPTUALIZATION, AND MEASUREMENT

Chapter 2 begins with a brief history of the field of traumatology and introduces stress as a general concept common to all human life experiences. Traumatic stress, presented in the form of posttraumatic stress disorder (PTSD), is also examined. PTSD diagnostic criteria are discussed, including the recent changes in the *Diagnostic and Statistical Manual for Mental Disorders* or DSM-5 (American Psychiatric Association, 2013).

Chapter 3 introduces the core concept of empathy as it relates to direct practice with vulnerable populations. The importance of regulating the appropriate use of empathy (described as empathy self-regulation) resources is discussed as a vulnerability factor for social workers and other human service professionals in direct practice. Conceptual and operational definitions for important concepts such as countertransference, vicarious traumatization, secondary traumatic stress, and compassion fatigue are introduced in this chapter as well. These concepts have the potential to make a psychologically consequential impact on providers as they employ empathy to engage with clients and their psychosocial problems in the treatment process.

Chapter 4 introduces the multidimensional construct of professional burnout and the vulnerability factors associated with experience of this condition as well as the vulnerability factors for the indirect forms of trauma. A detailed comparison between the experience of professional burnout and the experience of indirect trauma is included. Both are related to chronic direct practice interactions with clients and the emotionally challenging aspects of their psychosocial problems.

Chapter 5 concludes the first section and provides a discussion of the methodological issues and limitations for conducting accurate research in the areas of professional burnout and indirect trauma. This chapter includes descriptions of various scales used to measure stress, the primary and indirect forms of trauma, compassion fatigue, and professional burnout. Instruments commonly cited in the research literature as having the strongest psychometric properties are discussed in detail.

SECTION 2: A HOLISTIC FRAMEWORK FOR THE APPLICATION OF SELF-CARE PRACTICES

Chapter 6 begins this section with an introduction to the core concepts of resilience and self-care. Professional resilience is discussed as the outcome of compassion satisfaction, posttraumatic growth, and vicarious resilience.

The core concept of self-care is introduced as the "key to professional resilience" and is conceptualized holistically within the context of an ecological systems framework. Practical exercises include setting personal and organizational goals as components of the holistic approach for developing a functional plan for self-care.

Chapter 7 builds on the ecological systems framework for self-care presented in chapter 6 through the examination of the physical, organizational, interpersonal, familial, and spiritual aspects of the holistic self-care process.

Chapter 8 presents material on the ethical obligation of social workers, counselors, and other human service professionals to practice self-care. Direct practitioners are responsible for maintaining their own self-care practice, not only for themselves but also for the well-being of the clients they serve and their own families and loved ones (Carbonell & Figley, 1996; Waller, 2001). The ethical imperative of self-care is presented through examination of the ethics codes of the NASW and the American Counseling Association.

Chapter 9 addresses the importance of education, training, and professional development in the areas of stress management, trauma-informed practice, and professional self-care, particularly for students in practicum courses and recent graduates beginning their careers in direct practice. This chapter presents information on how material in self-care practice can be introduced across micro and macro curriculum in professional training programs. Application materials include case studies, competency-based assignments, and self-reflection exercises.

Chapter 10 concludes the application chapters of the book by discussing mindfulness approaches and practices, such as the use of attention, awareness, meditation, and self-compassion, as components of the self-care process.

BOOK FEATURES

CASE STUDIES

Case studies developed from my direct practice and professional training experiences have been incorporated in each chapter as teaching tools to illustrate the effects of professional burnout, secondary traumatic stress, and compassion fatigue in a pragmatic and more realistic way. These case studies help students develop their critical thinking and analytical abilities, assist with the practice skill of assessment and development of social case plans, support role-play with other students and faculty on social worker–client interactions, and work through potential ethical dilemmas that might occur in social work practice (Ruggiero, 2002).

Many books utilize case study methodology as an effective way to engage students in learning about topics such as professional burnout, vicarious trauma, secondary traumatic stress, and compassion fatigue (Black, 2006; Cunningham, 2004; Knight, 2010). Few books have incorporated case study assignments for assessment of the current standards for social work competencies in the way done here. The case studies are designed to be used simultaneously by students and faculty as part of course reading assignments, classroom discussions, and critical thinking. Following each case study, discussion and critical thinking questions are provided based on the newly revised Educational Policy and Standards from the Council on Social Work Education (table 1.1).

SELF-REFLECTION EXERCISES

As part of my work in this area, I have conducted numerous trainings for direct practitioners in child welfare, mental health, and other human service professions. Through this work, I have found it important to actively engage students and training participants in the process of their own self-reflection and correction. This is of particular importance when engaging the emotionally challenging aspects of human service work characteristic of practice with trauma-related disorders and other forms of human suffering. Self-reflection provides the opportunity for students and professionals to think critically about their interpersonal thoughts, feelings, and behaviors that manifest from the complex interactions with clients and their social problems. This includes helping students understand their own personal perspective on clients and their challenges and any interpersonal biases they may have toward the situation (Bean, Davis, & Davey, 2014). For some, this provides an opportunity for contemplative insight into the influence of personal life events, particularly past history of trauma exposure, on the problems of clients in the present moment. Self-reflection also is useful in the empathy self-regulation process, which contributes to the ongoing cultivation of professional resilience. Topics for personal reflection include resilience and self-appreciation, ethical dilemmas in direct practice, and engaging a group discussion on trauma-informed care.

WORKSHEETS AND SAMPLE ASSIGNMENTS

Along with the case studies materials and self-reflection exercises, worksheets and exercises for direct practice are included throughout the book. These application components provide an opportunity to use the material in a pragmatic way that reflects the "real world" of social work practice. Many of the application materials and exercises have been adapted from years of conducting training and professional development in this area. Specific application exercises include setting personal and professional goals for practice, conducting an assessment of organization strengths and challenges, conducting an assessment

TABLE 1.1 Council on Social Work Education

2015 EDUCATIONAL POLICY AND ACCREDITATION STANDARDS FOR BACCALAUREATE AND MASTER'S SOCIAL WORK PROGRAMS

Competency 1	**Demonstrate Ethical and Professional Behavior** • Make ethical decisions by applying the NASW Code of Ethics; • Use self-reflection and correction to manage personal values and maintain professionalism; • Demonstrate professional demeanor in behavior, appearance, and communication; • Use technology ethically and appropriately to facilitate practice outcomes; and • Use supervision and consultation to guide professional judgment and behavior.
Competency 2	**Engage Diversity and Difference in Practice** • Apply and communicate understanding of diversity in shaping life experiences at all practice levels; • Present themselves as learners and engage clients as experts of their own experiences; and • Apply self-awareness and self-regulation to manage the influence of personal biases and values.
Competency 3	**Advance Human Rights and Social, Economic, and Environmental Justice** • Apply understanding of social, economic, and environmental justice to advocate for human rights at the individuals an systems levels; and • Engage in practices that advance social, economic, and environmental justice.
Competency 4	**Engage in Practice-Informed Research and Research-Informed Practice** • Use practice expertise and theory to inform scientific inquiry and research; • Apply critical thinking to engage in analysis of quantitative and qualitative research methods; and • Use and translate research evidence to inform and improve practice, policy, and service delivery.
Competency 5	**Engage in Policy Practice** • Identify social policy at the local, state, and federal level that impacts well-being, service delivery, and access to services; • Assess how social welfare and economic policies impact the delivery of and access to social services; and • Apply critical thinking to analyze, formulate, and advocate for policies that advance human rights, and social, economic, and environmental justice.

(continued)

TABLE 1.1 *(continued)*

Competency 6	**Engage With Individuals, Families, Groups, Organizations, and Communities**
	• Apply knowledge of human behavior and the social environment, person-in-environment, and other multidisciplinary theoretical frameworks to engage with clients and constituencies; and
	• Use empathy, reflection, and interpersonal skills to effectively engage diverse clients and constituencies.
Competency 7	**Assess Individuals, Families, Groups, Organizations, and Communities**
	• Apply critical thinking to collect, organize, and interpret client data;
	• Apply knowledge of human behavior and the social environment, person-in-environment, and other multidisciplinary theoretical frameworks in the analysis of assessment data;
	• Develop mutually agreed-on intervention goals and objectives based on critical assessment of strengths, needs, and challenges; and
	• Select appropriate intervention strategies based on the assessment, research knowledge, values, and preferences of clients and constituencies.
Competency 8	**Intervene with Individuals, Families, Groups, Organizations, and Communities**
	• Critically choose and implement interventions to achieve practice goals and enhance capacities of clients and constituencies;
	• Apply knowledge of human behavior and the social environment, person-in-environment, and other multidisciplinary theoretical frameworks in interventions with clients and constituencies;
	• Use interprofessional collaboration as appropriate to achieve beneficial practice outcomes;
	• Negotiate, mediate, and advocate with and on behalf of diverse clients and constituencies; and
	• Facilitate effective transitions and endings that advance mutually agreed-on goals.
Competency 9	**Evaluate Practice With Individuals, Families, Groups, Organizations, and Communities**
	• Select and use appropriate methods for evaluation of outcomes;
	• Apply knowledge of human behavior and the social environment, person-in-environment, and other multidisciplinary theoretical frameworks in the evaluation of outcomes;
	• Critically analyze, monitor, and evaluate intervention and program processes and outcomes; and
	• Apply evaluation findings to improve practice effectiveness at all system levels.

Source: Council on Social Work Education. (2015). 2015 educational policy and accreditation standards for baccalaureate and master's social work programs. www.cswe.org/File.aspx?id=94704

of personal and professional strategies for self-care, and the application of mindfulness practice through deep breathing exercises. The appendixes include sample CSWE competency-based assignments for conducting an organizational assessment, developing a holistic plan of self-care, and completing a mindfulness-based journaling assignment. Each of these practice exercises and sample assignments is designed to assist students with their educational and professional development and are appropriate for students in practicum or in field seminar courses.

RECOMMENDED READINGS AND INTERNET RESOURCES

A list of recommended books in the chapter content area is provided as supplemental readings at the end of each chapter. The recommended readings come from my personal library of "go to" resources in the areas of stress, trauma, and self-care. Many of the suggested readings are authored by the foremost scholars in trauma-informed practice and are considered essential works in this area of study. A comprehensive bibliography of the recommended readings for each chapter is included in the appendixes for the text.

Following the recommended readings section, each chapter includes suggested Internet resources to supplement the chapter content. A brief description of each Internet site is included along with a list of useful site features and resources. Students have online access to valuable supplementary resources including additional bibliographic information, application materials, podcasts, hyperlinks to relevant YouTube videos and other related websites, PowerPoint

KEY TERMS

At the end of each chapter is a list of key terms defined in the chapter. Key terms help identify the major content areas in the chapter and their application to social work practice. It is suggested that students review their knowledge of the key terms at the completion of each chapter. Key terms are defined in the chapter in which they first appear and then are used consistently throughout the book.

Council on Social Work Education (CSWE)
Educational Policy and Accreditation Standards (EPAS)
ecological systems theory
empathy
National Association of Social Workers (NASW)
resilience
self-care
self-reflection
stress
traumatic stress

presentations, and information on professional conference venues. In some cases, bibliographies, handouts, presentations, and other educational resources can be downloaded at no cost.

A reference list and an inclusive bibliography of the recommended readings and suggested Internet resources from each chapter are included at the end of the book. Worksheets of application materials and self-reflection exercises for use in the chapters are also located at the back of the book.

CHAPTER SUMMARY

Social work practice is a career path rich with opportunities for reward through the professional practice of helping others who are underserved and in need. However, without proper knowledge of how to regulate the emotionally challenging aspects of direct practice, social workers and other human service professionals may experience erosion to their professional drive and spirit to continue in the work. It is of vital importance to the human service workforce that social workers providing direct services to vulnerable populations understand the emotional challenges associated with engaging the sometimes graphic details of clients and their experiences. The best way to create balance and equanimity for social workers, particularly those dedicated to providing services for trauma-related disorders, is to develop a holistic plan of self-care.

Self-care is an essential practice behavior for social workers and other human service professionals and should be interlaced into the curriculum of social work education. This book describes self-care as the key to professional resilience and to longevity in the human service workforce. Including the practice of self-care as a component of the knowledge base and skill set for professional social workers can decrease the psychological effects of direct practice described in the literature through terms such as *vicarious trauma, secondary traumatic stress, compassion fatigue,* and *professional burnout.* Based on the ecological systems perspective, a holistic approach to self-care is proposed as a model for developing an ongoing and effective plan of personal and professional self-care.

SECTION 1

THEORY, CONCEPTUALIZATION, AND MEASUREMENT

2

UNDERSTANDING THE CONNECTION BETWEEN STRESS AND TRAUMA

Stress is basically a disconnection from the earth, a forgetting of the breath. Stress is an ignorant state. It believes that everything is an emergency. Nothing is that important. Just lie down.

—NATALIE GOLDBERG

CHAPTER GOALS AND OBJECTIVES

1. Provide a general overview and definition of the various functions of stress as a pervasive and complex behavioral phenomenon.
2. Describe the neurobiology of stress as both a stimulus and a response to external cues in the social environment.
3. Provide a general conceptualization of stress using an ecological systems perspective focusing on the holistic effects of stress across biological, psychological, and social systems.
4. Review and summarize the clinical presentation of posttraumatic stress disorder (PTSD) including recent updates and limitations to the diagnostic criteria used in the *DSM-5.*
5. Demonstrate the presentation of symptoms for clients diagnosed with trauma-related disorders through the use of competency-based case study analyses, critical thinking, and discussion questions.

There is strong consensus among both researchers and practitioners in human service work regarding the potential impact of the relationship between occupational stress, empathy, resilience, and the practice of self-care—four essential constructs that lay the foundation for understanding and using the material in this book. This chapter focuses on the varied operational definitions of these terms as they apply to human behavior and to practice with vulnerable populations in later chapters. Using an ecological systems perspective, this chapter provides a general introduction and conceptualization of stress as a complex and dynamic presentation of human behavior with pervasive effects on individual, familial, social, spiritual, and organizational systems (Pardek, 2015). From the broad context of this approach, stress is also described from several perspectives as both stimulus and response to internal and external stimuli. The chapter concludes with an overview of trauma as a specific reaction to stress, outlining the complex processes by which traumatic experiences generate traumatic stress reactions in clients.

PART 1: WHAT IS STRESS? GENERAL DEFINITIONS

It is generally understood that stress and its effects can be pervasive, having holistic effects on the human body and all of its working systems. Hence, stress has been studied from a variety of perspectives and professional disciplines. For example, the neurobiological approach to stress focuses on the body's biological reactions to stressful events through the central nervous system (CNS), and the cognitive approach examines the brain's processing of stressful events and the corresponding influence of stress on patterns of thought, beliefs, and other areas of cognition. Because stress is such a broad and subjective construct dependent on the specific researcher's or author's perspective, this infinitely complex and omnipresent expression of human behavior can be conceptualized in multiple ways. Most people (including human service providers) probably do not have a concrete or working definition of stress, but they have no problem describing in detail what stress feels like and how stressful experiences routinely influence and change their thoughts, feelings, behaviors, and lives.

Using a clinical approach, stress is like many behavioral phenomena: people tend to know the diagnosis (e.g., "I am stressed" or "I am depressed") but are sometimes unfamiliar with the full range of symptoms. The term *stress* can be conceptualized as both environmental stimuli (also called stressors) such as individual or collective behavioral responses to environmental stimuli, stressors, or stressful events; or as biological stimuli such as the impact of a long-term illness on the working systems of the body (Berger, 2015). Focusing on the behavioral implications of stress, this book uses both of these conceptualizations of the term, referring to external stimuli as stressors or stressful life events and the internal or behavioral reactions to stressors as stress.

THE NEUROBIOLOGY OF STRESS

A simple explanation of the link between stressful events and stress behaviors begins in the moment a person is confronted with a stressful life event (or stressor), at which point there is an immediate and innate biological response to heighten awareness to the event as a method of self-protection.

The neurobiological response to stress is a function of the limbic system, a part of the CNS that shares in the regulation of emotion and behavioral reactions to both internal and external stimuli (Tyler, 2012). When people are confronted with any form of stress, the limbic system immediately generates an appraisal of the individual's internal and external coping resources, which in return generates an initial behavioral response through the functions of the autonomic nervous system (Rothschild, 2000). This is often called the "fight, flight, or freeze" response, which can be somewhat unpredictable and depends on the coping abilities of the individual and the nature of the stressful event. Why do some victims of physical assault try to run away from the perpetrator, why do some fight back in self-defense, and why do some go into a state of unresponsive shock?

From a broad perspective, stress can be conceptualized as the biological, psychological, and social responses by people to challenging or difficult stimuli in their physical and social environments. Behaviorally, human response to stress is subjective, and people and their abilities to process and cope with the effects of stress vary widely. Stress also can come from a variety of internal and external stimuli, or from a combination of both. For example, physical stressors affect the biological functions of the human body, leading to physical exhaustion, illness, or chronic fatigue (Kottler & Chen, 2011). Physical stress may come from working too many hours without proper rest and nutrition, not taking time to recover properly from a physical illness, chronic illness, losing sleep to care for an infant or sick child, chronic alcohol or drug use, or neglecting essential physical health care needs and positive health behaviors (diet, exercise, rest).

Psychological stress is related to an individual's internal abilities to process and cope with stressful life events. Psychological stress is much more subjective than physical stress and differs from person to person. Individuals experience psychological stress when they determine through their internal cognitive appraisal that they do not have the necessary coping resources to properly address the stressful event (figure 2.1). Psychological stress can generate a

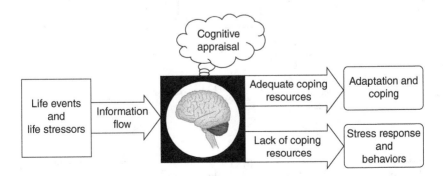

FIGURE 2.1 Internal cognitive appraisal of life events and life stressors

variety of behavioral reactions, including anger, fear, feeling overwhelmed, or even feeling helpless in a stressful situation. Chronic psychological stress, or "pile up," has the potential to lead to more pathological behaviors such as anxiety, panic, or mood disorders (Berger, 2015). I present a brief discussion of the physiological, cognitive, and other responses to stress in the social environment, but the primary focus is on the individual emotional and behavioral responses elicited as a result of stress or stressful events.

Social (or psychosocial) stressors consist of interactions among biological, familial, occupational, spiritual, community, and social systems (among others), as they intersect and integrate with one another and the inherent and often uncontrollable stress generated from these interactions. Social stressors may include the influence of ethnic, cultural, or spiritual values (and their corresponding systems) as they influence human behavior through the presentation of stress (figure 2.2). Social stressors also include myriad macro-level influences, such as the economy (economic recessions in particular); social politics and the influence of political leaders (both nationally and internationally); policy decisions; issues of social and environmental justice; poverty; racism, oppression and discrimination; and the corresponding shifts and adjustments in human behavior that occur as a result of the stress generated from these systems (Payne, 2002).

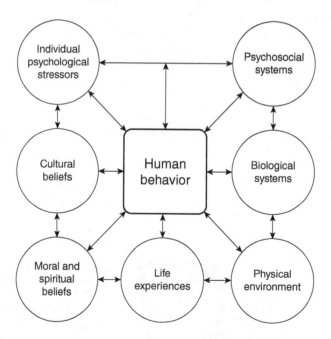

FIGURE 2.2 Ecological systems perspective on human behavior as it manifests through the complex intersection of multiple systems

STRESS FROM AN ECOLOGICAL SYSTEMS PERSPECTIVE

One useful and comprehensive context for understanding stress comes from the practice of social work and the influence and manifestation of human behavior as it interfaces with the various systems in the social environment. This fundamental perspective in social work practice is grounded in the field of ecology, which suggests that human behavior evolves as a living organism across the life span based on a combination of biological factors and nonbiological experiences that occur in the social environment (Payne, 2014). This combination of human experiences forms a biopsychosocial ecosystem, with all components of the system connected, interacting, and mutually influencing one another. The term *ecological perspective* (or "eco-systems") is used to describe this model of understanding human behavior and the impact of stress on systems of all sizes, whether it be an individual, a family, a small group, a larger group or community, or within a human service organization (Pardek, 2015).

The phrase *systems of all sizes* can be broken into three major categories (figure 2.3). The microsystem refers to an individual and his or her specific patterns of human behavior within a mesosystem, which is a larger system that interact with and has an influence on the behavior of an individual. Mesosystems

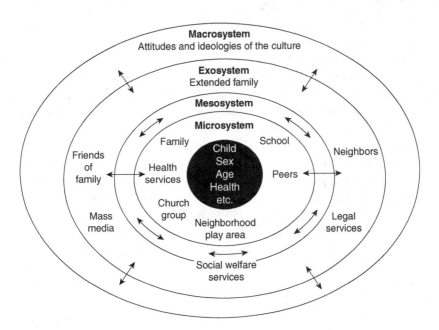

FIGURE 2.3 Model of ecological systems theory. Redrawn from Bronfenbrenner, U. (1979). The ecology of human development: experiments by nature and design. Cambridge, MA: Harvard University Press.

include family, peers, social organizations, cultural groups, religious or spiritual affiliations, workplaces, schools, and neighborhoods. The micro- and mesosystems occur within the broader context of various macrosystems, such as social politics, the economy, codes of civility and morality, social media, and national and world events (Payne, 2002, 2014).

THE CARSON FAMILY: A CASE STUDY ON THE SYSTEMIC EFFECTS OF STRESS

One way the impact of stress from the eco-systems perspective can be illustrated is in the context of the recent economic recession. A student visited my office and described a family she had encountered in field placement. The family was requesting emergency assistance for medication, overdue mortgage payments, and utilities. The family was upper-middle-class, and the father was the sole income earner for the home. He and his wife had one child who was born with a chronic and complicated medical condition that required full-time care. Historically, the client had been a substantial income earner, and the family was able to live comfortably on one income. He had spent his entire career working his way up the corporate banking ladder, but his position was cut when his bank "folded" and was purchased by a larger corporation. Because he was the sole income earner for the family, not only was the family in financial distress but they were also without health care. Without insurance, the child's medical bills and medications were approximately $2,000 a month.

Within six months the family was without severance pay, and within a year they had exhausted most of their savings. Due to the child's preexisting medical conditions and substantial medical bills, no insurance company was willing to provide the family with health care coverage at an affordable cost. Due to the economic recession and the failure of many corporate banks, the possibility for employment in the client's area of expertise was bleak and competition was high for the small pool of jobs. Many people had been laid off and replaced due to the buyout and merger, so many were looking for a job in banking in his area.

As a method of maladaptive coping with the financial stress, the father had begun using alcohol more frequently, which was putting additional strain on his marriage and his ability to adequately parent the complex medical needs of his daughter. When the father presented to my student for emergency assistance, he was overwhelmed with the guilt and shame of being unable to provide for his family, particularly his medically fragile daughter. They sold assets to get by and were now at risk of losing their home of 20 years. As the student practiced with the individual, she began to see how his current state of distress had unfolded over time, beginning with the economic recession, a macro-level social problem. The resulting stress of job loss, unemployment, lack of adequate health care coverage, and sudden loss of savings, property and other assets was directly affecting the family system (at the meso level) and his own individual mental health (at the micro level). Needless to say, there was much work to be done here; fortunately, enough resources were made available to resolve some of the immediate family stressors. The family that was historically a "contributor" to social programs through tax dollars and corporate and individual charity had become "consumers" of social welfare within one year.

DISCUSSION AND CRITICAL THINKING QUESTIONS

1. Using an ecological systems perspective, describe the collective impact of the economic recession and subsequent job loss on the familial well-being and quality of life of the Carson family across both micro- and macrosystems. (Social Work Competency 7: Assess Individuals, Families, Groups, Organizations, and Communities—through applied knowledge of human behavior and the social environment, person-in-environment, and other multidisciplinary theoretical frameworks.)

2. Conduct a comprehensive assessment of the needs of this family across systems of all sizes. In your assessment describe how you would engage interdisciplinary resources and service agencies to address issues of financial stress and burden, medical illness, mental health, and overall family well-being. (Social Work Competency 7: Assess Individuals, Families, Groups, Organizations, and Communities—through applied knowledge of human behavior and the social environment, person-in-environment, and other multidisciplinary theoretical frameworks; Social Work Competency 8: Intervene with Individuals, Families, Groups, Organizations, and Communities—through critically choosing and implementing interventions to achieve practice goals and enhance capabilities, and through the use of interprofessional collaboration as appropriate to achieve beneficial practice outcomes.)

3. Using a social justice perspective, appraise how a social worker would advocate for client services at both the micro and macro levels to effectively address the collective needs of this family. (Social Work Competency 3: Advance Human Rights and Social, Economic, and Environmental Justice; Social Work Competency 7: Assess Individuals, Families, Groups, Organizations, and Communities—through applied knowledge of human behavior and the social environment, person-in-environment, and other multidisciplinary theoretical frameworks.)

4. Conduct a brief search and critical analysis of current social policies at the national, state, and local levels addressing the service needs of this family. Identify and discuss the need for advocacy for social policies related to providing adequate services to the Carson family. (Social Work Competency 4: Engage in Practice-Informed Research and Research-Informed Practice; Competency 5: Engage in Policy Practice.)

PART 2: WHEN DOES STRESS BECOME TRAUMATIC STRESS?

The second major thematic construct in this book revolves around the concept of trauma and trauma-influenced behaviors. A fully comprehensive history of trauma and posttraumatic stress disorder (PTSD) is far beyond the scope of this book; please refer to the recommended readings and suggested Internet resources at the end of the chapter for additional resources. The References at the end of the book has additional entries on trauma-related disorders, and trauma-informed care exercises can be found in the worksheets.

STRESS AND TRAUMA IN COMBAT VETERANS: A BRIEF HISTORICAL CONTEXT

The seminal idea that neuroses could manifest based solely on life experiences outside of the biological mechanisms of the human brain and beyond the labyrinth of the unconscious mind was grounded in the examination of combat soldiers returning from war, particularly the First and Second World Wars (Birmes, Hatton, Brunet, & Schmitt 2003; Figley & Nash, 2007; van der Kolk, McFarlane, & Weisaeth, 1996). Although this era marked the first formal examination of what is now referred to and understood as posttraumatic stress disorder (PTSD), references to the impact of combat stress on the mind and soul of the soldier have been documented for as long as there have been written accounts of the tragedies associated with acts of war (Birmes et al., 2003; Figley & Nash, 2007). Although our contemporary diagnostic terminology and the use of a "clustering of symptoms" classification was not officially accepted in the *Diagnostic and Statistical Manual for Mental Disorders* until 1980 (American Psychiatric Association, 1980), the impact of combat stress and trauma had been described using a variety of terms such as *irritable heart, combat neuroses, war neuroses,* and *shell shock* (Gersons & Carlier, 1992; Figley & Nash, 2007; Friedman et al., 2007; van der Kolk et al., 1996).

UNDERSTANDING THE HUMAN EXPERIENCE AND RESPONSE TO TRAUMA

As professional understanding in the fields of traumatology have developed over time, the various psychological responses to combat stress first observed in soldiers have been generalized to other traumatic events, including natural disasters, fire or explosion, serious automobile or other moving vehicle accidents, exposure to a toxic substance, child sexual and physical abuse, severe child neglect, domestic violence, physical or sexual assault, torture, rape, sex trafficking, life-threatening illness, bearing witness to severe human suffering, homicide, suicide, or sudden unexpected death or serious injury to a significant person or persons (American Psychiatric Association, 2013; Figley, 2002b). Thus, primary traumatization or posttraumatic stress reactions are understood as the consequential, complex, and problematic patterns of behavior that result from the impact of a traumatic incident or event involving either actual or perceived threat to the obvious victim or victims of that incident (American Psychiatric Association, 2013; Friedman et al., 2007). Traumatic stress can occur at either the micro level, as in the case of a survivor of physical or sexual assault, or at the macro level, such as a community's response to a natural disaster.

This book focuses primarily on the individual or micro-level reactions to stress and trauma, but it is also beneficial to conceptualize the impact of traumatic events such as mass shootings, terror, or natural disasters at the macro or community level. Macro-level traumas are local community, national, or international events that involve a collective response of shock and horror, often resulting in large-scale consequences that affect large numbers of people. Macro-level events involving mass interpersonal violence or casualty—such as the terror attacks on the World Trade Center in 2001, mass shootings such as the one at Sandy Hook Elementary School in Connecticut in 2012, dramatic increases in gun violence on college campuses (among other public places) in the last three years across the United States, and police shootings of nonviolent offenders—have elicited a more collective or macro response at the community level, both positively and negatively (Harvey, 1996; Levers, 2012). Macro-trauma practice is discussed in greater detail in chapter 9.

PTSD: TRAUMATIC EVENTS (CRITERIA A)

At the micro or individual level, traumatic stress reactions, like stress itself, are subjective and are dependent on the psychological resources of the individual. Therefore, not all individuals who are confronted with a traumatic event will develop traumatic stress. Traumatic stress occurs when the psychological consequences of a traumatic event are such that an individual does not have the preexisting psychological coping resources to process and manage the impact of the event. The recently updated *DSM-5* defines a traumatic event in this way:

> Exposure to actual or threatened death, serious injury, or sexual violence in one (or more) of the following ways: (1) Directly experiencing the traumatic event(s); (2) witnessing, in person, the event(s) as it occurred to others; (3) learning that the traumatic event(s) occurred to a close family member or close friend—in cases of actual

or threatened death of a family member or friend, the event(s) must have been violent or accidental; (4) experiencing repeated or extreme exposure to aversive details of the traumatic event(s). (American Psychiatric Association, 2013, p. 271)

The language in the *DSM-5* outlining the diagnostic criteria A (1–4) for what constitutes a traumatic event is much more explicit than the language in the *DSM-IV* (American Psychiatric Association, 1994, 2013). Traumatic stress generally elicits feelings of both helplessness and hopelessness and may include intense shock and horror and a general disorganization in the behavioral response; however, the language describing a "subjective reaction" to trauma (formerly criteria A-2) has been removed from the *DSM-5* (American Psychiatric Association, 1994, 2013; Levers, 2012). It has been argued that the changes in language have made it more difficult to formally diagnose posttraumatic stress by underestimating the subjective impact of trauma experiences and limiting the criteria for trauma to "actual or threatened death, serious injury, and sexual violence" (American Psychiatric Association, 2013 p. 271; Briere & Scott, 2015). Further, the updated criteria limit the "impact assessment" of factors such as preexisting trauma history, the magnitude of the stressor or stressful event, and the level of preparation (if any) for the traumatic event, all of which contribute to an individual's response to a traumatic event (Figley & Nash, 2007; Quinn & Quinn, 2011; van der Kolk et al., 1996). In this book, a traumatic experience is defined as one that leaves an individual unable to cope with the psychological consequences of an atypically stressful event, resulting in chronic or pathological distress and marked impairment in psychosocial functioning.

In the *DSM-IV*, PTSD was classified as an anxiety disorder and the symptoms of PTSD were classified in three distinct clusters: reexperiencing or reliving the traumatic event or events; avoidance and emotional numbing; and increased arousal (American Psychiatric Association, 1994; Birnes et al., 2003; Friedman et al., 2007). In the *DSM-5*, PTSD is classified under the category "trauma and stress-related disorders" (American Psychiatric Association, 2013), which also includes acute stress disorder (ASD), adjustment disorders, reactive attachment disorder (RAD), and disinhibited social engagement disorder. There are now four clusters of systems; cluster C, formerly avoidance and emotional numbing, is now divided into two distinct clusters: avoidance and persistent negative alterations in both cognition and mood (American Psychiatric Association, 2013). The other clusters remain the same as outlined in the *DSM-IV*.

JONATHAN: A CASE OF COMBAT TRAUMA AND PTSD

Jonathan Adams is a 26-year-old Caucasian male Operation Iraqi Freedom (OIF) veteran who has presented to your agency requesting assistance with various emotional and physical complaints. Jonathan presents initially as somewhat quiet and shy, stating, "I have been having some problems, and my friend told me I could get some help here."

Jonathan comes from a military family and describes himself as a "military brat, we always moved around a lot when we were kids." His father is a retired Marine master sergeant; his mother was a military wife. Jonathan is the youngest of three children, and his two older brothers (ages 29 and 33) are both Marines and have also been deployed to Iraq. Jonathan is not full-time military, but he has been involved with the National Guard since he was in high school. Jonathan has completed two deployments and recently returned from his second 12-month tour of duty. Jonathan has a long-term relationship with his girlfriend, Melissa (age 24). They have maintained their relationship of five years through both deployments and are currently living together. However, Jonathan reports that "things are different now, we don't get along like we used to; I lose my temper all the time." Jonathan openly states that Melissa is the main reason he is coming in for help today.

After high school, Jonathan attended college briefly but never completed his college education. Jonathan secured employment driving a delivery truck and made enough money to support himself independently. Jonathan likes driving a truck because he "does not have to work with other people." Jonathan states that he drives the delivery truck to "pay the bills," but he loves to do woodworking projects in his spare time. Jonathan would like to use his GI Bill to attend trade school to learn more about woodworking, but he believes his parents will be disappointed if he doesn't go back to college to earn a professional degree. Since returning from his deployment, he reports that driving his truck has become more and more difficult. Jonathan finds himself "looking on the side of the road for IEDs" (improvised explosive devices) instead of paying attention to where he is going. Jonathan admits having more than one recent altercation with his coworkers and his boss. Jonathan reports feeling nervous and jumpy whenever he "hears loud noises in the warehouse," which makes other drivers laugh.

Prior to his deployments, Jonathan described himself as "fun-loving and very social." However, after his first deployment, he reports "feeling different" and now rarely wants to socialize with anyone. Jonathan gets nervous and anxious in large crowds and even in small group settings. Jonathan spends time alone in his garage, woodworking, instead of spending time with others. Jonathan admits that he prefers to spend time alone and that he and Melissa fight about spending time with their friends and family. Jonathan reports that even during family gatherings where he knows everyone, he finds himself retreating to a corner and standing alone.

Since his return home from his second deployment, Jonathan reports experiencing significant difficulties readjusting to his previous civilian lifestyle in more than one area. Jonathan denies having any severe physical injury but says, "I saw a lot of action over there." Jonathan was involved in an IED detonation, which "shook us around a little bit, but I wasn't really hurt." He and his troop fellows were riding in a HUM-V during a convoy mission when the IED was detonated. Jonathan reported being ordered to use his firearm to give "warning shots" to Iraqi civilians attempting to get into the military compound. Jonathan recalled witnessing many casualties during his deployment, including the death of two small Iraqi children who detonated an IED planted on the side of the road. Jonathan reported witnessing the death of two close friends after a HUM-V explosion; he and his unit were responsible for retrieving the bodies of the deceased soldiers and transporting them back to the military compound. One of the soldiers killed was Jonathan's long-time friend from high school and bunkmate (Mark). Jonathan reported that he typically would have been riding along with his friend, but he was assigned to a different transport at the last minute. Jonathan states that he feels like he "should have been with Mark when he died."

Jonathan admits that he spends a good deal of time alone "drinking" and searching the Internet for soldiers in his unit who may have been killed in action. Since he has been home, three soldiers from his unit have committed suicide. When asked if he (Jonathan) has firearms at home, Jonathan states, "Of course, I'm a soldier, why would I not have firearms at home?" When questioned about his alcohol use, Jonathan says he drinks approximately six to eight beers on weeknights and a bottle of whiskey every weekend. Jonathan describes himself as a "social drinker." However, he also describes drinking alone in his garage while woodworking. He reports having difficulty sleeping and states the alcohol helps him forget about his problems and rest at night, although he reports sleeping only three or four hours each night. Jonathan denies any other drug use, and he is frequently tested and could lose his CDL license if he tests positive on a drug screen.

Jonathan reports having chronic intrusive thoughts and images of the events that occurred while he was in Iraq and that he dreams about the events, often waking from his sleep startled and unable to rest again. Jonathan has extreme sensitivity to events or cues associated with the war. Jonathan admits to sometimes feeling like he is back in Iraq, especially when confronted with any trigger stimuli. He hears mortar fire in his head that sometimes becomes so loud he feels like he is reliving his experiences in the war. He admits feeling nervous and "on guard" most of the time. Jonathan denies ever discussing these events with anyone, not even Melissa.

Physically, Jonathan reports feeling "all right." He complains of difficulty remembering things and finds that he can't concentrate on reading. He reports having chronic headaches but attributes them to stress. Since his return from

Iraq, he suffers from knee and joint pain, which contribute to his difficulty sleeping. He also complains that he is experiencing hearing loss and has to ask others to repeat things. He reports infrequently experiencing rapid heartbeat and shortness of breath.

DISCUSSION AND CRITICAL THINKING QUESTIONS

1. Using the ecological systems perspective, describe the collective impact of Jonathan's history as a combat veteran on his biological, psychological, and social systems. (Social Work Competency 7: Assess Individuals—through applied knowledge of human behavior and the social environment, person-in-environment, and other multidisciplinary theoretical frameworks.)

2. Using a person-in-environment approach, describe how Jonathan's current psychosocial problems are influenced by his family of origin, his military culture, his relationship with Melissa, and his occupational situation. (Social Work Competency 2: Engage Diversity and Difference in Practice—by understanding the importance of diversity and difference in shaping life experiences; Competency 7: Assess Individuals—through applied knowledge of human behavior and the social environment, person-in-environment, and other multidisciplinary theoretical frameworks.)

3. Conduct a brief Internet search on the spectrum of trauma-related disorders; in your search, compare services for victims of physical assault to services for veterans and military families. (Social Work Competency 4: Engage in Practice-Informed Research and Research-Informed Practice.)

4. From an ethical and sociopolitical perspective, how would you manage any personal feelings you may have about this case, such as your political beliefs about the war? (Social Work Competency 1: Demonstrate Ethical and Professional Behavior—through the use of self-reflection and regulation.)

PTSD: INTRUSION AND AVOIDANCE (CRITERIA B AND C)

Criteria B, reexperiencing symptoms, includes intrusive thoughts and memories about the trauma experience(s); recurrent trauma-related nightmares; psychological and physiological sensitivity to trigger stimuli in the social environment either related to or reminiscent of the traumatic event; and in extreme cases, flashbacks in which traumatic memories manifest within the sensory mechanisms (seeing, hearing, tasting, and smelling) of the brain (Hackman, Ehlers, Speckens, & Clark, 2004). Dissociative reaction, more commonly referred to as flashbacks, are cognitive reactions to trauma memories that activate sensations such that the individual feels that the event is actually reoccurring in physical form rather than solely as a point of psychological distress.

Trauma survivors diagnosed with PTSD are often avoidant (criteria C) of thoughts, feelings, or conversations associated with their trauma experiences and may become detached or isolated from spouses, children, family, and friends as a part of conscious and subconscious efforts to avoid any dialogue or conversation related to the traumatic event (American Psychiatric Association, 2013; Galovski & Lyons, 2004; Nelson & Wright, 1996). This includes avoidance to the point of becoming numb or completely desensitized to any material or stimuli related to the traumatic event. Table 2.1 outlines the diagnostic criteria for PTSD.

TABLE 2.1 *DSM-5* Diagnostic Criteria for PTSD (abbreviated)

Criteria A: Traumatic event	Exposure to actual or threatened death, serious injury, or sexual violence
Criteria B: Intrusion	Intrusive thoughts or memories associated with the traumatic event; trauma-related nightmares; flashbacks; psychological or physiological distress when exposed to external trigger stimuli
Criteria C: Avoidance	Persistent avoidance of internal and external trigger stimuli associated with the traumatic event
Criteria D: Negative alterations in cognition and mood	Difficulty remembering important aspects of the traumatic event (dissociate amnesia); negative thoughts and beliefs about oneself and others; guilt, shame, and self-blaming associated with the traumatic event; social isolation and detachment from family and friends; lack of interest and ability to experience pleasurable activities (anhedonia)
Criteria E: Hyperarousal	Irritability and aggression; reckless or self-destructive behavior; hypervigilance; exaggerated startle response; difficulty with concentration and memory; insomnia
Criteria F: Duration of disturbance	One month or more
Criteria G: Functional impairment	Significant impact on familial, marital, social, occupational, spiritual, or other areas of psychosocial functioning.
Criteria H: Differential diagnoses	Symptoms are not attributed to an alcohol or substance use disorder or other medical condition(s).

Source: American Psychiatric Association (2013). *Diagnostic and statistical manual of mental disorders* (5th ed.). Washington, DC: Author.

This cluster of symptoms can be particularly difficult for the trauma practitioner as he or she attempts to engage the trauma survivor in any form of general or therapeutic dialogue regarding the traumatic event. Not only is this a significant barrier to treatment, this is also a deterrent for many trauma survivors who do not seek services. Clinical practitioners are essentially asking traumatized individuals to disclose information that is physiologically and psychologically distressing and otherwise avoided with the hope of a positive and efficacious outcome.

PTSD: NEGATIVE ALTERATIONS IN COGNITION AND MOOD (CRITERIA D)

Criteria D, formerly included as part of the avoidance and numbing cluster of systems, now stand alone as a cluster of systems associated with "negative alterations in cognition and mood associated with the traumatic event" (American Psychiatric Association, 2013, p. 271). This cluster is indicative of the substantial changes in cognition and behavior associated with the traumatic event. Cognitive symptoms include substantial changes in core schemas resulting from the traumatic event, such as beliefs about trust and safety in the world, self-blame, or blaming others. This cluster now includes the subjective reactions (described as "persistent negative emotional state") to trauma—such as fear, shock, horror, helplessness, and shame—as symptoms rather than as "qualifiers" for trauma injury. If negative alterations in both cognition and mood remain consistent, this could lead to cognitive distancing, detachment or complete isolation from others, and anhedonia. Anhedonia is characterized by marked impairment in the emotional ability to experience any type of joy, pleasure, or happiness in activities that were once enjoyable (American Psychiatric Association, 1994, 2013; Dekel, Peleg, & Solomon, 2013).

LIMITATIONS TO *DSM-5* UPDATES: RACE-BASED TRAUMATIC STRESS

One major limitation of the DSM-5 language regarding the definition and constitution of a traumatic event is that it does not engage the breadth of macro-level trauma at the sociopolitical level. For example, issues of race-related traumas that for many occur pervasively and progressively across the life course are not adequately addressed. Further, DSM-5 seems to omit the use of racial stressors across most psychiatric disorders and syndromes, a reflection of the dearth in psychological theory and in the treatment literature on the impact of racism on mental health (Carter & Forsyth, 2009). According the *DSM-5*'s criteria A, the continuous and compounding effects of racism in U.S. society do not qualify as a single and "unexpected" traumatic stressor. In contrast, the historical trauma narrative of discrimination, oppression, and racism and the resulting psychological, economic, social, and political impact constituted a complex trauma reaction (Carter & Forsyth, 2007; Lebron et al., 2015). Although the use of excessive force and other overt forms of racism certainly qualify as traumatic events, the underlying political ideologies and cultural values that drive this behavior and its omnipresence in the fabric of American culture is not addressed in *DSM-5* (Miller, 2009). This is despite data that suggest higher rates of trauma among minority groups including African Americans, Hispanics, Native Americans, Pacific Islanders, and Southeast Asians (Himle, Baser, Taylor, Campbell, & Jackson, 2009; Pole, Gone, Kulkarni, 2008). To address this important gap, researchers have suggested that a race-based traumatic stress category be added to the existing text as a form of complex PTSD (Carter, 2007; Miller, 2009).

GERALD: A CASE OF RACE-BASED TRAUMATIC STRESS

Gerald is a recent graduate with a master's in social work (MSW), and he has obtained a new position as a public child welfare worker in a small rural county. Gerald is originally from the southern part of the United States, but he grew up in a large urban city. After graduate school, Gerald decided to take a position in a small child welfare office located in an isolated rural area of his state. He has family in the area and was ready for a change after completing his internship in an inner-city placement. The population of the county is homogenous and is composed of mostly low-wealth white families living in isolation with very few resources. Nearly 30 percent of all families living in the county are in poverty. The child welfare office is one of the only social service agencies in the entire county covering a vast array of needs for children and their families. Despite the high rates of poverty, the department has only a small number of social workers to cover the myriad psychosocial needs of the county. Gerald is the only African American and the only male working in the office, but he felt welcomed by most of the social work and professional staff. He quickly realized this was going to be a big change from his previous job experiences.

Gerald was assigned to the investigation unit for child abuse and neglect. He had been an inner-city child welfare investigator with a bachelor's degree for four years before completing his MSW, and he felt ready for the challenge of this new office. Shortly after his start date, Gerald received an intake report from his supervisor from the elementary school principal who was concerned that an 8-year-old girl in the second grade was being neglected and possibly physically abused by her stepfather. The principal reported that the child looked malnour-ished, was in poor hygiene, and had some noticeable bruising on her face and arms. Feeling motivated, Gerald readily began preparation to do the initial visit at the elementary school.

When Gerald arrived at the school, he was greeted by Mrs. Phillips, the principal, who asked him to wait in conference room for over an hour before she would see him. When Mrs. Phillips returned, she commented that she had to call the child welfare office and verify that he was authorized to see the child. She then began to question Gerald's ability to adequately interview the student about "things of such a sensitive nature." Gerald quickly explained that he was an experienced child welfare investigator and had completed many hours of training and continuing education on forensic interviewing with abused and neglected children, not to mention that he had years of experience doing this work in another public child welfare office. Mrs. Phillips responded with, "yes, but you haven't worked here in our school; frankly, we don't have any teachers or students of color here." Gerald could sense that Mrs. Phillips was uncom-fortable with the situation and suggested that she walk him to the child's class-room and introduce him to the child. Mrs. Phillips asked if she could sit in on the interview, and Gerald reluctantly agreed. Upon meeting the child, Sarah, Gerald noticed that she was very shy and emotionally withdrawn. During the interview Mrs. Phillips kept assuring Sarah that Gerald was "not a scary man" and she had "nothing to worry about." Not surprisingly, Sarah did not disclose much information about her family situation; rather, she simply sat in the chair looking at the floor. When she did communicate, she always looked at Mrs. Phillips for confirmation before speaking.

Feeling that the interview was not very productive, Gerald decided to sched-ule a home visit with the family. He learned from Sarah that both her par-ents "stayed home all day." Gerald had the address of the family and called his supervisor to discuss conducting a home visit. His supervisor warned him that the home was in an isolated rural area at least 40 minutes away. She also warned Gerald that the community was known for both drug manufacturing and distribution. With his background in inner-city child welfare work, Gerald was no stranger to the drug culture and the correlation to incidents of child abuse and neglect. Gerald decided to see if he could locate the home to further inform his assessment at which point he could determine his comfort level with engaging the family. As he was driving, Gerald was fascinated by the lack of residential development in the rural area of the state. He counted only three houses for several miles down a long barely paved road that eventually became a dirt road. Gerald noticed that a large truck had been following him for several miles and continued to follow him up the driveway to the home. When Gerald stopped in the driveway, the truck pulled in behind him blocking his way out.

When he looked up, several men came out of the home, one with a firearm in his hand. All three men approached Gerald's car. Gerald felt uncomfortable and unsafe, but he cracked his window and stated that he was from the county child welfare office and had been working with a young girl named Sarah who lives at this address. The men looked at one another, the oldest of the group stated, "my daughter better not be talking to anyone like you." Gerald noticed one of the other men reaching in his pocket. Feeling threatened, Gerald rolled up his window and quickly drove away. For months after the incident, Gerald still replays this scenario in his head and feels very uneasy about conducting home visits in his new position. When he talked to his supervisor about the incident, she simply replied, "this is what child welfare work is like in this county, don't worry, people will get used to you at some point." Gerald begins to doubt his decision to do this work and is now reconsidering his effectiveness in the culture of this geographic environment.

DISCUSSION AND CRITICAL THINKING QUESTIONS

1. Critically analyze Gerald's experiences with racism and discrimination as he attempts to engage this family in social work practice. Describe how the homogeneity of the county, the rural culture of isolation, and the poverty of this family influences the perception of Gerald and his position of authority as a child welfare worker. (Social Work Competency 2: Engage Diversity and Difference in Practice—by applying and communicating understanding of diversity in shaping life experiences at all levels; Social Work Competency 6–7: Engage and Assess Individuals and Families—by applying critical thinking to collect, organize, and interpret client data.)

2. From an ethical perspective, how should Gerald negotiate his home visitation experience with his professional obligation to protect Sarah and other children in the county from parental abuse and neglect? Do you feel Gerald can effectively practice child welfare in this community? Why or why not? (Social Work Competency 1: Demonstrate Ethical and Professional Behavior—through the use of self-reflection and regulation.)

3. Describe the role of the supervisor in this situation. What is her responsibility in assisting Gerald as he adapts to his new role as a child welfare worker in this cultural environment? (Social Work Competency 1: Demonstrate Ethical and Professional Behavior—through the use of effective supervision and consultation; Social Work Competency 3: Advance Human Rights and Social, Economic, and Environmental Justice—by advocating for human rights at the individuals and systems levels.)

4. From a macro perspective, examine how the history of oppression, racism, and discrimination in the United States has influenced our collective

cultural belief system about race-related experiences. How does this influence the professional quality of life for all people of color in the human services workforce? (Social Work Competency 2: Engage Diversity and Difference in Practice—by applying and communicating understanding of diversity in shaping life experiences at all practice levels; Social Work Competency 3: Advance Human Rights and Social, Economic, and Environmental Justice—by advocating for human rights at the individual and systems levels; Social Work Competency 4: Engage in Practice-Informed Research and Research-Informed Practice.)

5. Critically examine the information in the chapter on the criteria A qualifiers for PTSD. Is Gerald's experience considered traumatic? Why or why not? Based on your examination, describe the limitations of the *DSM-5* diagnostic criteria for trauma as it applies to the experience of race-related traumatic stress. (Social Work Competency 2: Engage Diversity and Difference in Practice; Social Work Competency 4: Engage in Practice-Informed Research and Research-Informed Practice.)

KEY TERMS

anhedonia	ecological systems perspective
arousal	intrusion
avoidance	posttraumatic stress disorder (PTSD)
central nervous system (CNS)	race-based traumatic stress
cognitive appraisal	stress
dissociation	trauma-related disorders
depersonalization	traumatic stress

CHAPTER SUMMARY

This chapter provides a brief introduction to the complex behavioral phenomena of human stress reactions. The concept of stress is presented from various perspectives to provide a broad context for this dynamic construct. This includes a brief description of the neurobiology of stress. The ecological systems perspective is emphasized as a useful way to conceptualize the impact of stress on the "whole" person at the individual or micro level of practice or globally at the macro level. The conceptual difference between stress and traumatic stress is central to this book. This includes a summary of the diagnostic criteria and symptoms for presentation of PTSD. Recent changes to the diagnostic criteria for PTSD in the *DSM-5* are highlighted, including the limitations of these revisions with regard to race-related trauma experiences.

RECOMMENDED READINGS

American Psychiatric Association. (2013). *Diagnostic and statistical manual of mental disorders* (5th ed.). Washington, DC: Author.

Briere, J., & Scott, C. (2015). *Principles of trauma therapy: A guide to symptoms, evaluation, and treatment* (2nd ed.). Thousand Oaks, CA. Sage.

Figley, C. R., & Nash, W. P. (2007). *Combat stress injury: Theory, research, and management.* New York, NY: Taylor & Francis.

Friedman, M. J., Keane, T., & Resick, P. A. (2007). *Handbook of PTSD: Science and practice.* New York, NY: Guilford Press.

Rothschild, B. (2000). *The body remembers: The psychophysiology of trauma and trauma treatment.* New York, NY: Norton.

Rubin, A., Weiss, E. L., & Coll, J. E. (2013). *Handbook of military social work.* Hoboken, NJ: Wiley.

van der Kolk, B. A., McFarlane, A. C., & Weisaeth, L. (1996). *Traumatic stress: The effects of overwhelming experience on the mind, body, and society.* New York, NY: Guilford Press.

SUGGESTED INTERNET RESOURCES

Anxiety and Depression Association of America: http://www.adaa.org
The mission of ADAA is to promote the prevention, treatment, and cure of anxiety and mood disorders, OCD, and PTSD through education, practice, and research. The mission focuses on improving quality of life for children and adults affected with these disorders. The site features include educational resources (including podcasts and webcasts) for consumers and their families, treatment resources, and support information. The site includes excellent professional literature for consumers on understanding the facts about various forms of mental illness, including trauma-related disorders. For professionals, the site includes information on the empirically supported treatments and best practices across several professional disciplines.

McSilver Institute for Poverty Policy and Research: www.mcsilver.nyu.edu
Housed in the New York University Silver School of Social Work, the institute focuses on issues related to the "interrelatedness of race and poverty and is dedicated to dismantling structural racism and other forms of systemic oppression." The institute's research is guided by a collaborative interprofessional model with a systems framework to assess the root of macro-level social problems such as poverty and racism.

The site offers many useful features, educational opportunities, and research resources at no cost to the public. Under the "Research and Centers" tab, you can find brief descriptions of funded research studies in several areas including poverty, behavioral health, and public health. The "Policy and Publications" tab stores annual reports, legislative testimonies, research briefs, and embedded videos on topics such as racism and gender oppression in the workplace. Under the "News and Events" tab, a link to the report titled "Facts Matter! Black Lives Matter! The Trauma of Racism" is available at no cost.

National Center for PTSD: www.ptsd.va.gov

Managed by the U.S. government under the Department of Veterans Affairs, the site is largely dedicated to the treatment of veterans and military families, with an obvious emphasis on the treatment of combat-related trauma and PTSD. However, the trauma resources provided by this site are applicable to anyone either suffering from or treating the effects of trauma-related disorders. Features of the site include professional resources on the assessment, treatment, and research of trauma-related disorders, including a wealth of online continuing education and training at no cost. Two excellent resources, the "Clinician's Trauma Update" and the "PTSD Research Quarterly", can be accessed at no cost.

Sidran Institute: http://www.sidran.org/

This institute for traumatic stress education and advocacy is devoted to helping people who have experienced traumatic life events and to promote greater understanding of early recognition and treatment of trauma-related stress in children; understanding of trauma and its long-term effect on adults; strategies leading to the greatest success in self-help recovery for trauma survivors; clinical methods and practices leading to the greatest success in aiding trauma victims; and development of public policy initiatives responsive to the needs of adult and child survivors of traumatic events. Features of this site include links to training opportunities in the area of traumatology; a comprehensive Internet resource directory with links for trauma professionals, trauma survivors of all types, and loved ones; a help desk with contact information for those who are in crisis and searching for services; and a bookstore with audiovisual resources, books on trauma-related material, and assessment tools for purchase at reasonable cost.

3

CHRONIC EMPATHY AND TRAUMA IN HUMAN SERVICE WORK

Implications for Social Service Professionals

> *The most beautiful people we have known are those who have known defeat, known suffering, known struggle, known loss, and have found their way out of the depths. These persons have an appreciation, a sensitivity, and an understanding of life that fills them with compassion, gentleness, and a deep loving concern.*
>
> —ELISABETH KÜBLER-ROSS, 1975

CHAPTER GOALS AND OBJECTIVES

---

1. Discuss the conceptualization of human empathy from a broad-based biopsychosocial context.
2. Discuss the chronic use of empathy as a vulnerability factor to the vicarious effects of direct practice in social work and other human service professions.
3. Provide an in-depth and critical discussion of the most commonly cited terms and constructs describing the negative psychological and sometimes consequential impact of engaging clients and their emotionally challenging material in direct practice.
4. Illustrate one provider's experience of the indirect effects of trauma and compassion fatigue while in practice with a survivor of physical assault through a case study analysis and critical thinking questions.

Chapter 2 briefly introduced the concepts of stress and trauma, essential terms that help to lay the foundation for this book. Empathy, the second core concept, and in many ways the concept at the "heart and soul" of the book, is explored in this chapter. The appropriate self-regulation of empathy is essential to the practice skill set for any professional working with vulnerable or at-risk populations. Beyond this, the use of empathy serves as the primary conduit for engaging clients who are experiencing any form of emotional distress. Empathy is a finite psychological resource that requires self-regulation to prevent service providers from feeling overwhelmed or burdened by the emotional experiences of their clients. Although a great source of professional strength, empathy also presents opportunities for provider vulnerability due to the emotional effects of engaging clients in direct practice. This chapter discusses the concept of empathy both as an innate psychophysiological behavior and as an invaluable practice skill for developing efficacious communication pathways with clients. Without regulation, empathy may inhibit the practitioner–client relationship, leaving social workers vulnerable to the negative and sometimes consequential effects of vicarious traumatization, secondary traumatic stress, and compassion fatigue.

PART 1: UNDERSTANDING THE USE OF EMPATHY IN HUMAN SERVICE WORK

Similar to the inexact conceptualizations of stress discussed in chapter 2, empathy has been described in a variety of ways and is subject to the perspective and professional training of the individual. Descriptive language on the use of empathy in clinical practice settings is illustrated in the early literature referencing terms such as *empathic identification* and *empathic attunement* (Newell, Nelson-Gardell, & MacNeil, 2015). However, collectively, the literature reveals very little consistency regarding the operational definition of this construct; rather, the term *empathy* is often used interchangeably with other similarly ill-defined terms such as "warmth," and "genuineness" and "compassion." To further illustrate this point, compare this concept to the material on posttraumatic stress disorder (PTSD) in chapter 2, an example of a well-researched and articulately defined condition with an established standard for the presentation and measurement of diagnostic signs and symptoms.

The Social Work Dictionary defines empathy as "the act of perceiving, understanding, experiencing, and responding to the emotional state and ideas of another person" (Barker, 2014, p. 139). The synthesis of the various definitions of empathy in the literature describes a process of both intellectually (referring to the use of empathy as a practice skill or ability) and emotionally identifying with a client's current state of being, with the goal of eliciting an efficacious response within the feedback loop. In many settings (and in the informal dialogue of the social work profession), it is vaguely understood simply as "starting where the client is." The lack of clarity regarding the definition and meaning of empathy is remarkable given the frequent use of the term in the professional discourse of social work, counseling, and other human service professions (Thomas, 2013). In fact, the phrase "use of *empathy*, reflection, and other interpersonal skills" is cited in the 2015 version of the Council on Social

Work Education's (CSWE) "Educational Policy and Accreditation Standards" (EPAS) under Competency 6: Engage with Individuals, Families, Groups, Organizations, and Communities (CSWE, 2015, pp. 8–9).

THE PSYCHOPHYSIOLOGY OF EMPATHY

Empathy is common to the dialogue of the social work profession, but it also has been the subject of research in the biological and psychological sciences. Biologically, empathy has been described as an innate ability to relate and respond to the physical or emotional state of another person, a process that is essential to the survival of human beings (Rothschild & Rand, 2006). For example, most new parents can identify with the innate ability of parents to interpret their infant's "degrees of crying and wanting" despite the infant's inability to fully communicate them. Gender studies have suggested that females (compared to males) have an even greater biological predisposition for empathy to facilitate communication and attachment with infant children (Schulte-Ruther, Markowitsch, Shah, Fink, & Piefke, 2008). Using this example, empathy can be viewed as a biological predisposition to interpret and respond to the behavior of others, which can be used to alert one to a potentially dangerous situation as part of the human body's innate biological defense system (Rothschild & Rand, 2006).

Going beyond the biology of the human body and thinking in terms of human relationships, empathy may be described as both conscious and unconscious cognitive processes involving contemplative thinking while simultaneously sharing and communicating one's feelings and emotions (Smith, 2006). Empathy has been shown to elicit responses referred to as "somatic empathy," such as responding to a friendly smile and "hello" with a reciprocating smile or nod of the head (Rothschild & Rand, 2006). For those who are in close relationships with a significant other, somatic empathy can simply be a nonverbal response to a look or gesture from across the room. When working with clients, empathy is often used to facilitate the identification of outward or behavioral signs of chronic stress or crisis. Each of these examples describes the use of empathy as a component of the complex interchanges that occur in human behavior and as one of the many ways people verbally and nonverbally communicate their emotions, thoughts, feelings, and behaviors to one another.

Recent neurobiological research suggests that empathy is more than a combination of cognitive and emotional responses; it is the result of specific pathways created through neurotransmitters called "mirror neurons." Mirror neurons fire based on cues from the social environment, such as hearing people speaking, posturing, gesturing, and using facial expressions (Buccino & Amore, 2008; Gerdes & Segal, 2011). It is through this neurobiological process that people have the ability to act and respond in similar ways, or to mirror the behaviors of others. A simple way to illustrate this process is to visualize a profoundly sad and a funny moment from a favorite television show or movie and observe your response in mirroring the emotions depicted on the screen. The term *empathy* is used in this book to broadly describe the collective affective, emotional, cognitive, and somatic responses of practitioners to clients and their situations in an effort to appropriately engage the client in a helping relationship (Decety & Jackson, 2004).

THE VALUE AND IMPORTANCE OF REGULATED EMPATHY IN PRACTICE

For practitioners, empathy acts mutually as both conduit and catalyst to the formation of a helpful, healing, and meaningful human relationship. The ability of a practitioner to use empathy correctly and appropriately is vital to the provision of social services, particularly for those who are suffering from emotional trauma. Empathy can serve as a dynamic and transactional pathway for practitioners (and at first strangers) to bond with clients and to create a sense of emotional security during times of intense personal, familial, and communal crises (Gerdes et al., 2011). The proper use of empathy allows practitioners to understand, to the best of their ability, how a client is feeling at any given period of time in the helping process. Empathy is not sympathy, which is generally understood as feeling sorry for someone who has suffered in some way, although the two qualities do often intersect with one another in the defining literature (Thomas, 2013).

EMPATHY AS A COMPONENT OF HUMAN SERVICE WORK

One of my oldest and closest friends from college graduated with a degree in finance and subsequently went into the banking profession as I entered into the professional world of social work. For the better part of 20 years, my friend has been either in a small office or in a cubicle worrying only about the stock market and its impact on the global banking system. Whenever we discuss our work, he does not describe any form of human pain or suffering; rather, his occupational stress comes solely from "the market," essentially a ticker tape on his computer screen. As he says, "that is pretty much it." At some point during one of our conversations, I realized that at work my friend never worried about anyone but himself, an experience I knew nothing about in the practice of social work. However, when he gets home to his family at night, he has a nearly untapped reserve of empathy to dedicate to his wife, two children, and other family members. Needless to say, this was an interesting revelation for my work.

Through the process of conducting nearly 15 years of research, training, and education in this area, I have found one common denominator with regard to stress and stress reactions in human service work: the inherent demand for the chronic use of empathy as an essential practice skill and behavior (Newell et al., 2015). Metaphorically, I then began to think about empathy as a finite (rather than infinite) psychological resource. When conducting trainings on empathy and professional resilience, I often refer to one's psychological resources for the use of empathy as a reservoir, a natural energy source that can be used chronically but is subject to depletion if not properly cared for and replenished.

Unlike my friend in the banking industry, I allocate my empathy resources to myriad emotionally challenging situations with clients and their families, as part of daily practice. As a trauma professional dealing with clients in the aftermath of crisis, it seemed the conduit from which my empathy was being drawn was perhaps even larger than in other human service professions, and certainly larger than in professions where the use of empathy is nonessential. This led me to think more critically and empirically about the use of empathy in clinical practice and the importance of self-care in keeping my psychological resources "fully charged and flowing." This practice is beneficial not only for the clients served but for all of the functional components of the psychological ecosystem. Therefore, as we start to examine the relationship between clients and their stressors, and the use of empathy to foster and cultivate the dynamic exchange of information between client and practitioner, having a broad-based understanding of the meaning and uses of empathy is essential.

In sum, the appropriate use of empathy is the result of the collective cognitive, emotional, and somatic reactions to people, a biological phenomenon that when cultivated as a clinical skill is essential to the practitioner in meeting the needs of clients and their families (Gerdes et al., 2011). Work with those who are vulnerable and suffering, particularly those suffering from any form of psychological trauma, inherently requires service providers to be actively ready to use their own psychological resources in the form of empathy and compassion on a daily basis. However, unlike other professional disciplines, human service professionals are required to access and use their empathy resources and skills as an essential function of the work—a requirement that simply does not exist, at least to this degree, in non-human-service professions. Regardless of how the term is conceptualized or defined, empathy ultimately allows the practitioner to unlock other professional skills, such as the ability to be compassionate, genuine, nurturing, and caring toward others. Simply stated, empathy is an essential and invaluable component of the skill set of any human service professional and is sometimes part of the reason for selecting the pursuit of a career in social work or other human service profession.

MELANIE: A CASE STUDY ON PHYSICAL ASSAULT

Prior to her trauma experience, Melanie was a young, well-educated, vibrant professional in the community. Melanie enjoyed a successful career and often found herself going to the local shopping mall for what she called "retail therapy." One night as she was leaving her favorite department store, Melanie was physically assaulted in the parking lot. Fortunately, she was not sexually assaulted during the attack. The physical injuries that resulted from the attack were minimal and healed quickly; however, her emotional injuries were more longlasting and profoundly more difficult to treat.

As a result of this incident, Melanie's entire belief system about herself and the world was significantly altered and literally changed overnight. Prior to the traumatic incident, Melanie described herself as a woman of "confidence and control." After the incident, Melanie became so fearful and anxious that she developed a profound mistrust of people and of her physical safety in the world. Melanie began to see everyone as a perpetrator and every physical surrounding as a potential space for another assault. The intense fear generated in Melanie's psyche as a result of the physical assault was dominating her thinking, which was controlling her behaviors and her life. Because of her preexisting personality traits (confidence, self-control, high performer), Melanie also experienced intense feelings of self-blame, guilt, and shame surrounding the physical assault.

Melanie's persistent fear and marked disturbance in her feelings of emotional safety with others and the physical safety of the world led to resistance to any form of intimacy or emotional attachment, and eventually to personal isolation as a fear-driven mode of self-protection. Socializing and dating had once been a pleasurable activity for Melanie, one that often led her to the shopping center she enjoyed so much, but now she was afraid to establish any physical or emotional ties with a partner or a friend. She also experienced intense feelings of fear and panic when confronted with any situation involving her leaving from a crowded "place of safety" to a parking lot. This made even the most general daily routines, such as getting from her car in the parking garage to the safety of her office, profoundly difficult tasks. When Melanie finally presented for treatment, she was emotionally exhausted, avoidant of routine tasks such as going to the supermarket, having difficulty enjoying any part of her daily life, and nearly void of her ability to express even small feelings of positive affect and emotion. This case study illustrates how quickly a traumatic event can alter a survivor's orientation to the world and how pervasive the symptoms of trauma can be. Melanie is also a case study in the presentation of the significant changes in cognition and mood (criteria D; see table 2.1) that can result from the experience of a traumatic event.

This cluster of symptoms includes the presentation of dissociative amnesia, which is the inability to recall important aspects of the trauma experience. Other dissociative symptoms associated with PTSD (but not included in this cluster of symptoms) are depersonalization and derealization. Depersonalization is characterized by marked dissociation such that the trauma survivor feels as if she is outside of her current state of being. This symptom is more commonly described as an "out of body" experience. Derealization is associated with feeling that the world and its surroundings (space and time) are blurred, foggy, or even dreamlike rather than real. Symptoms of dissociation can include subconscious avoidance, which is essentially a method of coping and self-preservation by the mind to dissociate the trauma survivor from the negative emotional feelings resulting from the traumatic experience (Briere & Scott, 2015; Dorahy & van der Hart, 2015).

The final criteria or cluster of symptoms (E), including the symptoms of reactivity and arousal associated with the trauma experience. Symptoms of arousal include insomnia, hypervigilance, exaggerated startle response, impairment in concentration and memory, and chronic irritability (Krakow et al., 2004; Taft, Creech, & Kachadourian, 2012). The symptoms of irritability may be expressed as difficulty controlling impulsivity responses such as verbal or physical aggression toward others with little or no provocation, reckless behaviors, or behaviors of self-destruction (American Psychiatric Association, 2013). Symptoms should be present for a minimum of one month and have marked impairment in psychosocial functioning (Rodriquez, Holowka, & Marx, 2012).

DISCUSSION AND CRITICAL THINKING QUESTIONS

1. Using the simple model for stress and cognitive appraisal presented in figure 2.1, describe Melanie's psychological response to the physical assault in terms of her coping ability, resources, and adaptation to the physical and psychological stress of the assault. (Social Work Competency 7: Assess Individuals—through applied knowledge of human behavior and the social environment, person-in-environment, and other multidisciplinary theoretical frameworks.)

2. Using an ecological systems perspective for human behavior (see figure 2.2), describe how the incident of physical assault has systemically affected Melanie's well-being across multiple domains of her life. In your assessment, include how the trauma of the assault has affected Melanie's cultural, moral, and spiritual belief systems. (Social Work Competency 7: Assess Individuals—through applied knowledge of human behavior and the social environment, person-in-environment, and other multidisciplinary theoretical frameworks.)

3. Complete a brief trauma assessment of Melanie's behavior using the information provided on posttraumatic stress disorder in table 2.1. Describe Melanie's reaction to her physical assault as it relates to the presentation of PTSD signs and symptoms in the forms of intrusion, avoidance, negative alterations in cognitions and mood, and hyperarousal. (Social Work Competency 7: Assess Individuals—by applying critical thinking to collect, organize, and interpret client data.)

4. Conduct a brief Internet search of the trauma service agencies available in your community. Develop a list of trauma resources and include a brief description of trauma populations served by each agency on the list. Share this information with your instructor and classmates. (Social Work Competency 4: Engage in Practice-Informed Research and Research-Informed Practice.)

5. Briefly describe and assess how the presentation of Melanie's trauma symptoms differ from the case of Jonathan presented in chapter 2. Compare and contrast the two cases. (Social Work Competency 7: Assess Individuals—by collecting and analyzing data and through applied critical thinking to interpret information from clients and their constituencies.)

PART 2: EMPATHY AND THE PRACTITIONER RESPONSE TO CLIENT EMOTION AND TRAUMA

As stated in the opening of this chapter, the use of empathy as a function of direct practice is at the heart of this book, but the true purpose of this book is to support the theory that the use of empathy is both a valuable practice skill for engaging clients in the helping process as well as a significant vulnerability factor for practitioners themselves. Most social workers and human service professionals would agree that to effectively intervene with vulnerable clients, one must develop a strong working relationship. This involves knowing about the client's or the family's past and present life events and all of the corresponding (and often difficult) circumstances (Figley, 2002c; Pearlman & Saakvitne, 1995; Stamm, 1999). To best serve the needs of clients and their families, practitioners inevitably absorb some degree of the pain associated with the individual's, family's, or group's suffering (Morresette, 2004; Rothschild & Rand, 2006). Ideally, with the appropriate use of the collective forms of human empathy (described in part 1 of this chapter), a healthy and functional conduit for the flow and exchange of emotional energy and information lays the groundwork for efficacious practice. However, by virtue of this same metaphorical process, a functional pipeline also exists for the inappropriate or unregulated use of empathy, which may have negative implications for both clients and providers.

Research over the past 25 years has clearly established that chronic, day-to-day exposure to clients and the distress they experience has the potential to be emotionally taxing on helping professionals, particularly professionals working with trauma populations (Figley, 2002a; Pearlman & Saakvitne, 1995; Stamm, 1999). However, the synthesis of this research reveals a wide range of terminologies used to describe the maladaptive effects of providing services to at-risk client groups. The various terms and concepts in the literature range from early Freudian references to processes of countertransference to more contemporary terms such as compassion fatigue (Newell et al., 2015).

Much like the earlier discussion of the concept of empathy, multiple terminologies and a lack of consensus in the literature between these various terms has complicated the practice community's general understanding of these behavioral phenomena in direct practice. This chapter both critically and comparatively discusses the most commonly cited terminologies, describing the negative and sometimes consequential implications of providing direct (or micro-level) services to clients. Figure 3.1 provides a useful timeline illustrating the historical context of terms and constructs related to the deleterious effects of providing direct practice to vulnerable or at-risk populations.

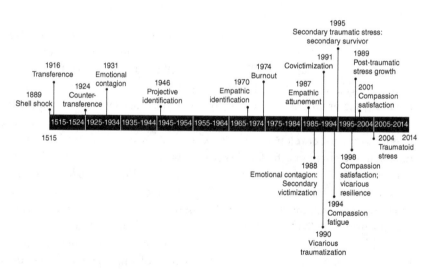

FIGURE 3.1 Terminology timeline
Source: Newell, J. M., Gardell, D. N., & MacNeil, G. (2016). Clinician response to client traumas: A chronological review of constructs and terminology. *Journal of Trauma, Violence, & Abuse,* 17(3), 306–313. doi:10.1177/1524838015584365.

PSYCHOANALYTIC BEGINNINGS: COUNTERTRANSFERENCE AND PROJECTIVE IDENTIFICATION

Research formally investigating the effects of direct practice on service providers is a comparatively recent area of empirical study, but the process by which the emotions of a client can be absorbed or "transferred" to the therapist was introduced in the early 1900s during the advent of Freudian theory and the corresponding practice of psychoanalysis (Clarkson & Nuttall, 2000; Freud, 1964; Hayes, Gelso, & Hummel, 2011; Orr, 1998). The transference process represents the client's unconscious projection of thoughts, feelings, and emotions based on past experiences onto the therapist or other individuals involved with the client, such as spouses, friends, or other people of significance (Freud, 1964; Jones, 2004). It was later observed that it would be nearly impossible to completely block all conscious and unconscious thoughts and feelings about the patient. This led to a change in both perspective and terminology, which Freud described as being a complementary pathway between the analyst and the client, called "transference neurosis" (Hayes et al., 2011). This process, by which client information and material presented to the analyst during psychoanalysis activates the analyst's own unconscious and unresolved childhood conflict, was referred to as "countertransference neurosis," and in later works simply as countertransference (Freud, 1964; Hacker, 1957). As it was first described by Freud, the phenomenon of transference neurosis from the client to the analyst was generally regarded as a positive and informative component of psychoanalysis (Rosenburg & Hayes, 2002; Jones, 2004). Classically, psychoanalysis depicts the mind of the analyst as a "blank slate," allowing the patient to both consciously and unconsciously project neurotic feelings onto the analyst for interpretation. Ideally, the transference interaction is uncomplicated by the analyst's own interpersonal conflicts and neuroses, a position that now generally is considered an impossibility (Appignanesi & Zarate, 1979; Freud, 1964; Rosenburg & Hayes, 2002).

DIFFERENT FORMS OF COUNTERTRANSFERENCE

The therapeutic process of countertransference has been described in two different ways: first, as the collective unconscious response a therapist has to his or her client, the client's clinical material, transference, and reenactments based on the therapists past life events; and second, as the therapist's conscious and unconscious defenses against the presentation of information and material by the client, including reactions such as avoidance, detachment, and overidentification with the client and his or her situation (Pearlman & Saakvitne, 1995; Wilson & Lindy, 1994). This distinction between the two types of countertransference reactions has been referred to as Type I and Type II countertransference (Wilson & Lindy, 1994). The contemporary view of countertransference is typically not viewed as a positive or helpful part of the psychoanalytic process; rather, it is potentially harmful or even destructive to the analyst's ability to objectively analyze and interpret the client's information and situation (Clarkson & Nuttall, 2000). Freud's identification of the counter-transference relationship between client and therapist later influenced similar developments in psychoanalytic theory and process in concepts such as projec-tive identification. Projective identification (Klein, 1946) is said to occur when a therapist experiences emotions or feelings similar to those of the client due to the client's projection of these feelings onto the therapist. The occurrence of projection identification has been described as an antecedent behavior to the countertransference relationship (Greatrex, 2002; Rothschild, 2006).

A PARADIGM SHIFT FROM COUNTERTRANSFERENCE

The use of the Freudian references and terminologies related to countertrans-ference remained consistent in the practice literature until the late 1970s and early 1980s (see figure 3.1). It was during this time that research on the orga-nizational behaviors associated with the phenomena of professional burnout, a construct discussed in detail in chapter 4, introduced a new and focused area of empirical inquiry (Maslach, 2003a). It was not until the early 1990s that an important shift in thought and in the research literature occurred with regard to the empathetic responses direct practitioners have to clients and their physical and emotional circumstances (Brend, 2014). This paradigm shift, deeply rooted in the historical context of countertransference, suggested that direct practice with individuals and their emotional traumas could have a negative impact on the behavior of the practitioner beyond the macro-oriented conceptualization of professional burnout.

This change in thought had a significant effect on the way the professional community conceptualized the impact of direct practice on practitioners, and it ushered in a new era of research based on the theory that there is great poten-tial for maladaptive emotional reactions (and associated behaviors) to occur in helping professionals due to chronic exposure. It was posited that these practi-tioners' responses to clients and their emotional material and information were not countertransference reactions , nor were they the result of professional burnout (Newell et al., 2015). Practitioners in direct practice with trauma pop-ulations, such as survivors of child physical and sexual abuse, rape, natural disaster, or combat, were proposed to be at the greatest risk in terms of their vulnerability to these conditions. Refer to the material in part 2 of chapter 2 for a detailed explanation of stress, trauma, and posttraumatic stress. A review of the

TABLE 3.1 Search Terminologies Cited for Vicarious Trauma, Secondary Trauma, and Compassion Fatigue

Compassion Fatigue	Empathic Identification	"Traumalike" Experience
compassion stress injury	empathic attunement	traumatoid stress
countertransference	projective identification	traumatization "by concern"
covictimization	secondary survivor	vicarious traumatization
emotional contagion	secondary traumatic stress	
empathic engagement	secondary victimization	

literature in this area reveals three key terms used to describe the negative and potentially "contaminating" psychological reactions direct practitioners may experience when working with clients and their trauma-related material: vicarious traumatization, secondary traumatic stress, and compassion fatigue. Other terms having similar connotations, such as covictimization, secondary survivor, emotional contagion, secondary victimization, and traumatoid stress, were also cited in the literature less frequently. Table 3.1 presents a summary of various terms and constructs cited in the literature for describing these phenomena in direct practice.

VICARIOUS TRAUMATIZATION

The term *vicarious traumatization* (VT) was first introduced into the literature in the early 1990s, largely influenced by the work of Laurie Anne Pearlman with survivors of sexual abuse and incest. Pearlman defined vicarious trauma as "the transformation in the inner experience of the therapist that comes about as a result of empathic engagement with client's trauma material" (Pearlman & Saakvitne, 1995, p. 31). Providers could experience emotions and trauma-related behaviors similar to those of their clients indirectly or "vicariously" in the process of treatment as a result of chronic empathic engagement (McCann & Pearlman, 1990; Pearlman & MacIan, 1995; Pearlman & Saakvitne, 1995).

Grounded in the theory of constructivist self-development, vicarious trauma represented the potential cognitive changes in the therapist's collective frame of reference both intrinsically and extrinsically—such as the therapist's sense of self; worldviews regarding issues such as safety, intimacy and trust; and spirituality—as a result of chronic exposure to and the treatment of trauma-related disorders (McCann, Sakheim, & Abrahamson, 1988; McCann & Pearlman, 1990; Pearlman, 1998; Pearlman & Saakvitne 1995). Other psychological resources vulnerable to disruption by work with trauma victims include disruption in ego resources and cognitive schemata. *Ego resources* refer to an individual's ability to manage both one's own intrinsic psychological needs and the extrinsic interpersonal needs of others (Young, Klosco, & Weishaar, 2003). *Cognitive schema* refers to practitioners' interpersonal feelings about the self, including their general orientation to the world around them (Young, Klosko, & Weishaar, 2003). Over time, the cumulative effects of VT may result in an erosion of the practitioner's value and spirit to do the work or spiritual frame of reference, a phenomenon described in the literature as moral or spiritual injury (Cunningham, 2003; Kopacz, Simons, & Chitaphong, 2015). If left untreated or unacknowledged, it has been suggested that vicarious traumatization could result in a complete disruption in the therapist's ability to provide care for both him- or herself and the client, essentially depleting psychological resources of the professional (Pearlman & Saakvitne 1995; Stamm, 1999).

SECONDARY TRAUMATIC STRESS

Secondary traumatic stress was first cited in the literature in the mid-1990s and was largely influenced by the work of Charles Figley, who grounded this concept in his early works examining the psychiatric symptoms associated with PTSD (Figley, 1995). References to terms such as *secondary victimization, compassion stress injury, catastrophic stress reaction,* and *traumatization by concern* (see table 3.1) further illustrated the notion that close interpersonal relationships with individuals suffering from trauma could have both a negative and an infectious impact on the service provider (Brend, 2014; Figley, 1995). Figley later defined secondary traumatic stress (STS) as the "natural and consequential behaviors and emotions resulting from knowing about a traumatizing event experienced by a significant other (or client) and the stress resulting from helping or wanting to help a traumatized or suffering person" (Figley, 1995, p. 7).

Similar to the work of McCann and Pearlman (1990) and Saakvitne and Pearlman (1996) and their conceptualization of vicarious traumatization, Figley suggested that secondary traumatic stress reactions also may result from engaging in an empathic relationship with a client (or other close associate) suffering from a traumatic experience and bearing witness to the intense or horrific experiences of that particular person's trauma (Figley, 1995). However, rather than focusing on the cognitive shifts in thinking that could potentially occur when treating trauma disorders, Figley's early conceptualization of secondary traumatic stress suggested that the clinician could mirror the symptoms of a primary trauma survivor, albeit to a lesser degree (Figley, 1995). This approach to trauma suggested that the manifestation of a secondary traumatic stress reaction could potentially include a full range of PTSD symptoms (see chapter 2, part 2), including intrusive thoughts, traumatic memories, nightmares associated with client traumas, insomnia, chronic irritability or angry outbursts, fatigue, difficulty concentrating, avoidance of clients and client situations, and hypervigilance toward trigger stimuli as a reminder of clients and their trauma material (American Psychiatric Association, 2013; Figley, 1995).

The symptoms associated with exposure to a traumatic event include intrusive memories and reexperiencing the traumatic event, avoidance of trigger stimuli associated with the traumatic event, and increased arousal upon exposure to reexperiencing symptoms or trigger stimuli (American Psychiatric Association, 2013). In addition to direct exposure to a traumatic event or events, the DSM-5 stipulates that the diagnostic criteria for PTSD also indicates that trauma reactions can occur based on "experiencing repeated or extreme exposure to aversive details of the traumatic event(s)" (p. 271). In other words, these parts of the diagnostic criteria suggest that traumatic reactions may occur as a result of hearing or experiencing trauma indirectly through the suffering of someone else, as in the case of social service professionals or family members who are responsible for providing care to the individual who is suffering. However, it was not until recently that the indirect form of posttraumatic stress was identified as a separate issue of concern.

ERIN: A CASE STUDY ON THE EFFECTS OF PHYSICAL AND SEXUAL ASSAULT COUNSELING

Erin practices social work at a nonprofit agency providing services to female victims of domestic violence and sexual assault. The agency is located centrally to the college campus where she completed her social work program and caters to many young college women her age. As the agency is nonprofit and has few staff members, Erin is very busy and has the opportunity to work in several different areas including intake, victim counseling and advocacy, support group facilitation, and community/campus awareness.

Erin's supervisor, who is a seasoned social worker, received a phone call from Erin requesting to speak with the supervisor about Erin's new job position during the lunch break. This seemed odd to the supervisor because Erin had been consistently excited about working with this population and had been very positive about her experiences. Erin reported that she is having some "strange thoughts and feelings" about one of her clients. Erin explains that last week she saw a client who was physically assaulted at a local shopping mall, a place Erin frequently visits herself. Erin openly admits that she was shocked during the intake interview and found herself preoccupied with thoughts of her own safety because she goes in and out of the shopping mall at least three times a week. As Erin was discussing the situation, she became tearful, stating "I just can't get that girl out of my head, I mean, she was my age and she even looked like me."

Erin reports that she has had nightmares about the client's assault and even intrusive thoughts about the incident during her waking hours. She also reports that she refuses to go to the shopping mall alone now because she is fearful this could happen to her. She also becomes worried and anxious when she and her friends visit the shopping mall; she is currently avoiding this place at all cost. Erin admits this is distressing because the shopping mall was once a very positive and enjoyable place for her.

Erin hesitantly discloses to the supervisor that she has avoided talking with anyone else at the agency about this because she does not want to appear incapable or inefficient. She also doesn't want to jeopardize her new position in any way. At the end of the meeting, Erin very hesitantly and tearfully discloses that she was date raped in high school and fears this may be part of the reason she is having this reaction. She states this was the reason she felt so strongly about working with this population to begin with, but now she is beginning to doubt herself and her capability to do this work.

DISCUSSION AND CRITICAL THINKING QUESTIONS

1. Take a moment to critically reflect on Erin's psychological reactions to the physical assault and victimization of her client. Based on your readings, which of the concepts discussed in this chapter most relate to Erin's behavioral response to her client's situation? Does one conceptualization seem more appropriately applied to this case study? (Social Work Competency 1: Demonstrate Ethical and Professional Behavior—through the practice of self-reflection and regulation; Competency 9: Evaluate Practice with Individuals and Families.)

2. Compare and contrast the similarities in behavior between this case study and the earlier case study of Melanie, who is the primary victim of this assault (Social Work Competency 9: Evaluate Practice with Individuals and Families.)

3. Based on your critical analysis of this case study and your review of the professional literature in this area, describe your perceptions of this case as they relate to practice with victims of physical and sexual assault. (Social Work Competency 1: Demonstrate Ethical and Professional Behavior—through the practice of self-reflection and regulation; Competency 4: Engage in Practice-Informed Research and Research-Informed Practice.)

4. Based on your critical analyses from questions 1 and 2, was Erin's reaction to her client reasonable? Why or why not? Describe the important aspects of your analysis. (Social Work Competency 1: Demonstrate Ethical and Professional Behavior—through the practice of self-reflection and

regulation; Competency 4: Engage in Practice-Informed Research and Research-Informed Practice.)

5. Based on your understanding of the NASW Code of Ethics and the core values of the social work profession, critically assess the potential impact of Erin's past history with sexual trauma on her work with survivors of physical and sexual assault. Describe any potential ethical dilemmas that may occur in this case. (Social Work Competency 1: Demonstrate Ethical and Professional Behavior—through the application of the NASW Code of Ethics.)

6. Evaluate Erin's decision to openly and directly disclose her feelings about the client to her agency supervisor. What are the possible implications of this decision? (Social Work Competency 1: Demonstrate Ethical and Professional Behavior—through use of professional supervision and consultation.)

COMPASSION FATIGUE

Perhaps the most contemporary and commonly used term regarding clinicians' psychological reactions to their clients is compassion fatigue (CF), a concept based on the earlier proposed concepts of vicarious trauma and secondary traumatic stress. Compassion fatigue has been cited in the literature and frequently used interchangeably with both VT and STS, although it has been suggested that secondary or vicarious reactions to clients and their traumas and the manifestation of compassion fatigue are two independently occurring phenomena (Adams, Boscarino & Figley, 2006; Newell & MacNeil, 2010). The term *compassion fatigue* was first described by Figley (1995) as synonymous with secondary traumatic stress but was less stigmatizing than the trauma-focused concept of STS. Compassion fatigue has been both conceptualized and measured as a component of overall professional quality of life and as a syndrome consisting of a combination of the symptoms of secondary traumatic stress and professional burnout (Figley, 1995; Stamm, 1999, 2010).

Compassion fatigue has been cited in the literature as describing a more general and perhaps user-friendly concept that describes the overall experience of emotional and psychological fatigue human service providers experience due to the chronic use of empathy when treating individuals who are suffering in some way (Figley, 1995; Stamm, 2005). The concept of compassion fatigue suggests that providers of trauma-related services may experience a significant level of stress associated with the trauma work, but may or may not become "traumatized" by the work as is implied by secondary and vicarious trauma.

KEY TERMS

cognitive schemata   mirror imaging
compassion fatigue   projective identification
constructivist self-development theory   secondary traumatic stress
countertransference   somatic empathy
ego resources   vicarious trauma
empathy

Also, unlike the concepts of secondary and vicarious trauma, the potential triggers for compassion fatigue are not solely reliant on the primary trauma of the client but rather on the combination of psychological stressors that present themselves in daily practice in human service organizations and with those who are vulnerable or suffering.

CHAPTER SUMMARY

This chapter introduces the second core concept in this book, the use of empathy. Empathy is conceptualized from a broad-based psychophysiological context as the collective cognitive, emotional, and somatic reactions to people and their emotions. Empathy is discussed as an essential practice skill to anyone serving clients in the various human service professions. Part 2 stresses the importance of appropriately regulating the use of empathy in human service work, particularly in work with clients who have trauma-related material or who have been diagnosed with trauma-related disorders.

The personal and professional impact of daily practice in the fields of human services is of central importance to both the content and application of the materials and resources presented in this book. Guided by a terminology timeline (see figure 3.1), the literature reveals various terms and constructs related to the behavioral implications of providing direct client services to practitioners. Countertransference, vicarious traumatization, secondary traumatic stress, and compassion fatigue are compared and contrasted in detail. Each of these terms (and others) attempt in some way to describe practitioners' potential reactions to clients, their situations, and the corresponding emotions involved with engaging and cultivating a practice relationship through the use of empathy, among other clinical and organization skills. However, these various defining terms have notable and distinguishable differences that have complicated the professional community's understanding of these phenomena.

RECOMMENDED READING

Breggin, P. R. (1997). *The heart of being helpful: Empathy and the creation of a healing presence.* New York, NY: Springer.

Figley, C. R. (1995). *Compassion fatigue: Coping with secondary traumatic stress disorder in those who treat the traumatized.* Levittown, PA: Brunner/Mazel.

Pearlman, L. A., & Saakvitne, K. W. (1995). *Trauma and the therapist: Countertransference and vicarious traumatization in psychotherapy with incest survivors.* New York, NY: Norton.

Stamm, B. H. (1999). *Secondary traumatic stress: Self-care issues for clinicians, researchers, and educators.* Baltimore, MD: Sidran Press.

Young, J. E., Klosko, J. S., & Weishaar, M. E. (2003). *Schema therapy: A practitioner's guide.* New York, NY: Guilford Press.

SUGGESTED INTERNET RESOURCES

Compassion Fatigue Awareness Project: www.compassionfatigue.org

The project mission is to promote awareness and understanding of compassion fatigue and its effect on caregivers under the vision and belief that compassion fatigue for those in caregiving roles (including that of animal caregivers) can be alleviated through education and the practice of authentic self-care. This site is tailored to anyone in a personal or professional caregiving role. Features of the site include pages dedicated to recognizing compassion fatigue, steps for the path of wellness, and promotion of compassion satisfaction for caregivers. The site includes a resources page with information on general caregiving, animal caregiving, family caregiving, and traumatic stress caregiving. The Suggested Readings tab has a directory of printable resources in the area of compassionate caregiving available at no cost.

Figley Institute: http://www.figleyinstitute.com/indexMain.html

The institute's mission is to alleviate human suffering resulting from traumatic life experiences by providing laypeople and professionals with high-quality traumatologist training. This site provides excellent resources for professional training, certification, and development and offers a complete catalog of online training sessions and certification programs (with continuing education credits) in the areas of psychological trauma, disaster trauma, compassion fatigue, and professional self-care. The site includes a link to other public resources related to the field of traumatology at no cost. A companion site for additional resources related to the scholarly work of Charles Figley can be accessed at www.charlesfigley.com.

4

UNDERSTANDING AND PREVENTING THE EFFECTS OF PROFESSIONAL BURNOUT AND INDIRECT TRAUMA

An Individual and Organizational Challenge

Do not assume that he who seeks to comfort you now, lives untroubled among the simple and quiet words that sometimes do you good. His life may also have much sadness and difficulty that remains far beyond yours. Were it otherwise, he would never have been able to find these words.

RAINER MARIA RILKE, *LETTERS TO A YOUNG POET*

CHAPTER GOALS AND OBJECTIVES

1. Provide a detailed description of the process of professional burnout as a multidimensional construct.
2. Present professional burnout as a dynamic behavioral phenomenon in human service related to the individual, the service organization, and the clients served.
3. Differentiate the behaviors associated with professional burnout from those associated with vicarious traumatization, secondary traumatic stress, and compassion fatigue.
4. Summarize the research on the vulnerability factors associated with professional burnout, vicarious traumatization, secondary traumatic stress, and compassion fatigue in direct practitioners.
5. Illustrate the organizational effects of professional burnout on a new social worker in child welfare practice through a case study.
6. Synthesize the strategies for preventing professional burnout, vicarious traumatization, secondary traumatic stress, and compassion fatigue at the individual and the organizational levels.

THE NATURE OF HUMAN SERVICE WORK

A major premise of this book is the idea that those who choose careers in the fields of human service should consciously work to cultivate and regulate the appropriate use of empathy as a defined practice skill. At the same time, practitioners also need to be keenly self-aware that unregulated (or overuse) of empathy resources can serve as a vulnerability factor for vicarious trauma, secondary traumatic stress, and compassion fatigue. The various constructs and terminologies used to describe the potential behavioral reactions some practitioners have as a consequence of their work (vicarious trauma versus secondary traumatic stress) have been debated, but all agree that emotional stress is a pervasive component of any career path in the fields of human services. The greatest risk factor for vicarious traumatization, compassion fatigue, or any of the other emotional stress-related conditions is at the very nature of human service work itself. Simply stated, the professional commitment to help others through their problems requires a deep commitment to doing very difficult work, particularly for those in direct contact with the intense emotions and behaviors associated with survivors of trauma-related experiences.

Part 1 of this chapter provides a detailed discussion of the concept of professional burnout. Professional burnout is a multidimensional phenomenon in human service work that is distinctly different from the empathic stress responses described earlier. Part 2 describes the vulnerability factors associated with vicarious trauma, secondary traumatic stress, and compassion fatigue for providers in direct practice with clients in a variety of agency practice settings. This includes a summary of the various individual and organizational strategies presented in the research literature as possible preventative and mitigating methods for the effects of these experiences for direct practitioners.

PART 1: PROFESSIONAL BURNOUT: A CONCEPTUAL PERSPECTIVE

Professional burnout related to human service work was first introduced in the literature in the early 1970s (Freudenberger, 1974). The number of community-based social service agencies increased substantially during this time, a trend that both influenced the growth of the human service professions and generated job opportunities for career human service professionals. As the breadth and outreach of social services grew, social workers and other human service professionals became responsible for large numbers of cases. All of these factors influenced the introduction of a new term and the subsequent description of the phenomenon of becoming "burned out" as it relates to the high-stress demands involved with human service work (Freudenberger, 1974). One of the first qualitative descriptions of professional burnout depicted professional social workers as

> idealistic young men and women who, while working harder and harder, were sacrificing their own health in the process of meeting ideals larger than themselves, and reaping few rewards for their efforts. Despite all their energetic and

enthusiastic labor for the larger good, the human service worker often failed to make a difference in the lives of their clients. (Freudenberger, 1974, p. 160)

The concept of professional burnout introduced a new orientation for understanding the influence of stress when working with the challenging demands of human service agencies. Both the interpersonal relationship between the human service professional and the client and the relationship between the professional and the social service agency were accounted for in this new orientation (Maslach, 2001). Since first defined, the breadth and applicability of professional burnout has reached far beyond the fields of human services. Professional burnout has been cited in the fields of nursing, medicine, management, technology, education, and within military populations (Maslach, 2001).

PROFESSIONAL BURNOUT: A MULTIDIMENSIONAL CONSTRUCT

The synthesis of the defining literature describes professional burnout as a cumulative state of physical, emotional, psychological, and spiritual exhaustion resulting from chronic exposure to (or practice with) populations that are vulnerable or suffering (Pines & Aronson, 1988). The process and experience of professional burnout historically has been described as a progressive state occurring over time with contributing factors related to the individual, the populations served, and the organization (Maslach, 2001, 2003a, 2003b). The most widely accepted conceptualization of burnout is as a multidimensional construct with three distinct domains: emotional exhaustion, depersonalization, and marked reduction in one's sense of personal accomplishment (figure 4.1).

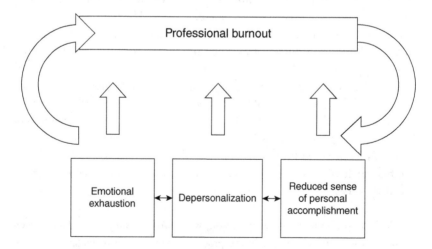

FIGURE 4.1 Maslach's conceptual model of professional burnout

However, some studies have suggested other affect, social, and cognitive dimensions of the burnout construct (Baldschum, 2014; Maslach & Goldberg, 1998). This multidimensional approach to burnout, based on the pioneering work of Christina Maslach, provides a holistic conceptualization of this complex organizational and behavioral phenomenon (Lee & Ashworth, 1996; Maslach, 2001; Maslach & Jackson, 1981; Maslach & Leiter, 1997).

Emotional exhaustion occurs when a practitioner's emotional resources become depleted by the chronic needs, demands, and expectations of his or her clients, supervisors, and organization (Maslach, 2001; Maslach & Goldberg, 1998). Depersonalization (also referred to as cynicism) refers to negative, cynical, or excessively detached responses to coworkers, job task, or to clients and their situations (Maslach, 2001; Maslach & Goldberg, 1998). This domain represents the change in interpersonal thoughts and feelings regarding practice with clients that may occur in the process of professional burnout. Professional helpers may feel inadequate when clients do not respond to interventions, despite practitioners' diligent efforts to help them. This domain of the burnout phenomenon may also occur in response to bureaucratic constraints and administrative demands that often accompany social service practice, such as dictating client records or completing required administrative documentation.

INDIVIDUAL VERSUS ORGANIZATIONAL VULNERABILITY FACTORS

Factors contributing to professional burnout may occur at the individual, organizational, or client level and often are a result of a combination of these factors. A simple online search for the phrase "professional burnout in human service or social work" will easily produce a wealth of empirical study data (Mor Barak, Nissly, & Levin, 2001; Font, 2012; Lizano & Mor Barak, 2012; Lloyd, King, & Chenoweth, 2002). Professional burnout has been studied in numerous public and private service fields including child welfare, mental health, nursing, hospital social work, and education, to name a few. One major factor that emerges from the literature on professional burnout across settings and populations is the finding that human service organizations play a key role in the professional burnout process. Maslach and Leiter (1997) identify six major organizational factors contributing to the experience of professional burnout in human service work; these factors include excessive workload, lack of control over agency policies and procedures, insufficient reward from the work, unfairness in organization structure and discipline, low peer and supervisory support, and role conflict or ambiguity.

Elaborating on the organization factors proposed by Maslach and Leiter (1997), studies have validated that excessive workload, specifically the number of assigned cases, is a significant contributing factor both to professional burnout and to provider intention to leave an employment setting, particularly for providers in public child welfare positions (Mor Barak et al., 2001; Cyphers, 2001;

Zlotnick, DePanfilis, Daining, & Lane, 2005; Yamatani, Engel, & Spjeldnes, 2009). Because of the bureaucratic nature of many state and federally funded human service agencies, providers may find they have little control or influence over agency policies and procedures regulating caseload size and assignment (Kim, 2011). For employees with less work experience and training, excessively high caseloads create an even greater vulnerability factor to the effects of professional burnout (Bennett, Plint, & Clifford, 2005; Boyas, Wind, & Kang, 2012). Higher caseloads may require providers to take on additional work hours, have more dedicated on-call time, and have increased documentation time, which may lead providers to feel poorly or inadequately compensated for their time and efforts (Lloyd et al., 2002). The profession of social work often requires direct practice from multiple roles (court advocate, therapist, case manager, legal guardian, teacher, coach, etc.), which sometimes creates complex intersections with organization policy, personal values, and professional ethics. For example, a child welfare worker may be directed by a court official to remove a child from an at-risk home when he or she truly feels the child is safe and would like to continue practice to preserve the biological family. Role confusion as a source of ethical dilemma has been shown to influence social workers' perception of personal and professional well-being and to influence burnout and agency retention (Graham & Shier, 2014).

Individual provider personality attributes or characteristics may increase vulnerability to the effects of professional burnout. Neophyte professionals are often younger, have less organizational training, and have fewer years of direct practice experience; these workers are more vulnerable than those with organization tenure and experience (Boyas et al., 2012; Boyas, Wind, & Ruiz, 2013; Cyphers, 2001; Hamama, 2012; Lizano & Mor Barak, 2012). Younger professionals with less direct practice experience may have difficulty navigating and understanding conflicting relationships with coworkers while at the same time learning to interact with and understand clients and their situations, factors that may lead to the premature experience of the effects of professional burnout (Barak, Nissly, & Levin 2001; Lloyd et al., 2002; Thorton, 1992). Some studies have shown that individual personality and coping styles may influence the effects of professional burnout, suggesting that those with a cognitive or contemplative personality are more resilient to the effects of human service work and burnout than those with an emotive personality (Mandell, Stalker, de Zeeuw-Wright, Frensch, & Harvey, 2013; Medina & Beyebach, 2014; Zosky, 2010). It also has been suggested that an active style of coping, such as the use of a planful approach to problem solving rather than an avoidant coping style, might mitigate the effects of burnout (Anderson, 2000; Stevens & Higgins, 2002; Thorton, 1992). Other individual factors, such as gender (females are at greater risk) and race (minorities are at greater risk) have been correlated with some dimensions of the professional burnout phenomenon (Newell & MacNeil, 2011; Sprang, Craig, & Clark, 2011). Finally, and not surprisingly, the emotional expectations involved with human service work, such as requirements to either repress or display emotions routinely as well as the chronic use of empathy, are strongly associated with the experience of professional burnout (Wagaman, Gieger, Shockley, & Segal, 2015).

PREVENTING BURNOUT: THE IMPORTANCE OF SUPERVISION AND PEER SUPPORT

The literature across professional settings and populations indicates that the existence of a strong organizational support system from agency administrators, supervisors, mentors, and colleagues has a significant impact on buffering the effects of professional burnout. Some studies have suggested that effective supervision has a significant impact on the intention of many providers to remain committed to the work, even when the stresses of the job seem overwhelming (Bennett et al., 2005; Hamama, 2012; Mor Barak et al., 2001). As stated earlier, the combination of chronological age and professional work experience is a significant vulnerability factor for new social service professionals, particularly those choosing careers in public child welfare (Dill, 2007). However, in any social service setting, the role of the direct service supervisor, ideally in a positive organizational climate, is a vital aspect to social worker retention, commitment to the agency, and overall job resiliency (Cahalane & Sites, 2008; Lizano, Hsiao, Mor Barak, & Casper, 2014; O'Donnell & Kirkner, 2009).

Creating effective agency models for new employee supervision, peer support, and training may serve to increase worker retention over time (Boyas et al., 2012). Effective supervision also has been shown to positively influence professional self-esteem and empowerment to practice and problem solve efficaciously, even in difficult client and family situations, qualities that have potential over time to serve as buffers to the effects of professional burnout and increase the likelihood of employee retention (Lee, Weaver, & Hrostowski, 2011; Medina & Beyebach, 2014; Stevens & Higgins, 2002). Significant evidence suggests that support from professional colleagues may help mitigate the effects of professional burnout (Hamama, 2012; Lizano & Mor Barak, 2012; Lloyd et al., 2002). Simple examples of social support from professional colleagues may include concrete support such as assisting with excess clerical work or taking on a particularly difficult client, or emotional support such as comfort, insight, comparative feedback, personal feedback, and humor (Maslach, 2003b).

In addition to mentoring supervisees directly, organization managers may have influence on work conditions that are contributing factors to professional burnout, such as work or caseload allocations, the use (or misuse) of overtime and on-call time, and job autonomy (Stalker, Mandell, Frensch, Harvey, & Wright, 2007). Agency supervisors and administrators also may have influence in creating positive changes or restructuring organization policies and procedures related to professional burnout within the agency. Changing agency policy is typically a challenging and time-consuming task, but some more reasonable efforts can be made. Developing additional staff resources, restructuring the division of workload, advocating to agency officials and board members for policy change, limiting job spillover, and encouraging more professional training and staff development may help to buffer or prevent the long-term effects of professional burnout (Bennett et al., 2005; Lizano et al., 2014; Maslach & Leiter, 1997; Medina & Beyebach, 2014).

INDIVIDUAL STRATEGIES FOR BURNOUT PREVENTION

Despite the wealth of empirical data supporting the existence of professional burnout across human service workers and agency settings, there are surprisingly few well-tested models for the prevention of burnout and even fewer suggestions for how to treat those who have experienced the cumulative effects of burnout over a long period of time. Hence, there seems to be a substantial gap in the literature between research and practice. Several individual, social, and institutional strategies have been proposed as useful in either preventing or intervening with the effects of professional burnout. Strategies for positive changes in work patterns within the organization include setting realistic goals with regard to workload and client care, brainstorming to find different ways to approach the same task, taking coffee and lunch breaks, and avoiding taking client problems personally (Maslach, 2003b; Maslach & Goldberg, 1998). Positive lifestyle and health behaviors outside of the agency setting, such as maintaining adequate rest and relaxation, leaving work-related problems at the office, and maintaining positive connections with close friends and family, may be beneficial in buffering the effects of professional burnout (Maslach, 1998). Once burnout becomes chronic, some human service workers consider vacating their current job or beginning an active search for other employment as a solution to their burnout experiences and also as a method of professional self-preservation (Maslach, 2001, 2003a, 2003b).

LESLEY: A CASE STUDY IN CHILD WELFARE PRACTICE

Lesley recently graduated with a bachelor's degree in social work and has been hired for her first professional position at a local child welfare agency. Lesley has been assigned to a seasoned social worker as both mentor and supervisor as she adjusts to the demands of her new position. In her first supervision session,

Lesley shares with her supervisor that, during her first week on the unit, she was told by several of the other social workers that "staff turnover is high around here, so I hope you are prepared to do this kind of work." As part of her agency orientation, she was placed on unit rotation for two weeks to gain exposure to the different unit areas within the agency. During her unit rotation, she was allowed the opportunity to practice in an assessment unit where she learned about the interviewing process and policies used to determine child abuse and neglect. She also shadowed and participated in independent living /case management services to a teenager in foster care, and spent time working in a resource unit recruiting and developing foster homes in her local community.

After a month of orientation to agency policy, practice, and general proce-dure, the supervisor tells Lesley that she is doing an excellent job performing multiple duties and is glad that her time and skills are being used by several members of the agency. The supervisor tells Lesley that the agency has several openings, and many other supervisors have indicated that she would be an asset to their units. The supervisor feels confident that Lesley is ready to take on a full caseload of child welfare clients and their families. Upon hearing this, Lesley hesitantly discloses to her supervisor that she often feels pulled in many different directions and, in her words, "stretched very thin." She reports that she has overheard the other social workers discussing openly amongst themselves "who will get to use Lesley for the day," which makes her feel like an intern rather than a full-time professional. Lesley tells her supervisor that she often has mixed feelings of both "being taken advantage of and at the same time being a burden to the workers." She informs her supervisor that she has been staying in the office until 10 o'clock every night auditing charts and archiving old client records because there is not time to do these tasks during the day. She will not be compensated for this time because the agency does not approve overtime for newly hired professional staff members. Lesley reports spending most of the day floating from unit to unit and attending to client transportation needs rather than learning how to practice effectively with the children and families served by the agency. She has already clocked over 200 miles on her private vehicle, creating a financial burden as she will not be reimbursed for mileage until the following month. Because she is a new employee, according to state policy, her first full paycheck will be held, so she will not be paid for another 30 days.

Despite positive feedback from both her supervisor and from other agency employees, Lesley is feeling apathetic about her potential as a child welfare worker and thinks she might just go to work for her father's business. Her first impression of the job is that this work is too stressful, and she doesn't think she is "cut out" for it because she finds it difficult to be pulled in so many directions. Lesley openly expresses to her supervisor that she feels emotionally drained and that it is taking all of her energy to complete the full array of her tasks each day. She feels as if her "wheels are spinning" and "nothing ever gets accomplished." She ends the supervision session by saying there is "too much paper work, too little time, and not enough resources to truly help these families." Her supervisor is both surprised and bewildered by Lesley's statements and wonders how to handle this situation with the new social worker whose well-being she is responsible for, with the other contributing agency professionals, and within the organization itself.

DISCUSSION AND CRITICAL THINKING QUESTIONS

1. Based on your reading of this case study and your review of the professional literature in this area, analyze what circumstances and factors exist related to whether Lesley is at risk of professional burnout. (Social Work Competency 4: Engage in Practice-Informed Research and Research-Informed Practice—through the use and translation of research evidence to inform and improve practice, policy, and service delivery.)

2. Based on the information presented in the chapter, assess Lesley's vulnerability to the effects of professional burnout from both an individual and an organization perspective. (Social Work Competency 9: Evaluate Practice with Individuals and Organizations—by critically analyzing, monitoring, and evaluating intervention, program processes, and outcomes, and by applying evaluation findings to improve practice effectiveness at the micro, mezzo, and macro levels.)

3. Consider the statement by Lesley's new colleague that "staff turnover is high here, so I hope you are prepared to do this kind for work." What influences could this statement have on Lesley's perception of the organizational culture of this agency or her supervisor's expectations? (Social Work Competency 7: Assess Organizations—by applying knowledge of human behavior and the social environment, person-in-environment, and other multidisciplinary theoretical frameworks in the analysis of organizational assessment data.)

4. If you were Lesley's supervisor, how would you introduce her to the organization? What aspects of the agency and the organizational culture would you consider more or less important, and why? (Social Work Competency 2: Engage Diversity and Difference in Practice—by applying self-awareness and self-regulation to manage the influence of personal biases and values in working in diverse organizations.)

5. Applying knowledge of human behavior and how the social environment affects behavior, analyze how Lesley's reaction to the stress of the social work agency setting may be expected for a new social work field student. (Social Work Competency 7: Assess Organizations—by applying

knowledge of human behavior and the social environment, person-in-environment, and other multidisciplinary theoretical frameworks in the analysis of organizational assessment data.)

6. Should Lesley directly disclose her feelings about the agency to her field supervisor? Why or why not? Compare and contrast the possible implications of this decision. (Social Work Competency 1: Demonstrate Ethical and Professional Behavior—through the use of supervision and consultation to guide professional judgment and behavior.)

7. How might Lesley's feelings of apathy affect her ability to practice in the child welfare agency setting? Describe at least one example of a potential ethical dilemma that might occur if Lesley does not address these feelings with her agency and field supervisor. (Social Work Competency 1: Demonstrate Ethical and Professional Behavior—by making ethical decisions by applying the NASW Code of Ethics, relevant laws and regulations, models for ethical decision making, ethical conduct of research, and additional codes of ethics as appropriate to context.)

PART 2: DIFFERENTIATING PROFESSIONAL BURNOUT FROM INDIRECT TRAUMA EFFECTS

Professional burnout has often been the subject of study in combination with vicarious trauma (VT), secondary traumatic stress (STS), compassion fatigue (CF), and other conditions related to the experiences of clients, particularly those suffering from trauma-related disorders (Baird & Kracen, 2006; Craig & Sprang, 2010; Sprang, Clark, & Whitt-Woosley, 2007). Although there are clearly emotional components related to the cumulative effects of professional burnout, the literature is consistent in describing the source of components of stress leading to burnout as being rooted in human service organizations. Burnout has been closely linked to organizational challenges, and in combination with individual personality factors it may progressively leave providers vulnerable to the cumulative effects of burnout over time (Conrad & Keller-Guenther, 2006; Font, 2012; Lizano & Mor Barak, 2012; Maslach & Goldberg, 1998). Organizational factors were discussed in detail earlier in the chapter: high caseloads, lack of personal time away from work, and the lack of supportive supervision. Other specific organizational behaviors linked to burnout include intention to quit the job, lack of commitment to clients and to the organization, chronic absenteeism, and tardiness (Lloyd et al., 2002; Maslach, 2003a; Maslach & Leiter, 1997; Shinn, Rosario, Morch, & Chesnut, 1984).

The emotional stressors related to the experience of VT, STS, and CF manifest as a result of indirect exposure to the intense emotion and suffering some clients experience as a result of their presenting problems and treatment situations (see figure 4.2). These conditions are more closely associated with the client and with providers' expectations to meet the emotional demands of their situation through efforts to help and provide services rather than with the bureaucratic constraints of human service organizations (Figley, 1995; Stamm, 1999). Professional burnout has been generalized to organizational settings in a variety of fields and disciplines, including the business world, but VT, STS, and CF are phenomena unique to direct practice with vulnerable populations and the cognitive and behavioral changes in the provider that occur as a result of the dynamic exchange of human emotion and dialogue required to create therapeutic or helping relationships (Pearlman & Saakvitne, 1995; Stamm, 1999).

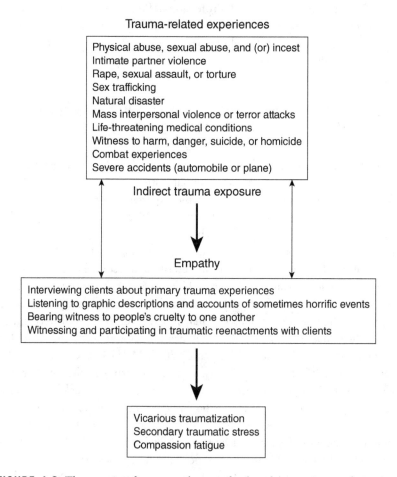

Trauma-related experiences

Physical abuse, sexual abuse, and (or) incest
Intimate partner violence
Rape, sexual assault, or torture
Sex trafficking
Natural disaster
Mass interpersonal violence or terror attacks
Life-threatening medical conditions
Witness to harm, danger, suicide, or homicide
Combat experiences
Severe accidents (automobile or plane)

Indirect trauma exposure

Empathy

Interviewing clients about primary trauma experiences
Listening to graphic descriptions and accounts of sometimes horrific events
Bearing witness to people's cruelty to one another
Witnessing and participating in traumatic reenactments with clients

Vicarious traumatization
Secondary traumatic stress
Compassion fatigue

FIGURE 4.2 The emotional stressors that can lead to the experience of vicarious trauma, secondary traumatic stress, or compassion fatigue

VT, STS, and CF have all been described as "traumalike" in the literature and may present behaviors similar to those who have either survived a traumatic event or who have been diagnosed with a trauma-related disorder (Bride, 2007; Figley, 1995; Thomas & Wilson, 2004). Studies have indicated that direct practitioners experiencing VT, STS, or CF may have recurrent and intrusive recollections of clients and their traumas, distressing dreams or nightmares associated with client traumas, and physiological reactivity upon exposure to internal or external stimuli that resemble an aspect of client traumas (Bride, 2007; Figley, 1995 Collins & Long, 2002; Palm, Polusny, & Follette, 2004).

There was a time when these conditions were described in the literature as being exclusive to work with trauma-related disorders. However, the recent use of a more generalized orientation suggests that any human service job requiring the chronic use of empathy to meet the emotionally demanding needs of clients who are suffering in some way may leave providers vulnerable (Newell et al., 2015). It is possible and likely in some settings that these conditions interact and co-occur with professional burnout, and it has been suggested that VT, STS, or CF may serve as a significant vulnerability factor leading to the development of professional burnout as an overall final outcome (Conrad & Keller-Guenther, 2006; Sprang et al., 2011).

VULNERABILITY FACTORS FOR INDIRECT TRAUMA EXPOSURE

Unlike the construct of professional burnout, VT, STS, and CF have been used both synonymously and interchangeably in the research literature. As described in detail in chapter 3, there are both similarities and differences with regard to the defining features of these conditions. For the purposes of this chapter, these three terms will be used in a similar amalgamation to refer to the negative and often consequential effects clients and their emotional or trauma-related material have on direct service providers. One similarity between professional burnout, VT, STS, and CF is that these behavioral phenomena have been documented in a variety of agency settings. Providers working in agencies treating survivors of sexual assault and incest, veterans and military families, survivors of natural disasters (disaster relief workers), the mentally ill, and chronically ill patients including paramedic and emergency care workers have all been linked with experiences of indirect forms of stress as a result of their work with these client populations (Barak et al., 2001; Bennett et al., 2005; Bride, 2007; Farrell & Turpin, 2003; Newell & MacNeil, 2011; Palm et al., 2004; Regehr, Goldberg, & Hughes, 2002; Trippany, Wilcoxin, & Satcher, 2003).

For those looking forward to careers in the fields of human service, or for those already in direct practice, it is important to understand vulnerability factors that may contribute to the development of VT, STS, and CF. The single greatest risk factor for the experience of these conditions is clearly the work itself; in other words, any direct practice with clients who are suffering from emotional pain or trauma experiences, and who are exchanging trauma material through therapeutic or helping processes, places providers at risk (Figley, 1995; Pearlman & Saakvitne, 1995; Stamm, 1999). Some studies have suggested that practitioners with a preexisting anxiety disorder, mood disorder, or with their own histories of personal trauma (particularly child abuse and neglect) may be at greater risk of experiencing these conditions (Lerias & Byrne, 2003; Dunkley & Whelan, 2006; Nelson-Gardell & Harris, 2003; Trippany et al., 2003). Professionals with high caseloads of trauma-related situations and those with less professional work experience and training with trauma clients are particularly vulnerable to the effects of these conditions (Baird & Kracen, 2006; Bell, Kulkarni, & Dalton, 2003; Lerias & Byrne, 2003; Pearlman & McIan, 1995). The use of maladaptive coping skills in response to trauma work, such as suppression of emotions, distancing from clients, and reenacting abuse dynamics, as well as the use of poor professional boundaries, have all been identified as vulnerability factors for the effects of VT, STS, and CF (Dunkley & Whelan, 2006; Farrell & Turpin, 2003; Lerias & Byrne, 2003; Schauben & Frazier, 1995).

ORGANIZATIONAL PREVENTION OF VT, STS, AND CF

The synthesis of the research literature reveals that specific features in human service organizations serving trauma populations also serve as vulnerability factors for these conditions. Much like the findings from the literature on professional burnout, the importance of institutional support in the form of direct practice supervision, mentorship, and collegiality may have a significant mitigating effect on the experience of VT, STS, and CF (Baird & Kracen, 2006; Catherall, 1995, 1999; Dunkley & Whelan, 2006; Farrell & Turpin, 2003; Pearlman & MacIan, 1995). There is a strong agreement across studies that education, training, and professional development are vital components of the prevention of these conditions (Figley, 1995; Harrison & Westwood, 2009; Pearlman & MacIan, 1995; Pearlman & Saakvitne, 1995; Stamm, 1999). Several studies have proposed professional development and continuing education as the natural "first line" in prevention (Zimering, Munroe, & Gulliver, 2003; Hesse, 2002; O'Halloran & O'Halloran, 2001).

Practitioners and agency administrators alike must consider organizational culture and the impact of agency culture on the well-being of providers and the clients they serve as a method of promoting practitioner resilience and well-being. Generally, organizational or agency culture is comprised of the assumptions, values, norms, and tangible signs (artifacts) of agency members and their behaviors (Catherall, 1995). This is of particular importance to social workers practicing in agencies catering specifically to trauma populations (Bell et al., 2003). An important component of organization support is the simple acknowledgment of the existence of VT, STS, and CF as normal reactions to clients and their trauma material (Pryce et al., 2007). An accepting organizational culture helps to alleviate stigmas service providers may have about experiencing these normative reactions to trauma material—such as feeling inadequate or incapable of completing work responsibilities effectively—and may significantly contribute to professional self-esteem and coping ability (Bell et al., 2003). Finally, organizations driven by a supportive culture promote the importance of a clear understanding among agency providers that the indirect effects of trauma are not reflective of an inability to perform job responsibilities adequately or professionally; rather, they are a very real, and sometimes underestimated, occupational hazard associated with trauma work (Catherall, 1995; Pryce et al., 2007).

INDIVIDUAL STRATEGIES FOR PREVENTING INDIRECT TRAUMA RESPONSE

In addition to the organizational methods suggested, various individual strategies have been proposed as useful in preventing the effects of VT, STS, and CF. Similar to the research on professional burnout, there is little literature on rigorously tested models of prevention or intervention for the effects of these conditions on direct service providers. Models such as Critical Incident Stress Debriefing (CISD) have been cited, but have not been shown to be consistently efficacious. CISD and other proposed methods such as mindfulness techniques are discussed in greater detail in chapter 10.

At the individual level, efforts to maintain a healthy personal and professional work–life balance, including maintaining clear professional agency and client boundaries, are essential components for sustaining resilience in human service work, particularly for those engaged in trauma practice (Pearlman & Saakvitne, 1995). Positive health behaviors such as maintaining a balanced diet, an adequate sleep schedule, and a reasonable exercise routine may serve to buffer the effects of VT, STS, and CF (Zimering et al., 2003; O'Halloran & O'Halloran, 2001; Pearlman, 1999; Pearlman & Saakvitne, 1995). Recreational activities involving the use of positive forms of self-expression such as drawing, painting, sculpting, cooking, and outdoor activities may help to mitigate the effects of trauma work (Hesse, 2002). Maintaining spiritual connections through church, meditation, yoga, philanthropic activities, and self-revitalization also have been suggested as important factors in creating a healthy balance between personal and professional obligations, and they can act as buffers to the indirect effects of stress and trauma (Pearlman & Saakvitne, 1995).

Similar to the importance of organization mentorship, supervision, and peer support, the emotional and social support from close family and friends is a useful defense against the effects of VT, STS, and CF (O'Halloran & O'Halloran, 2001; Ray & Miller, 1994). Conscious efforts to address feelings of anxiety associated with clients and their situations, such as the use of mindful awareness, self-talk, positive imagery, and maintaining a realist worldview about the impact of trauma work on both the client and the self, may have possible mitigating effects (Harrison & Westwood, 2009; Pearlman & Saakvitne, 1995). Finally, for those who feel they already may be experiencing significant psychological effects as a result of their direct practice, psychotherapy is a reasonable treatment option, particularly for those with past trauma history (Hesse, 2002).

KEY TERMS

avoidant coping style
cynicism (as depersonalization)
emotional exhaustion
indirect trauma exposure
organizational culture

personal accomplishment
planful problem solving
professional burnout
professional self-esteem
role confusion

CHAPTER SUMMARY

This chapter describes the vulnerability factors associated with the forms of indirect trauma response previously described as vicarious traumatization, secondary traumatic stress, compassion fatigue, and professional burnout. Professional burnout is best conceptualized as a meta-construct with dimensions related to emotional exhaustion, depersonalization, and a reduction in one's sense of personal accomplishment. Based on a thorough synthesis of the research literature, individual and organizational factors cited as contributing to the experience of professional burnout are discussed at length. This chapter also provides an important discussion of the key differences between professional burnout and the indirect forms of traumatic stress including the vulnerability factors related to both the individual service provider and the human service organization. Surprisingly, there are no rigorously tested models for either preventing or intervening with the effects of burnout, VT, STS, and CF. Rather, the literature suggests that a combination of individual strategies related to professional self-care and strong organization support in the form of peer mentorship and supervision are useful at preventing the effects of these conditions. A case study describing the effects of professional burnout on a new social worker in a child welfare agency illustrates the organizational effects of professional burnout.

RECOMMENDED READING

Clow, J. (2012). *The work revolution. Freedom and excellence for all.* Hoboken, NJ: Wiley.

Maslach, C. (2003). *Burnout: The cost of caring.* Cambridge, MA: Malor.

Maslach, C., & Leiter, M. P. (1997). *The truth about burnout.* San Francisco, CA: Jossey-Bass.

Morrissette, P. (2004). *The pain of helping: Psychological injury of helping professions.* New York, NY: Taylor & Francis.

Pines, A., & Aronson, E. (1988). *Career burnout: Causes and cures.* New York, NY: Free Press.

Rothschild, B. (2006). *Help for the helper: Self-care strategies for managing burnout and stress.* New York, NY: Norton.

SUGGESTED INTERNET RESOURCES

Helpguide.org: http://www.helpguide.org/home-pages/work-career.htm
    This site is hosted by a nonprofit driven by the mission that people can affect fundamental changes in their emotional and physical health with the aid of appropriate online resources. The main site offers a variety of resources related to the emotional and physical aspects of well-being. The site provides free online materials for mental illness, family development across the life span, stress, and suicide prevention. The Work and Career page includes resources related to effective workplace communication, finding the right job, and preventing job burnout. The job burnout link, embedded in the Work and Career page, includes information on the warning signs for professional burnout, the differences between stress and burnout, and several practical strategies for preventing and recovering from the effects of stress and burnout.

Professional Burnout: http://maslach.socialpsychology.org/
    This site provides information on Christina Maslach and use of the Maslach Burnout Inventory (MBI). An overview of Dr. Maslach's career includes a short history of the burnout construct as well as a complete review of her research and publication history. The MBI is available for use by purchase by contacting info@mindgarden.com. A lecture by Dr. Maslach on the burnout process and construct is available at no cost on YouTube at https://www.youtube.com/watch?v=4kLPyV8lBbs.

5

ASSESSMENT AND MEASUREMENT OF OCCUPATIONAL STRESS AND TRAUMA

The study of trauma confronts one with the best and worst in human nature and is bound to provoke a range of intense personal reactions in the people involved.

—VAN DER KOLK, MCFARLANE, & WEISAETH, 1996, P. 6

CHAPTER GOALS AND OBJECTIVES

1. Discuss the importance of proper assessment and measurement of the primary and secondary effects of traumatic stress, compassion fatigue, and professional burnout.
2. Define the methodological terms used to evaluate and determine the psychometric properties of measurement instruments including the various forms of scale reliability and validity.
3. Provide an overview and discussion of the scales cited in the literature as reliable and valid measures of generalized stress, traumatic and posttraumatic stress, and professional burnout.
4. Discuss the methodological challenges with the construct validity of similar terms used interchangeably to describe the indirect or secondary effects of trauma.
5. Provide an overview and discussion of the psychometric properties of the scales cited in the literature as measures of vicarious traumatization, secondary traumatic stress, and compassion fatigue.

Chapters 1 through 3 provide an introduction to the effects of both direct and indirect forms of traumatic stress on direct practitioners involved in human service work. Chapter 4 introduces the concept of professional burnout and the myriad stressors associated with direct practice in human service organizations. This chapter discusses the importance of accurate assessment and measurement of the primary and secondary forms of traumatic stress and professional burnout. Scales designed to measure trauma exposure and the resulting behavioral pathologies that may eventually manifest as PTSD have been in existence for quite some time. Since the diagnosis of PTSD was formally included in the *Diagnostic and Statistical Manual* in 1980, there has been an exponential growth in the field of traumatology in the United States and internationally (Dalenburg, 2002; Birmes et al., 2003; Figley, 2002a). The field of trauma study has continued to grow in recent times. The expansion of this research in the United States has been fueled in part by the increase in number of terror attacks, mass shootings, and combat deployments to Operation Enduring Freedom and Operation Iraqi Freedom (OEF/OIF) and other combat theatres (CSWE, 2010; Figley & Nash, 2007).

Professional burnout has been the focus of extensive conceptual and empirical study since the 1980s and has been examined across human service, education, organizational management, and other occupational and professional settings in the United States and internationally (Schaufeli & Maslach, 1993). However, the empirical literature lacks conceptual clarity with regard to the indirect effects of chronic exposure to survivors of the primary forms of traumatic stress (and their trauma material) on the providers who treat them. The only consensus in the literature seems to be that there is indeed no consensus. The terms *vicarious traumatization, secondary traumatic stress,* and *compassion fatigue* are often used interchangeably in the research literature, which has further complicated the accurate measurement of these constructs. Further, the common usage of terms such as "burnout" and "traumatized" in the lay vocabulary of many social service agencies has created confusion in many professional ranks (Newell et al., 2015). This chapter reviews the measures of stress, traumatic stress, VT, STS, and CF most commonly cited in the research literature, including the challenges with the operational definitions and construct validity of these behavioral phenomena. Part 1 provides a brief overview of important psychometric terms related to scale reliability and validity to assist understanding of these measures. Part 2 reviews some of the commonly used measures of stress and primary trauma and their psychometric properties. Part 3 discusses measures of professional burnout and indirect or secondary trauma experiences.

PART 1: UNDERSTANDING THE PSYCHOMETRIC PROPERTIES OF SCALES AND ASSESSMENT TOOLS

This chapter focuses on the assessment and measurement of the concepts and constructs discussed in earlier chapters. The utility of various scales and measures of traumatic stress, burnout, and secondary or vicarious trauma experiences is explained, beginning with some basic knowledge of the terminologies used to discuss the psychometric properties of measurement tools and instruments.

Scales used to collect data can be administered in more than one way. For example, some scales are administered as structured interviews and are rated by the person delivering the scale items within the context of the interview. Some scales involving structured interviews, particularly those with a diagnostic component, require special training to administer. Scales completed by the respondent with little or no influence by an outside rater with formal training are called self-report measures. One commonly used and understood scale methodology is the Likert scale (Rubbin & Babbie, 2010), which involves rating a particular quality or experience based on degree of agreement ("strongly disagree" versus "strongly agree") or exposure ("happens to me every day" versus "never happens to me"). Qualitative data collection may include information from focus groups or structured interviews without the use of standardized or quantitative measures.

Scale reliability refers to the amount of random error in a measurement instrument and whether the instrument is consistently useful across populations and over time (Barker, 2014). Scale reliability can be determined in several ways. Interrater reliability refers to the amount of consistency between or among observers or raters completing the scales. Test-retest reliability is determined by administering a scale to the same participants on at least two separate occasions and comparing the scores for consistency. Sometimes more than one instrument intended to measure a behavioral construct is used comparatively with the same group of participants; this is referred to as parallel-forms reliability. When discussing the psychometric properties of scales, the term *internal consistency* is used to reference the reliability of the correlation between individual items on a scale used to produce an overall or combined score (Rubin & Babbie, 2010). Some scales have items that correspond with specific components or elements of a behavioral construct; these are commonly referred to as the scale domains, which are added together as a measure of the holistic presentation of the behavior. For example, the diagnosis of PTSD consists of various symptoms related to intrusion, avoidance, affect, and arousal (American Psychiatric Association, 2013). Each domain has specific indicators or symptoms that correspond with that specific element of the PTSD behavioral construct as a whole. For example, trauma-related nightmares are part of the intrusion domain of the PTSD construct. The most commonly used statistical method for calculating internal consistency is the coefficient alpha, referred to as the alpha level.

Instrument or scale validity, a psychometric quality different from reliability, refers to an instrument's ability to reasonably measure and reflect the intended behavioral construct realistically and accurately (Barker, 2014). In simplest terms, instrument validity is a measure of whether a scale or instrument fulfills the purpose of its intention; this is often referred to as face validity. Because the validity of scales relates to accurate measurement of an intended construct, it is important to examine the individual items of an instrument to determine whether the items represent the construct in its entirety. This comprehensive measurement property is referred to as construct validity. One way to assess the construct validity of an instrument is to compare the scores from one instrument to another intended to measure the same construct, which is called convergent validity. Another way to measure scale validity is to assess the degree to which a scale measures the intended construct as opposed to another unintended construct; this is referred to as discriminant validity. Finally, criterion validity references a scale's ability to accurately reflect some external criteria believed to be another indicator of the measure (Rubbin & Babbie, 2010); for example, SAT scores predict college success rates.

PART 2: MEASURES OF STRESS AND TRAUMA EXPERIENCES

GENERAL STRESS MEASURES

Not all stress is traumatic stress. From an ecological systems perspective, stress can be conceptualized as a complex and dynamic presentation of human behavior consisting of the biological, psychological, and social responses by people to challenging or difficult stimuli in their physical and social environments (see chapter 2). Several instruments are cited in the literature that purport to measure generalized or everyday stressors that do not constitute traumatic stress. However, the perception of non-trauma-related stressors is quite subjective, and accurately measuring and determining levels of stress has proven to be difficult (Rush, First, & Blacker, 2008).

The original Daily Hassles Scales was developed as a 117-item self-report measure of the impact of life events and environmental stressors on overall physical and mental health. Respondents rated impact of the stressor on both severity and frequency using a 4-point Likert-type scale with 0 = "None" and 3 = "extremely severe." The developers of the scale later shortened the original version to 53 items, which they combined with a parallel measure of positive life events (Maybery & Graham, 2001). The Perceived Stress Scale (PSS) was developed to measure rater perception of the severity of stressful life events across four domains: unpredictability, lack of control, burden overload, and stressful life circumstances. The PSS includes 14 self-report items rated for intensity and frequency on a 5-point Likert-type scale ranging from 0 = "never" to 4 = "very often" (Cohen, Kamarck, & Mermelstein, 1983). Other self-report measures of stress and stressful life events include the Derogatis Stress Profile (DSP), the Coddington Life Events Scale (CLES), the Life Experiences

Survey (LES), the Recent Life Changes Questionnaire, and the Life Stress Test (Rush et al., 2008).

MEASURES OF TRAUMATIC STRESS

See chapter 2 for an in-depth discussion of the etiology and symptomologies associated with PTSD. A thorough discussion of the measure of this construct is beyond the scope of this book, but a general discussion of trauma scale reliability and validity is relevant to the core trauma content. The scientific rigor with regard to the measurement of PTSD has clearly helped to establish the linear relationship between clients with PTSD and the resulting psychological effects on direct practitioners of interacting with primary trauma material. Much of the work on the conceptualization and measurement of PTSD occurred in the 1980s and has since become an important area of specialization in clinical practice and research (Gersons & Carlier, 1992; Figley & Nash, 2007; van der Kolk et al., 1996).

As the professional understandings of the field of traumatology have developed, various psychological responses to combat stress first observed in soldiers have been generalized to other traumatic events including natural disasters; fire or explosion; serious automobile or other moving vehicle accidents; exposure to a toxic substance; domestic violence and physical or sexual assault; rape; life-threatening illness; bearing witness to severe human suffering, homicide or suicide; or sudden unexpected death or serious injury to a significant person or persons (American Psychiatric Association, 2013). Thus, primary traumatization or posttraumatic stress reactions are understood as the consequential, complex, and problematic patterns of behavior that result from the impact of a traumatic incident or event involving an actual or perceived threat on the obvious victim or victims of that incident (American Psychiatric Association, 2013; van der Kolk et al., 1996).

A useful measure of the experience of personal exposure to trauma can be assessed using the Life Events Checklist (LEC) taken from the Clinician Administered PTSD Scale (CAPS), a clinician-administered structured interview for PTSD. This instrument was developed concurrently with the CAPS by the National Center for Posttraumatic Stress Disorder (Blake et al., 1995). The LEC lists multiple examples of traumatic events (natural disaster, rape, combat exposure) in which participants are asked to rate the extent to which they have been exposed to each traumatic event on a 5-point Likert-type scale: (1 = "happened to me"; 2 = "witnessed it"; 3 = "learned about it"; 4 = "not sure"; 5 = "does not apply"). Although not as rigorously tested as the PTSD domains of the CAPS, the LEC has proven to have strong psychometric qualities (Blake et al., 1995; Gray, Litz, Hsu, & Lombardo, 2004).

Another measure of trauma exposure cited in both the primary and secondary trauma literature is the Impact of Event Scale–Revised (IES-R). The IES-R is a 22-item self-report instrument measuring the PTSD symptom domains of intrusion, avoidance, and arousal (Weiss & Marmar, 1995). Items are rated on a 4-point Likert-type scale ranging from 0 = "not at all " to 4 = "extremely." The measure has demonstrated strong psychometric properties including internal validity, clinical utility, and test-retest reliability (Rush et al., 2008; Buchanan, Anderson, Uhlemann, & Horwitz, 2006). In addition to measuring primary trauma in combat veterans, survivors of sexual assault, and victims of domestic violence, the IES-R has been cited in a number of studies measuring the secondary or indirect provider effects of trauma work with these populations (Buchanon et al., 2006; Creamer & Liddle, 2005; Hyman, 2004; Pearlman & MacIan, 1995).

The Clinician Administered PTSD Scale for *DSM-5* (CAPS-5) is a 30-item scale designed to be used in structured interviews as a diagnostic assessment of the 20 criteria presented in the *DSM-5* (American Psychiatric Association, 2013). The CAPS is supported by the National Center for PTSD as the "gold standard" in PTSD assessment. Detailed information about the CAPS, including an interview with one of the scale developers, Frank Weathers, training information, and measure availability can be found at the Department of Veterans Affairs National Center for PTSD (U.S. Department of Veterans Affairs, 2017). Each of the 20 established *DSM-5* diagnostic criteria for PTSD are rated by the clinician based on both intensity and frequency. Intensity is rated based on five anchors ranging from 0 = "Absent"; 1 = "mild or subthreshold"; 2 = "Moderate"; 3 = "Severe or markedly elevated"; and 4 = "Extremely incapacitating." The CAPS has been used extensively as a measure of PTSD, has been translated into several different languages, and is also available in a child and adolescent version. The CAPS has consistently demonstrated strong psychometric properties including reliability, validity, and clinical utility (Carlson, 1997; Rush et al., 2008; Weathers, Keane, & Davidson, 2001). The current *DSM-5* criteria do not address the issue of race-based traumatic stress, but the Race-Based Traumatic Stress Scale (RBTSS) purports to measure this construct. The RBTSS is a 52-item measure consisting of seven subscales: depression, anger, physical reactions, avoidance, intrusion, arousal, and self-esteem (Carter et al., 2013). Table 5.1 provides a useful list of other scales that are valid measures of either traumatic or posttraumatic stress.

PART 3: MEASURING PROFESSIONAL BURNOUT AND INDIRECT TRAUMA EXPERIENCES

The literature reveals few validated measures of occupational stress as it relates to professional burnout. The Job Content Questionnaire (JCQ) measures the

TABLE 5.1 Measures of Primary Trauma Experiences (Adult and Child)

Trauma Scale or Measure	Author(s)	Administration
Acute Stress Disorder Interview (ASDI)	Richard Bryant	structured interview
Children's PTSD Inventory	Phillip A. Saigh	clinician administered
Child PTSD Symptom Scale	Edna Foa	structured interview
Childhood Trauma Interview	Laura Fink	self-report (adult)
Davidson Trauma Scale (DTS)	John Davidson	self-report
Mississippi Scale for Combat-Related PTSD	Keane, Caddell, & Taylor	self-report
Posttraumatic Stress Diagnostic Scale (PDS)	Foa, Cashman, Jaycox, & Perry	self-report
Posttraumatic Stress Inventory for Children (PTSIC)	Mitchell Eisen	structured interview
Posttraumatic Stress Disorder Checklist	Nat. Center for PTSD	self-report
Posttraumatic Symptoms Scale (PSS-I)	Edna Foa	semi-structured interview
Race-Based Traumatic Stress Symptoms Scale (RBTSS)	Carter et. al.	self-report
Structured Interview for PTSD (SI-PTSD)	John Davidson	structured interview
Trauma Assessment for Adults (TAA)	Resnick et. al.	self-report
Trauma History Questionnaire	Bonnie Green	self-report
Trauma Symptom Checklist for Children (TSCC)	John Briere	structured interview
Trauma Symptoms Inventory (TSI)	John Briere	self-report
Traumatic Stress Schedule	Frank Norris	self-report
UCLA Posttraumatic Stress Disorder Reaction Index	Melissa Brymer	self-report for children

physical and psychological health risks associated with the demands of stressful work environments but does not purport to measure burnout. The scale consists of 49 items rated across five occupational stress domains: decision latitude, psychological demands, social support, physical demands, and job insecurity. The measure has shown relatively strong psychometric properties and clinical utility and has been translated into several languages (Rush et al., 2008).

The most commonly cited and well-tested measure of professional burnout is the Maslach Burnout Inventory (MBI). The MBI has been tested extensively since the 1980s and has shown strong psychometric qualities including reliability and construct validity. The instrument has been tested in the United States and internationally and has been translated into several languages (Drake & Yadama, 1995; Schaufeli, Bakker, Hoogduin, Schaap, & Kladler, 2001). Studies have used the MBI as a measure of burnout in various professional settings including human service organizations, education, and in the business world. The MBI is considered the "gold standard" for measurement of the burnout construct (Drake & Yadama, 1995; Schaufeli et al., 2001; Um & Harrison, 1998).

The MBI is designed to assess professional burnout in each of three separate domains: emotional exhaustion; depersonalization or job cynicism; and reduced sense of personal accomplishment, which is also referred to as lack of professional efficacy (figure 5.1). The MBI contains 22 self-reported items, which are coded into the three subscales: emotional exhaustion, depersonalization, and reduced sense of personal accomplishment and professional efficacy (Maslach, 1998; Taris, LeBlanc, Schaufeli, & Schreurs, 2005).

Respondents indicate the frequency of burnout related job experiences over the last year on an 8-point Likert-type scale ranging from 0 = "never" to 7 = "every day." Each subscale of the MBI is coded separately; the instrument does not yield a composite score. Scores from each subscale are coded as "low," "moderate," or "high" range for burnout (Maslach, 2001; Schaufeli et al., 2001). A "higher" degree of burnout is indicated by higher scores on the emotional exhaustion and depersonalization scales and low scores on the personal accomplishment scales. The scoring range for each domain of the MBI is presented in table 5.2.

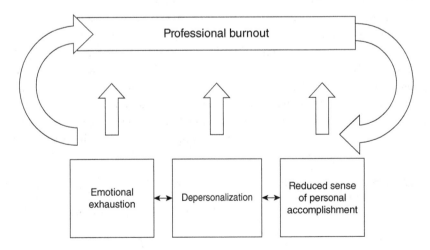

FIGURE 5.1 Conceptual model of the Maslach Burnout Inventory domains

TABLE 5.2 Psychometric Properties for the Maslach Burnout Inventory (MBI)

	Maslach Burnout Inventory (MBI)			
	Range	Low	Moderate	High
Emotional exhaustion	0–63	0–16	17–26	27–63
Depersonalization	0–28	0–6	7–12	13–28
Personal accomplishment	0–56	39–56	32–38	0–31

MEASURES OF INDIRECT TRAUMA EXPERIENCES

The Secondary Traumatic Stress Scale (STSS) is a 17-item instrument designed to measure symptoms associated with STS in three specific domains related to the experience of PTSD (intrusion, avoidance, and arousal) framed in the form of client exposure rather than direct or primary exposure (Bride, Robinson, Yegidis, & Figley, 2004; Bride, 2007). Respondents rate the frequency with which they have experienced each symptom or indicator in the last seven days on a 5-point Likert-type scale ranging from 1 = "never" to 5 = "very often." The scores for each domain are summed to yield a composite score. There is a maximum possible score of 85 on the STSS (table 5.3). A total score of 28 or less is considered subthreshold for symptoms of STS, and scores ranging from 29 to 37 are considered mild, 38 to 43 moderate, 44 to 48 high, and 49 and higher severe (Bride, Radey, & Figley, 2007). The STSS has demonstrated strong psychometric qualities including convergent and discriminate validity and factorial validity across several populations of trauma professionals including child welfare workers, mental health professionals, and trauma specialists (Bride, 2007; Bride et al., 2004; Ting, Jacobson, Sanders, Bride, & Harrington, 2005).

The Professional Quality of Life scale (ProQOL) has recently been revised in a fifth version and was originally the Compassion Fatigue Self-Test (Figley & Stamm, 1996; Stamm, 2010). Items on the ProQOL measure the effects of burnout and secondary trauma in two specific domains. Stamm (2010) suggests the combination of professional burnout and secondary trauma constitute the cumulative effects of compassion fatigue. The ProQOL also includes a third subscale or domain measuring compassion satisfaction, which relates to the positive and

TABLE 5.3 Scoring Range for the Secondary Traumatic Stress Scale (STSS)

	Range	Subthreshold	Mild	Moderate	High
Secondary Traumatic Stress Scale	0–85	0–28	29–37	38–43	44–85

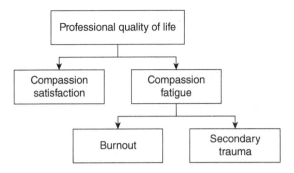

FIGURE 5.2 Conceptual model for the Professional Quality of Life Scale (ProQOL)

rewarding experiences associated with human service work. A conceptual model of the domains of the ProQOL is presented in figure 5.2. The ProQOL contains 30 items, which participants are asked to rate on a 5-point Likert-type scale ranging from 1 = "never" to 5 = "very often." Each subscale of the ProQOL is coded separately; the scores from each subscale can be converted into "low," "moderate," and "high" for each domain. The ProQOL is a popular measure of the combined effects of burnout and trauma and the mediating effects of compassion satisfaction (table 5.4). The measure demonstrates strong reliability and validity for each of the subscales using the Cronbach's Alpha test (compassion satisfaction = .87; burnout = .90; and compassion fatigue = .87) (Stamm, 2010). The measure has been administered across a variety of human service professionals including child welfare workers, mental health professionals, and other micro and macro trauma specialists and has been translated into more than 20 languages (Adeyemo et al., 2015; Ray, Wong, White, & Heaslip, 2013; Stamm, 2010).

The Traumatic Stress Institute Belief Scale Revision-L (TSIBS-L) is an 80-item self-report measure of vicarious trauma. The instrument is based on the constructivist self-development theory, which frames vicarious traumatization as disruptions in cognitive schemata in major areas including safety, trust, esteem, intimacy, and control (McCann & Pearlman, 1992; Pearlman & MacIan, 1995; Pearlman & Saakvitne, 1995). Items are rated on a 6-point Likert-type scale ranging from 1 = "disagree" to 6 = "strongly agree." Scores obtained include

TABLE 5.4 Scale Ranges for the ProQOL Domains

Domain	Low	Moderate	High
Compassion satisfaction	0–42	23–41	42 or more
Burnout	0–42	23–41	42 or more
Compassion fatigue	0–42	23–41	42 or more

a total score calculated from the sum of all responses; a higher score indicates greater cognitive schema disruption. The scale items have demonstrated strong internal consistency, and the scale has been administered to a variety of trauma professionals including those working with survivors of sexual trauma and incest (Jenkins & Baird, 2002: Trippany et al., 2003; Pearlman & MacIan, 1995; Schauben & Frazier, 1995).

QUALITATIVE ASSESSMENTS

Some studies have attempted to measure the effects of burnout, vicarious trauma, and secondary traumatic stress from a qualitative approach without the use of standardized scales or measures. Research using qualitative assessment methodology can be conducted in a number of ways. One way to gather qualitative data is to facilitate a group of participants in some form of human service or trauma-related work and initiate a semistructured dialogue or conversation without the use of a specific set of questions or a plan for the inquiry. This method allows the observer to capture phenomenological data in the form of a subjective narrative in the moment as it emerges in conversation (Iliffe, 2000; Kapoulistas & Corcoran, 2015). Other methods of qualitative inquiry involve a more formal interview process with a set of standardized open-ended questions such as, "Describe the most difficult and the most rewarding aspects of your job" (Schauben & Frazier, 1995). Interviews may be recorded and transcribed for analysis of common themes that emerge from the structured interviews (Rubbin & Babbie, 2010). Qualitative studies on the effects of trauma work have been conducted with direct practitioners serving child welfare clients, perpetrators and survivors of domestic violence, sexual assault survivors, the

KEY TERMS

burnout	open-ended question
compassion fatigue	posttraumatic stress disorder (PTSD)
compassion satisfaction	psychometric properties
convergent validity	qualitative assessment
construct	range
content validity	reliability
criterion validity	scale
discriminant validity	secondary traumatic stress
domain	self-report measure
face validity	structured interview
internal consistency	test-retest reliability
interrater reliability	vicarious trauma
item analysis	

mentally ill, and with survivors of mass interpersonal violence (Anderson, 2000; Collins & Long, 2002; Dane, 2000; Harrison & Westwood, 2009; Iliffe, 2000; Jankoski, 2010; Schauben & Frazier, 1995).

CHAPTER SUMMARY

The focus of this chapter is on the importance of accurate assessment and measurement of the primary and secondary forms of traumatic stress, compassion fatigue, and professional burnout. The chapter provides a brief overview of the methodological terms associated with instrument reliability and validity. The constructs of PTSD and professional burnout have been accepted in the professional literature for some time and have been the subject of empirical study validating the measurement of these constructs. However, the construct validity of the indirect effects of trauma has been challenging. Terms such as vicarious traumatization, secondary traumatic stress, and compassion fatigue have been blended together in the research literature, which has inhibited the operational definitions and construct formation of these behavioral entities. The only consensus in the literature seems to be that there is indeed no consensus.

Parts 2 and 3 of this chapter highlight specific scales used to measure both the existence and the effects of stress, primary trauma, indirect trauma, and burnout. Specific trauma measures discussed include the Life Events Checklist (LEC), the revised Impact of Events Scale (IES-R), and the Clinician Administered PTSD Scale (CAPS). Other validated measures of primary trauma are listed in table 5.1. Part 3 discusses quantitative and qualitative measures of professional burnout and secondary trauma. There are fewer validated measures of these constructs, partly due to significant issues of construct validity with regard to the sometimes synonymous use of terms such as vicarious trauma and secondary traumatic stress in the empirical literature. Therefore, the content in this section includes more detail regarding the scales that purport to measure these constructs. Specific scales reviewed include the Maslach Burnout Inventory (MBI), the Secondary Traumatic Stress Scale (STSS), the revised Traumatic Stress Institute Belief Scale (TSIBS-R), and the Professional Quality of Life scale (ProQOL). This section also includes a brief review of studies that have attempted to measure these constructs from a qualitative perspective.

RECOMMENDED READINGS

Berg, B. L., & Lune, H. (2012). *Qualitative research methods for the social sciences.* Boston, MA: Pearson.

Carlson, E. B. (1997). *Trauma assessments: A clinicians guide.* New York, NY. Guilford.

Rubin, A., & Babbie, E. (2010). *Essential research methods for social work* (2nd ed.). Belmont, CA: Brooks/Cole: Cengage Learning.

Rush, J. A., First, M. B., & Blacker, D. (2008). *Handbook of psychiatric measures* (2nd ed.). Washington, DC: American Psychiatric Publishing.

Russell, A. C. (2014). *A hands on manual for social work research.* Chicago, IL: Lyceum Books.

SUGGESTED INTERNET RESOURCES

Maslach Burnout Inventory (MBI): http://maslach.socialpsychology.org/

For more information on Christina Maslach and the use of the MBI, visit the website hosted by the Social Psychology Network. The site provides an overview of Dr. Maslach's career, including a short history of the burnout construct and a complete overview of her research and publication history. The MBI is available for use by purchase by contacting info@mindgarden.com. A lecture by Dr. Maslach on the burnout process and construct is available at no cost on YouTube at https://www.youtube.com/watch?v=4kLPyV8lBbs.

International Society for Traumatic Stress Studies: www.istss.org

This is the premier society for the exchange of professional knowledge and expertise in the field of traumatology. Membership is international and open to anyone practicing or interested in trauma work. The site includes a wealth of resources on the assessment, treatment, and research of trauma-related disorders. Features include public resources on trauma-related practice at no cost, including a comprehensive list of scales measuring trauma experiences with psychometric data included, teaching resources, access to a trauma blog, and links to the publication *Stress Points.*

National Child Traumatic Stress Network (NCTSN): http://www.nctsnet.org/

The mission of NCTSN is "to raise the standard of care and improve access to services for traumatized children, their families and communities throughout the United States." This is an excellent resource on trauma-related disorders and treatment in children and adolescents. The site contains portals with information for parents and families, professionals, military families, and educators. Specific features include an online learning center for professional development in the area of child traumatic stress and a comprehensive review of the measures of childhood trauma complete with psychometric information. Other resources include handouts on the presentation of child traumatic stress disorders and a toolkit for natural disaster or terrorist attack response and recovery.

Professional Quality of Life Scale (ProQOL): www.proqol.org

Developed by Dr. Stamm, this is the most comprehensive source of information on the ProQOL scale. The site includes extensive information on the theoretical development, conceptualization , and psychometric qualities of ProQOL. The cite provides a complete bibliography on studies utilizing ProQOL and a recently updated comprehensive bibliography on the secondary aspect of caring, citing 2,000 related materials. Additional materials include handouts, PowerPoint slides, and pocket guides related to compassion fatigue. All of the resources are downloadable and provided at no cost.

SECTION 2

A HOLISTIC FRAMEWORK FOR THE APPLICATION OF SELF-CARE PRACTICES

6

THE ESSENTIAL PRACTICE OF PROFESSIONAL SELF-CARE
Cultivating and Sustaining Professional Resilience

Rest and self-care are so important. When you take time to replenish your spirit, it allows you to serve others from the overflow. You cannot serve from an empty vessel.

—ELEANOR BROWN

CHAPTER GOALS AND OBJECTIVES

1. Introduce the concept of resilience from a multidisciplinary approach as a dynamic construct that has been studied across professional disciplines at the micro and macro levels of practice.
2. Describe the conceptualization of professional resilience and other associated terms, including posttraumatic growth, vicarious resilience, and compassion satisfaction, as they apply to efficacious practice with human service populations.
3. Discuss professional self-care from a holistic perspective as an essential practice behavior for the resilience of social workers and other human service professionals.
4. Provide a comprehensive framework outlining the development of a plan of self-care using an ecological systems framework.
5. Illustrate the holistic process of developing a plan of self-care using a case study exercise and a sample plan of care.

The first half of the book focuses on providing education and awareness of the emotionally challenging aspects of human service work and the potential (and sometimes consequential) effects of daily practice with individuals who are vulnerable or suffering in some way. The second half focuses on maintaining professional resilience through various strategies of personal and professional self-care. In simple terms, these chapters attempt to bridge the identified gap between research in the area of professional resilience and self-care (i.e., knowing compassion fatigue exists) and the real world of practice (i.e., what social workers and other human service professionals can do to prevent this from happening).

Part 1 of this chapter describes resilience as a dynamic construct with application to multiple areas of professional practice including neurobiology, psychology, psychiatry, and social work (at both the micro and macro levels of practice). Part 2 discusses self-care as both a practice and a process essential to the maintenance of personal and professional resilience. Using an ecological systems perspective, the practice of self-care is conceptualized as a multidimensional process related to the care and maintenance of multiple aspects of the psychosocial self.

PART 1: THE IMPORTANCE OF CULTIVATING RESILIENCE

A DYNAMIC CONCEPT

A simple definition of resilience is "the ability to become strong, healthy, or successful again after something bad happens" or "an ability to recover from or adjust easily to misfortune or change" (Merriam-Webster, 2017). In clinical terms, the American Psychological Association (APA, 2016) describes resilience as "the process of adapting well in the face of adversity, trauma, tragedy, threats or significant sources of stress—such as family and relationship problems, serious health problems or workplace and financial stressors." The empirical work on defining human *resilience* or *resiliency* is similar to the material describing empathy in chapter 3; the defining literature on the construct validity of resilience reveals no universally agreed-upon or clearly defined operational definition for this term. Rather, the works examining resilience, often as a personal characteristic, use resilience interchangeably with other similar concepts such as hardiness, personal growth, positive adaptation, and psychological well-being (Luthar, Cicchetti, & Becker, 2000). Alternatively, resilience has been described as an overall process of well-being consisting of intrapersonal, interpersonal, and social dimensions rather than solely as a function of personality (Kent et al., 2014). Using a multidimensional approach, resilience has been described as "a sustained adaptive effort that prevails despite challenge, as a bouncing back or recovery from a challenge, and as a process of learning and growth that expands understanding, new knowledge, and new skills" (Kent et al., 2014, p. xii).

From an ecological systems perspective, personal resilience may occur at the individual or micro level of practice as the ability to recovery from crisis or human tragedy such as sexual assault, rape, child sexual abuse, combat exposure, or mass acts of violence (Easton, Coohey, Rhodes, & Moorthy, 2013; Schok, Kleber, & Lensvelt-Mulders, 2010; Simon, Smith, Fava, & Feiring, 2015; Waller, 2001). Resilience may also occur at the macro level in the context of larger community events such as the global response to the citizens of New York in the aftermath of the September 11 terrorist attacks (Cicchetti, 2013; van der Walt, Suliman, Martin, Lammers, & Seedat, 2014). This process is eloquently described by Victor E. Frankl, who during World War II lost his father, mother, and brother while being held prisoner in a Nazi concentration camp:

> We who lived in the concentration camps can remember the men who walked through the huts comforting others, giving away their last piece of bread. They may have been few in number, but they offer sufficient proof that everything can be taken from a man but one thing: the last of the human freedoms—to choose one's attitude in any given set of circumstances, to choose one's own way. (Frankl, 1984, pp. 65–66)

Resilience has been shown to occur across multiple domains of psychosocial systems while simultaneously and mutually influencing the overall functioning of the person (Berger, 2015; Payne, 2014; Waller, 2001). Chapter 2 has a detailed discussion and illustration of the ecological systems approach to human behavior. For example, an individual's biological resilience to human disease and infection (or lack thereof) may affect resilience in other key areas of psychosocial functioning, including the developmental, professional, marital, familial, social, and community domains of the ecological system, a process referred to as system homeostasis (Payne, 2014; Southwick, Liz, Charney, & Friedman, 2011). Based on the holistic perspective of the ecological model, Walsh (2003, 2015) proposes a multidimensional framework for conceptualizing family resilience consisting of family belief systems (making meaning out of diversity, positive outlook, and transcendence and spiritually), organizational patterns (flexibility, connectedness, and social and economic resources), and communication and problem solving (clarity, open emotional expression, and collaborative problem solving).

Human resilience has been examined both as an innate biological adaptive response to stressful external stimuli (passive resilience) and as the use of coping skills (active resilience) as moderators or buffers to the effects of stress and trauma (Kent et al., 2014; van der Walt et al., 2014; Yehuda, Flory, Southwick, & Charney, 2006). Human resilience has been studied from a variety of perspectives, including neurobiology, as an adaptive and sometimes anticipatory reaction to change and the biological predisposition to recover (also referred to as allostasis) in the wake of chronic stress or trauma (Russo, Murrough, Han, Charney, & Nestler, 2012; Stix, 2011; van der Walt et al., 2014). Resilience has been examined as a function of healthy human development across the life span in infants, children, adolescents, adults, and in families both biologically and as a coping skill (Masten, 2001, 2014; Masten & Coatsworth, 1998;

Ryff, 2013; Walsh, 2003). Cognitively, resilience has been studied as the various ways people appraise, process, and regulate the emotions attached to external stimuli, with emphasis on the application of positive thoughts and emotions to promote psychological well-being (Duckworth, Steen, & Seligman, 2005; Frederickson, 2004). Finally, as a function of spirituality, resilience may include the use of compassion for the care of others, honoring one's personal and spiritual sense of morality, and adhering to personal and professional values and ethics (Seagar, 2014; Wicks & Maynard, 2014).

In summary, resilience is a dynamic concept defined in a similar way across multiple disciplines, but it has yet to be clearly defined or measured from one perspective (Rutter, 2013; Southwick, Bonanno, Masten, Panter-Brick, & Yehuda, 2014). Like other terms discussed in this text, the lack of a universally accepted approach to human resilience creates challenges in the measurement and validation of the specific elements or components of the resilience construct. However, the breadth of multidisciplinary research in this area is timely and is an indicator that the functions of human and community resilience are varied and can occur across the micro and macro dimensions of psychosocial systems (Southwick et al., 2011, 2014; Walsh, 2015).

PROFESSIONAL RESILIENCE AS THE POSITIVE ASPECTS OF HUMAN SERVICE WORK

Resilience (framed as "professional resilience") has been used in the human service fields, including counseling, social work, education, psychotherapy, nursing, medicine, and other health-related professions, to describe the process by which those who provide services to vulnerable or at-risk populations thrive in these inherently stressful work conditions (Hegney, Rees, Eley, Osseiran-Moisson, & Francis, 2015; Hernandez, Gangsei, & Engstrom, 2007; Skovholt & Trotter-Mathison, 2011). A recent shift in the professional literature, particularly in the area of traumatology, reveals a stronger focus on defining and measuring the positive aspects and experiences contributing to the motivational resilience of direct practitioners to continue their work over time. A review of the literature on the various approaches to defining professional resiliency once again reveal one common denominator—the use of empathy and compassion as the driving force to do this work. Examination of recent empirical studies in the area of professional resilience shows an attempt to bring balance to previously discussed constructs such as vicarious traumatization, secondary traumatic stress, and compassion fatigue; these constructs have focused solely on the emotionally challenging and sometimes consequential aspects of providing direct services to those who are vulnerable and suffering in some way, particularly professionals involved in any form of trauma-related practice.

Studies examining the positive aspects of trauma work suggest that the chronic use of compassion and empathy in the context of practice can be a great source of stress, but it also has the potential to be a great source of strength and fulfillment (Radey & Figley, 2007; Stamm, 1999). Moreover, developing the professional skills to regulate empathy while engaging clients and their experiences in the helping process may foster the growth of practice wisdom and expertise over time (Linley, 2003).

The terms and concepts have emerged in the professional literature in a linear fashion, originating in the traumatic stress literature. Much like the concept of vicarious traumatization, which was originally proposed to describe the consequential changes in behavior and cognition experienced by providers treating clients with emotional traumas, the same is true of the literature on positive adaptation (Berger, 2015; Linley, 2003; Newell et al., 2015). Refer to the timeline in figure 3.1 for a chronological orientation to the terms discussed here. For example, posttraumatic growth (PTG) was first cited in the late 1980s, but it became a more researched and measured construct in the 1990s. Posttraumatic growth describes the positive changes in the self, in relationships with others, and in the overall outlook and philosophy of life that occur for many individuals when confronted with challenging life situations such as physical and sexual assault, major medical illness, natural disaster, and combat stress (Easton et al., 2013; Saimos, Rodzik, & Abel, 2012; Tedeschi & Calhoun, 1996, 2004). The early literature on PTG focused solely on the ability of the trauma survivor to experience positive growth after a traumatic experience, but it has also been found in those who work with trauma populations (Samios et al., 2012; Engstrom, Hernandez, & Gangsei, 2008). The review of studies during this time period revealed an important and positive change in the use of client-centered language (rather than perpetrator or incident centered) to describe trauma experiences; for example, framing clients as "survivors" of sexual assault rather than as "victims."

Much like the review of the literature on the other terms and constructs, the review on posttraumatic growth revealed terms such as *stress-related growth* and *transformational coping*, which have been used interchangeably with PTG (Linley, 2003). A similar and more recently cited term is *vicarious resilience* (VR). Adapted from the literature on vicarious trauma, VR describes the process of trauma recovery as having the potential to foster resilience and growth not only in the client but in the clinician as well (Hernandez et al., 2007). The process of VR occurs through witnessing and participating with clients who are suffering from the effects of crisis, trauma, or another human tragedy and who overcome these circumstances while rediscovering the meaningful aspects of life through the healing process (Engstrom et al., 2008; Hernandez et al., 2007).

The most commonly cited term in this area is *compassion satisfaction*, which refers to those aspects of human service work that provide professional success, reward, and fulfillment (Conrad & Keller-Guenther, 2006; Stamm, 2010). Elements of compassion satisfaction include positive interactions with clients such as celebrating client successes, the formation of meaning and supportive relationships with colleagues, the personal and spiritual satisfaction or being in a helping profession, and the positive professional interactions that occur in human service organizations and as benefits of membership in a helping community (Kapoulistas & Corcoran, 2015; Stamm, 2010). The professional experiences of compassion satisfaction and the similar concept of VR have been shown to mitigate the effects of indirect trauma and burnout in psychotherapists, child welfare workers, nurses, and other human service professionals (DePanfilis, 2006; Hegney et al., 2015; Hernandez et al., 2007; Ray et al., 2013). Empathy is the driving force behind posttraumatic growth, compassion satisfaction, and vicarious resilience. Witnessing and interacting with clients as they overcome adversity and experience positive personal growth and healing despite hardships and suffering enables the clinician to experience professional and spiritual satisfaction in a unique way (Engstrom et al., 2008). This type of personal and professional growth can and should be considered both a unique reward of clinical practice and an opportunity to truly appreciate the importance and value of this work (Pooler, Wolfer, & Freeman, 2014).

Take time to complete the first worksheet at the end of the book, titled Personal Refection Exercise: Resilience and Self-Appreciation, before reading part 2 of this chapter.

PART 2: PRACTICING SELF-CARE: THE KEY TO PROFESSIONAL RESILIENCE

WHAT IS PROFESSIONAL SELF-CARE?

A well-defined and operational plan of self-care is the key to a positive outcome for professional resilience in human service work. The need for professional self-care as a component of daily practice for social workers and other human service professionals involved with clients who are vulnerable or suffering has been overlooked in professional development, training, and education for some time (Cunningham, 2004; Courtois, 2002; Dunkley & Whelan, 2006; Newell & MacNeil, 2010). Only in the last two decades has the professional community, particularly those treating trauma-related disorders, acknowledged the existence of these risks and the possibility that these risks may be underestimated occupational hazards for human service workers (Pryce et al., 2007). The research over a 30-year span confirms that many social service professionals are unable to meet the emotional and professional demands associated with direct practice. Further, the literature clearly reveals that those who are new to social service work are the most vulnerable to the psychological effects of treating consumers with myriad challenges and treatment needs.

The research literature is rich in our knowledge of the emotional effects of working with vulnerable clients through provider experiences such as counter-transference, vicarious trauma, secondary traumatic stress, compassion fatigue, and professional burnout. However, little empirical literature supports the use of validated models, methods, and strategies to address this important issue of the preservation of the social service workforce. Perhaps this is due to the primary emphasis in the field of traumatology in recent years on treatment for those in direct contact with trauma-related experiences (Figley, 2002a). Interest, concern, and formal investigation of the indirect or secondary effects of human service work on direct service providers is recent (Newell et al., 2015). A second speculation is that the methodological challenges in the construct development and measurement of the various defining terms in the literature has overshadowed outcome studies on the resolution of these conditions. Regardless of the reason behind the challenges, the research literature across professional disciplines in human services and other allied health professions clearly consistently suggests (if not mandates) that it is essential for professionals to commit themselves to their own professional resilience as an ongoing function of self-care (Figley, 2002b).

SELF-CARE AS A HOLISTIC PROCESS

Self-care has been described as both a process and a defined set of practice skills and strategies to mitigate the emotionally challenging effects of providing services to individuals, families, and communities (Skinner, 2015). Professional awareness of the importance of self-care in the practice community has been acknowledged and supported by the National Association of Social Workers (NASW, 2009), who define self-care as "a core essential component to social work practice that reflects a choice and commitment to become actively involved in maintaining ones effectiveness as a social worker in preventing and coping with the natural, yet unwanted, consequences of helping" (p. 246). A synthesis of the various definitions and recommendations for professional self-care can be summarized as social workers and other human service professionals using skills and strategies to maintain their own personal, familial, emotional, physical, and spiritual needs to actively and consciously promote holistic well-being and professional resilience while attending to the complex emotional needs and demands of their clients (Cox & Sterner, 2013b; Lee & Miller, 2013; Pearlman & Saakvitne, 1995; Stamm, 2010). The amalgamation of the various definitions and approaches to self-care support a comprehensive approach to self-care with physical, interpersonal, organizational, and spiritual components (Lee & Miller, 2013; Pearlman & Saakvitne, 1995). This holistic interpretation of self-care practice is consistent with the ecological systems perspective discussed earlier in the chapter to describe the concept of human resilience. Refer to chapter 2 for a detailed outline of this approach to conceptualizing social problems.

Although *professional self-care* is used extensively in the research literature, the responsibility for this practice largely falls on the individual (i.e., the worker) and requires efforts that go far beyond the confines of social service agencies and the borders of that individual's chosen profession (Bressi & Vaden, 2016). From the ecological systems perspective, the term *self-care* encompasses multiple dimensions across psychosocial systems and is not simply a function of professional behavior. A holistic view of the practice of self-care as the pathway to professional resilience is illustrated in figure 6.1, which diagrams the various domains of self-care from an ecological systems perspective.

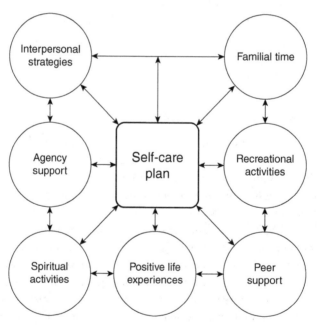

FIGURE 6.1 Ecological systems framework for the practice of holistic self-care

APPLYING EXISTING PROFESSIONAL KNOWLEDGE
TO SELF-CARE PRACTICE

Professional resilience is the positive outcome of human service work that has the potential to bring balance to the negative and sometimes deleterious outcomes resulting in professional burnout. Human service professionals, particularly those trained in social work education programs, garner the professional education, skills, and abilities to practice self-care, but the biggest challenge for many social service professionals is simply to make a commitment to embrace self-care as an essential and ongoing practice behavior. One valuable qualitative theme (and lesson) gathered from conducting professional trainings in this area is the realization that practicing self-care is often counterintuitive for those who have dedicated their lives to caring for others. The ability to practice self-care is almost always present, but it may be overlooked by the professional. Therefore, training in the practice of self-care becomes a matter of cultivation.

Using the social work profession as an example, maintaining a plan of professional self-care requires little more than applying the basic theories, skills, and knowledge used to facilitate clients through the process of case management and treatment planning. Fundamental to the practice of social work is the assessment of human behavior as it interfaces with the social environment; this core competency can be applied to the practitioner (as in to oneself) to gain valuable insights into both personal and professional patterns of behavior. Other mainstays of social work practice, such as problem-solving and task-centered approaches, can easily be applied when creating a useful, functional, and ongoing plan of professional self-care. Strengths-based practice can be used to identify areas of professional or client success in analyzing the positive aspects of working in human service organizations (see the Personal Reflection Exercise worksheet at the end of the book), Finally, psychosocial assessment skills can be used to comprehensively examine personal and professional areas in need of improvement, which may prove helpful in determining future self-care goals and objectives. Saakvinte and Pearlman (1996) provide an instrument for the comprehensive assessment of self-care activities across the physical, psychological, emotional, spiritual, relational, and occupational domains. Once a self-assessment is made, human service professionals can begin to conceptualize and develop their own functional and holistic self-care plan based on the strategies provided in table 6.1. Worksheets at the end of the book also include exercises on setting personal and professional goals for the self-care process.

TABLE 6.1 Suggestions for Developing a Comprehensive Plan of Self-Care

Self-Care Domain	Suggested Strategies
Biological	Balanced diet and nutrition; adequate sleep schedule; regular exercise regime; moderation in alcohol use; use health and mental health days to recover from physical or emotional illness including grief work
Interpersonal	Maintain professional boundaries with clients; create a healthy balance between personal and professional obligations; use adaptive rather than maladaptive coping skills; actively engage anxiety associated with clients through techniques such as mindfulness, self-talk, and self-awareness; use psychotherapy, counseling, or support group help (particularly for those with a personal trauma history)
Organizational	Seek out organizations with missions consistent with personal values and career aspirations; participate in education, training, and professional development opportunities; participate in active supervision and ongoing mentorship; engage in supportive relationships with professional colleagues; set realistic goals and objectives for the workday or workweek; use coffee and lunch breaks for non-work-related activities; participate in the celebration of client success and fulfillment; maintain a realistic worldview about the impact of client-work on the self
Familial	Use social support from family and close friends; participate in nonstressful family events; engage in "no-technology" dinners and family time; schedule family and couples vacation time; participate in children's activities, school functions, and sports events (if applicable); protect time to celebrate special family events, birthdays, or anniversaries; schedule nonfamily time to catch up with close friends; enjoy time caring for and spending time with family pets
Spiritual	Attend church regularly; engage in positive forms of self-expression and self-revitalization; yoga; meditation; philanthropic activities
Recreational	Read; draw; paint; sculpt; participate in team sports; cook; hike; swim; go to movies; find other outdoor activities or forms of positive self-expression; participate in any activity personally or professionally that fosters joy, humor, or laughter

DEVELOPING A PLAN OF SELF-CARE: AN ECOLOGICAL SYSTEMS FRAMEWORK

Using the holistic approach to self-care proposed by the ecological systems framework, positive activities across several domains—biological, interpersonal, organizational, familial, peer-related, spiritual, and recreational—all contribute to a comprehensive plan of self-care. This approach allows for a broader view of self-care and does not focus solely on the professional aspects of this practice. One of the major premises of the ecological systems theory is the idea of *homeostasis*, which refers to a human system's drive and collective ability to maintain its fundamental nature, even during times of sudden or intense change (Payne, 2014). Another principle of systems theory suggests that the collective system and all of its domains naturally adapt and adjust to maintain balance or equilibrium in a homeostatic state. The occupational domain directly influences all other domains in the collective system, and too much human energy expended in the stress of work activities takes valuable energy and resources away from other areas (positive health behaviors, time with family and friends, and spiritual and recreational activities). Maintaining an ongoing plan of self-care helps to create a healthy work–life balance, which contributes to professional resilience and overall well-being.

Simple strategies for self-care at the individual level range from maintaining positive health behaviors, to spiritual activities, recreational activities, positive forms of self-expression, and connections with family members and close friends. At the organizational level, substantial evidence suggests that self-care can be augmented through support from professional colleagues and supervisors in assisting with documentation and administrative duties, conducting client interviews, or providing emotional support such as comfort, insight, or humor (Maslach, 2003b).

OLIVER: A CASE STUDY IN PRACTICE WITH VETERANS AND MILITARY FAMILIES

Oliver is working in the mental health clinic at a VA Medical Center, and his primary duty is to screen patients as an intake worker and connect them to other resources in the hospital including primary care, counseling, vocational rehabilitation, and disability.

Oliver is often the first mental health professional the veteran meets. In supervision, Oliver reports that during interviews he is often exposed to the graphic details of soldiers' experiences in combat. Many soldiers have experienced life-threatening circumstances and have subsequent trauma that inhibits their readjustment to civilian life. In addition to exposure to soldiers' emotional injuries, Oliver often is exposed to the long-term effects of their physical injuries.

More than 30 percent of the soldiers returning from combat have some form of mental illness, and many of Oliver's clients are quickly referred to PTSD, substance abuse, vocational rehabilitation, and treatment programs.

Oliver reports that the combination of physical and emotional injury makes it difficult for many veterans to readjust to their spouses, children, extended family, jobs, and friends. One soldier lost both of his legs during an IED bombing, during which he also witnessed the death of his best friend and bunkmate. When the soldier returned home, he discovered that his wife was having an affair with a neighbor and was planning to divorce him. Oliver reports that veterans often become tearful and anxious during their interviews, which makes the intake process even more difficult. He openly admits to excusing himself from sessions on more than one occasion to "pull it together" because the veterans' stories are often disheartening and difficult to hear.

Oliver actively pursued a career in military social work because he has great compassion for this population and comes from a military family. However, at the end of the day, he often feels emotionally drained due to using his empathy skills as he listens to veterans' issues and makes effective recommendations and connects them to the right resources. He admits that the struggles veterans experience often weigh heavily on his heart, and he finds himself thinking and worrying about his patients during nonworking hours. Oliver states that he sometimes wakes up tired and fears that the chronic, day-to-day exposure to these clients and their problems is affecting his ability to use empathy effectively.

DISCUSSION AND CRITICAL THINKING QUESTIONS

1. Take a moment to reflect on Oliver's psychological reactions to the emotional and physical trauma of his clients. Which of the concepts discussed so far seem to best fit Oliver's reactions to his practice with veterans and military families? (Social Work Competency 1: Demonstrate Ethical and Professional Behavior—through the practice of self-reflection and regulation; Competency 9: Evaluate Practice with Individuals and Families.)

2. Based on your critical analysis of this case study and your review of the professional literature in this area, describe your perceptions of this case as they relate to practice with veterans and military families. Do you feel these reactions are normal? Why or why not? (Social Work Competency 1: Demonstrate Ethical and Professional Behavior—through the practice of self-reflection and regulation; Competency 4: Engage in Practice-Informed Research and Research-Informed Practice.)

3. Using the ecological systems framework for self-care, outline a holistic plan of self-care for Oliver with recommendations for personal and professional activities that may enhance Oliver's resiliency in his practice. (Social Work Competency 1: Demonstrate Ethical and Professional Behavior—through the practice of self-reflection and regulation; Competency 4: Engage in Practice-Informed Research and Research-Informed Practice; Competency 9: Evaluate Practice with Individuals—through the application of knowledge of human behavior and the social environment, person-in-environment, and other multidisciplinary theoretical frameworks.)

4. Professionally evaluate Oliver's decision to openly and directly disclose his feelings about the clients to his agency supervisor. What are the possible implications of this decision? Appraise the potential impact of the military culture on his supervisor's perception of his emotional reactions to his clients. (Social Work Competency 1: Demonstrate Ethical and Professional Behavior—through use of professional supervision and consultation; Competency 2: Engage Diversity and Difference in Practice—through application and communication of the importance of diversity and difference in shaping life experiences in practice at the micro, mezzo, and macro levels.)

5. Applying a strengths-based approach, conduct a brief assessment of the potentially positive aspects of Oliver's work with veterans and military families. In your assessment, include any implications for posttraumatic growth, vicarious resilience, or compassion satisfaction from this work. (Social Work Competency 1: Demonstrate Ethical and Professional Behavior—through the practice of self-reflection and regulation; Competency 4: Engage in Practice-Informed Research and Research-Informed Practice; Competency 9: Evaluate Practice with Individuals—through the application of knowledge of human behavior and the social environment, person-in-environment, and other multidisciplinary theoretical frameworks.)

KEY WORDS

compassion satisfaction	practice wisdom
ecological systems perspective	professional resilience
holistic	self-appreciation
homeostasis	self-care
posttraumatic growth	vicarious resilience

CHAPTER SUMMARY

This chapter presents a detailed discussion on the use of the term *resilience* as it applies to human behavior and to practice in the human service professions. Resilience is a dynamic construct with dimensions examined in the fields of neurobiology, life-span development, cognitive and social psychology, and spirituality. Given the breadth of study regarding the construct of personal and professional resiliency, it is helpful to conceptualize resilience from the multidimensional approach of the ecological systems perspective. The concept of professional resilience relates to the positive and growth-promoting aspects of direct practice with those who are vulnerable or suffering in some way. Ideas such as posttraumatic growth, vicarious resilience, and compassion satisfaction have introduced a welcome and greatly needed balance to the empirical work on the deleterious effects of human service work through vicarious traumatization, secondary traumatic stress, compassion fatigue, and professional burnout.

In part 2, the practice of self-care is described as the key to professional resilience. The practice of self-care has generally been described as professional self-care, but that term fails to acknowledge that self-care is a holistic practice with domains that move beyond the professional setting. An ecological systems perspective conceptualizes self-care as both a personal and a professional practice that includes aspects related to physical health behaviors, interpersonal coping, organization strategies, time with family and friends, recreational activities, and spirituality. This holistic approach to self-care allows for the application of various strategies to promote a positive professional quality of life and an overall sense of physical and emotional well-being. Using the ecological systems perspective, table 6.1 summarizes the specific domains of self-care and provides sample goals and objectives for maintaining self-care over time. Finally, a case study describing one social worker's practice experience with veterans and military families is presented. The discussion and critical thinking questions about the case study highlight the need for a plan of self-care as an essential component of social work practice to cultivate and maintain professional resilience.

RECOMMENDED READINGS

Berger, R. (2015). *Stress, trauma, and posttraumatic growth: Social context, environment, and identities.* New York, NY: Routledge.

Cox, K., & Sterner, S. (2013). *Self-care in social work: A guide for practitioners, supervisors, and administrators.* Washington, DC: NASW.

Frankl, V. E. (1984). *Man's search for meaning: An introduction to logotherapy* (3rd ed.). New York, NY. A Touchstone Book, Simon & Schuster.

Kent, M., Davis, M. C., & Reich, J. W. (2014). *The resilience handbook: Approaches to stress and trauma*. New York, NY: Routledge.

Meichenbaum, D. (2012). *Roadmap to resilience: A guide for military, trauma victims and their families*. Williston, VT: Crown House.

Skovholt, T. M., & Trotter-Mathison, M. (2011). *The resilient practitioner: Burnout prevention and self-care strategies for counselors, therapists, teachers, and health professionals* (2nd ed.). New York, NY: Routledge.

Wicks, R. J., & Maynard, E. A. (2014). *Clinician's guide to self-renewal: Essential advice from the field*. Hoboken, NJ: Wiley.

SUGGESTED INTERNET RESOURCES

Self-Care Starter Kit: https://socialwork.buffalo.edu/resources/self-care-starter-kit.html
This site offers excellent resources for students and professionals as they begin to develop their own self-care plans. The site describes the resources as a "Self-Care Starter Kit." Additional resources are helpful no matter where you are on your self-care journey. A link for beginners introduces the concept of self-care with embedded hyperlinks to additional resources for the development of a holistic approach to self-care practice. Other pages include developing individual goals and objectives for the plan of self-care, self-care assessments, exercises, activities, and community resources. Under the Additional Self-Care Resources tab are links to inspiration materials, suggested readings, and a comprehensive bibliography. Most of the materials on this page can be downloaded and printed for distribution at no cost.

The Melissa Institute: www.melissainstitute.org
This nonprofit organization is dedicated to the study and prevention of violence through education, community service, research support, and consultation. Their mission is to prevent violence and promote safer communities through education and application of research-based knowledge. The institute was set up in memory of Melissa Aptman, who was murdered in St. Louis. This site is an excellent resource for those working with survivors of physical and sexual assault. The Resources tab includes quick links to a variety of helpful resources for treating aggressive an anxious children, bullying, faith and family-based interventions, family violence, and suicide. The resilience resources include hyperlinks to useful information on resilience as it relates to military populations, children and adolescents, practice interventions, human development, and political decision making. Most of the documents can be downloaded at no cost.

7

PRESERVING PROFESSIONAL RESILIENCE

The Ongoing Practice of Holistic Self-Care

I don't know what your destiny will be, but one thing I do know, the only ones among you who will be really happy are those who have sought and found how to serve.

—ALBERT SCHWEITZER

And we can only serve others and society well if we can cultivate the resilient life.

—ROBERT WICKS, 2008

CHAPTER GOALS AND OBJECTIVES

1. Provide a thorough review and discussion of the effects of work-related stress on physical health, emotional health, and overall well-being.
2. Build on the ecological systems framework for holistic self-care by presenting self-care strategies from various domains of the biopsychosocial self.
3. Present application strategies for the development of a productive and time-efficient organizational plan of self-care.
4. Discuss the use of self-compassion as a component of the ongoing practice of interpersonal self-care.
5. Present strategies for maintaining the familial, social, and spiritual components of the interpersonal self-care process.

INTRODUCTION

The ongoing practice of self-care is key to maintaining both personal and professional resilience. There is little empirical data to suggest that any one strategy or combination of strategies represent the best practices in self-care. This chapter provides several strategies for organizational and interpersonal self-care for use individually or collectively to develop an individually unique plan for ongoing self-care and resilience. Using the ecological systems framework, the chapter explores various strategies for the practice of holistic self-care across biological, interpersonal, organizational, familial, spiritual, and recreational domains. Part 1 expands the discussion in chapter 6 on the impact of occupational stress on overall physical health and emotional well-being. Part 2 discusses the organizational components of holistic self-care, which includes individual strategies for effective time management and productivity and efforts by the organization to maintain a healthy and supportive work environment. Specific strategies for managing work-related stress, such as using a task-centered approach for time management and project completion, are discussed. Part 3 explores the interpersonal domain of self-care, including the use of self-compassion, the maintenance of familial and social support systems, and the use of spirituality. Specific content addresses those in direct practice who are traumatized or otherwise vulnerable or suffering in some way.

PART 1: THE IMPACT OF STRESS ON WELL-BEING

It is generally understood that chronic stress is pervasive, having cumulative effects on the human body and all of its working systems. Sources of stress include various components of the biopsychosocial self, including physical health, mental health, family well-being, and spirituality (see chapter 2). Stress is "any influence that interferes with the normal functioning of an organism and produces some internal strain or tension" (Barker, 2014 p. 414). From the human systems perspective, one of the most commonly cited sources of stress comes from the occupational or professional domain of life. At the micro level, work-related stress has the potential to pervasively affect physical, emotional, familial, and spiritual well-being, and it has been linked to a variety of mental health conditions including anxiety and mood disorders as well as physical illnesses such as heart disease, hypertension, digestive disorders, and fibromyalgia (Leka, Griffiths, & Cox, 2003). At the macro level, stress-related health conditions globally cost billions of dollars each year in health care and missed days from work.

The *Social Work Dictionary* defines psychological stress as "environmental demands or internal conflicts that produce anxiety; people tend to seek an escape from the sources of these influences (or stressors) through means such as defense mechanisms, avoidance of certain situations, phobia, somatization, rituals, or constructive physical activity" (Barker, 2014, p. 414). In 2014, the American Institute of Stress (AIS) cited job pressure as the most significant cause of stress-related illness, both physical and emotional. It is estimated that three-quarters of working Americans seek either medical (77 percent) or psychological (73 percent) care due to work-related stress. Nearly half of all working Americans (48 percent) feel that occupational stress has had a negative impact on their personal lives, including the quality of marital and parenting relationships, and has resulted in neglecting important family obligations (AIS, 2015). This is evidenced by the substantial increase and expansion of employee assistance programs in the United States over the past four decades, many of which are now moving to more comprehensive models of service to cover a variety of work-related stress conditions (Hughes, 2013). Occupational stress has been associated with higher rates of maladaptive coping behaviors in the form of alcohol, tobacco, caffeine, and other substance use disorders and addictions (Kottler & Chen, 2011).

For some, the work itself can become an addiction; hence, terms such as "workaholics" or "workaholism" are framed in the diagnostic context of biological addictions like alcoholism. With regard to mental health, occupational stress has been correlated with anxiety disorders, sleep disorders, eating disorders, and depression, among other emotional health concerns (Kurzman, 2013; Leka et al., 2003). Given the higher incidence of occupational stress conditions such as vicarious trauma and compassion fatigue, which pave the way for professional burnout, professionals in social work, counseling, and other human service careers are at even greater risk for developing stress-related physical or emotional health conditions (Graham & Shier, 2014). To protect and preserve our human service workforce, self-care should be understood as an ongoing effort to maintain both personal and professional resiliency over time.

This chapter addresses approaches to maintaining self-care as a mainstay for the cultivation of professional resilience. Given the breadth of the concept of stress and its application across micro and macro domains, the ecological systems perspective provides a pragmatic way of thinking, understanding, and conceptualizing the impact of stress on our personal and professional lives. A synthesis of the research literature suggests that the best approach to professional resilience is through an individualized combination of strategies at the personal and the organization levels.

There are no specific formulations for how to prepare or construct a self-care plan, although various components have been recommended. The term *self-care* in many ways defines itself: this practice is specific to the interpersonal and physical needs of the individual, the demands of the organization, and balancing family responsibilities and other life dimensions. Finding the right combination of activities to promote a healthy balance between personal and professional obligations is the overarching goal in developing an ongoing plan of self-care. Additional resources and supplemental materials can be found in the worksheets at the end of the book.

PHYSICAL SELF-CARE

The logical place to begin talking about self-care is with the basics—assessing activities related to physical well-being, such as eating, sleeping, physical activity, and leisure time (Wicks, 2008). For some, chronic stress can be a pathway for the use of maladaptive coping in the form of unhealthy physical behaviors, such as abuse of alcohol (to calm down), use of caffeine, nicotine, and other stimulants (to stay awake), and use of other recreational or addictive substances. For those using alcohol or other substances chronically or who have developed substance dependency, seeking treatment from employee assistance or another treatment program may be the first step in treating the physical, emotional, and familial consequences of substance abuse (Kurzman, 2013). Once substance abuse becomes addiction, it is no longer an issue of self-care; it is a serious medical condition that often requires intensive treatment.

Outside of behaviors that require more targeted interventions, maintaining a balanced diet is the most basic positive health behavior, yet that appears to be difficult for many. In 2010, a National Institutes of Health (NIH) report estimated that two-thirds (68.8 percent) of adults in the United States were considered to be overweight or obese, a factor that contributes to other major health conditions such as diabetes, heart disease, stroke, and some types of cancer (National Institute of Diabetes and Digestive and Kidney Disease, 2010). The report goes on to suggest that physical exercise, even in small amounts, combined with a nutritious diet helps with weight management as well as with the prevention of other health-related conditions. The benefits of physical exercise go far beyond weight management and have been linked to other key areas of physical and emotional health, such as regulating sleep patterns, reducing anxiety and depression, improving cardiovascular health, and increasing self-confidence and a healthier libido (Balch, 2010; Lustyk, Widman, Paschane, & Olson, 2004). It should come as no surprise that exercise and nutrition contribute to improved physical and mental health and an overall state of well-being. The bigger question is why maintaining a balanced meal plan and exercise program is such a difficult regimen to maintain. Many reasons for this have been suggested, with the most obvious being that many professional jobs, even those in the sometimes chaotic environments of human service agencies, no longer require the use of physical energy to be productive. In fact, it can be argued that quite the opposite is true in many office settings. A brief assessment of the amount of time spent each day attending to professional tasks through the use of computerized or virtual interfaces can be very telling in this regard.

Using myself as example, I would quickly lose count of the number of hours spent returning emails each week, many of which are pushed out to colleagues who are located in the same building if not on the same office floor or just a few doors down. Sometimes it is simply easier and more efficient to initiate an email response than to get up and walk down the hall to initiate a personal dialogue. With this all too common mind-set, the opportunities to take a break from work by leaving my computer, to take a brief walk to clear my mind, and the opportunity to engage in a potentially enjoyable and helpful dialogue with a colleague, are lost with a short response and a key stroke.

Each of these "missed opportunities" had the potential to provide some form of stress relief (however minor) as a function of self-care as well as to introduce a physical activity to balance the sedentary time spent in front of a computer screen. For some, adding cardiovascular activity to a day when the brain is occupied with job-related duties that are sometimes mentally exhausting can be challenging. For human service professionals, who often have an added layer of emotional exhaustion due to their use of empathy and other psychological resources, this can be an even greater challenge. This compounds the ever-present challenges of simply finding and prioritizing the time for exercise and balancing the needs and demands of family and other activities.

If the need for an improved meal plan and an exercise routine are identified areas of self-care, it is best to start with one reasonable health behavior goal or objective. Avoid "pie in the sky" goals. For example, setting a goal to complete a marathon is only reasonable for someone interested in training to be a marathon runner. Completing a marathon is a reasonable long-term goal, whereas a reasonable short-term goal is to make time to take a brisk walk at least once each workday for one month. Once this benchmark has been achieved, it is feasible to set a loftier goal. Although it may be challenging at first, getting up 30 minutes earlier and starting the day with a physical activity may prove helpful for maintaining an exercise routine over time. This is also true when setting food intake and food behavior goals. Healthy eating goals can be as simple as making a commitment to buying healthy food items and packing a sensible lunch rather than relying on vending machines or fast food as daily sources of nutrition; substituting water in the place of soda, coffee, or other caffeinated beverages; or leaving one's office or computer space to eat lunch in a nonworking space for a mental break.

In addition to regulating diet and exercise, maintaining a regular sleep schedule is important to the maintenance of overall physical and emotional health. Using earned leave time from work to properly maintain outside primary and specialty care appointments such as wellness visits, dental care, optometry, and other forms of needed professional care should not be neglected. This may involve taking leave time as needed to properly recover from any emotional or physical illness, including adequate time to grieve if necessary. Neglecting to schedule or canceling medical appointments due to busy work schedules should be avoided unless absolutely necessary. The basic premise for each of the elements of physical self-care discussed in this section is the same: success in the form of resilience is largely based on the commitment of the individual to establish reasonable goals and to maintain them over time.

PART 2: STRATEGIES FOR ORGANIZATIONAL SELF-CARE

PERSONAL EFFICIENCY AND TIME MANAGEMENT

Human service organizations play a key role in the practice of self-care. The biggest challenge to organizational self-care lies in the functions of the organization that are bureaucratically out of individual (and often agency administrator) control, sometimes despite genuine efforts for change. There is very little evaluation data on organizational models of excellence in resiliency; however, the synthesis of the research literature in this area suggests that the organizational component of self-care consists of two key elements. The first involves individual efforts made by service professionals to meet the demands of the service organization as they meet the needs of the consumers of the agency's services. The second element consists of the organization's commitment to mitigate demands fairly and with equanimity while promoting a supportive work environment and organizational culture that sustains the organizational mission, services to consumers, and the providers and administrators of those services (Leka et al., 2003).

One significant challenge to direct practitioners, and to maintaining the organizational components of self-care, is preventing the effects of professional burnout. Professional burnout is an organizational phenomenon with factors related primarily to the accumulation of stressors associated with practice in human service agencies (Maslach, 2001). Professional burnout is a multidimensional construct with domains related to emotional exhaustion, depersonalization, and professional inefficiency (see chapter 4). Several factors are associated with the experience of professional burnout in human service work, and table 7.1 summarizes the most commonly cited individual and organization factors associated with the experience of burnout. Six major organization factors have been identified as contributing to the experience of professional burnout in human service work: excessive workload, lack of control over agency policies and procedures, insufficient reward from the work, unfairness in organization structure and discipline, low peer and supervisory support, and role conflict or ambiguity (Leiter & Maslach, 2005). Without the proper methods of self-care, the cumulative effects of organizational stress may lead to professional burnout, which results in many human service professionals vacating positions as a form of personal and professional self-preservation (Maslach, 2001, 2003b).

TABLE 7.1 Vulnerability Factors for Professional Burnout

Individual	Organizational
Lack of professional work experience	Number of assigned cases
Age (younger professionals at greater risk)	Lack of control over agency policy
Gender (females at greater risk)	Poor supervision
Difficulty regulating emotional demands	Poor collegiality and peer support
Lack of professional training and education	Role conflict or ambiguity
Avoidant coping style	Poor compensation
Difficulty understanding client challenges	Excessive overtime or on-call hours
Poor conflict management skills	Excessive documentation requirements

Suggested strategies at the individual level include engaging workload demands with active and contemplative approaches to problem solving rather than avoidant coping styles (Anderson, 2000; Stevens & Higgins, 2002; Thorton, 1992). For example, avoiding habits such as procrastination, which often leads to feeling overwhelmed by project tasks and deadlines, can be achieved by allocating sufficient work time to complete assignments, reports, and documentation. Protecting calendar time, which for some is simply learning to control one's calendar, is an essential time management skill that includes not only setting reasonable deadlines but actively prioritizing personal and professional obligations. Using a task-centered approach by setting specific goals and objectives (framed in the form of tasks) for each day of the week and remaining dedicated to these tasks when at all possible may be useful in developing time management skills.

Maslach and Leiter (2005) propose a four-step model for addressing issues of occupational stress and work overload: (1) define the organizational challenges; (2) set positive and practical objectives for addressing the challenges; (3) develop a strategy for taking action; and (4) track progress. Maintaining effective time management practices is often challenging in human or social service organizations, particularly for those providing services to clients in crisis or emergency situations. Therefore, part of developing effective time management skills may involve elements of preplanning for unexpected breaks in daily or weekly schedules. A thorough assessment of "out of office" calendar time versus time spent working in the office may prove useful in determining areas where time may be used inefficiently. One helpful time management strategy is to create an ongoing folder with a list of tasks and assignments to be completed during periods of downtime. Finally, once task work begins, consciously avoid distractions from phone calls, answering emails, office chatter, and text messaging, and stay "on task" as much as possible.

ORGANIZATIONAL SUPPORT

The second major component of self-care in human service organizations involves the infrastructure, bureaucracy, leadership, policies, and procedures of the organization itself. This area of self-care is much more difficult to develop and maintain because most employees have very little (if any) control over these elements of the organization. Many social service agencies are funded by state, federal, or philanthropic bureaucracies, and management policy and procedure often are developed outside of the organization. It is important to learn as much as possible about the organization's structure and management, particularly for those who are new to human service work or who are job searching. Finding a position with an organizational mission congruent with your personal values and professional goals may help to bring meaning and value to the ever-present challenges that accompany most human service jobs. The ability of an organization to empower meaningful work with consumers is valuable in the cultivation of professional resilience, particularly for human service professionals (Pooler et al., 2014).

One of the first steps in this process is to conduct an informal organization assessment of the professional work environment, starting with a review of the organization's purpose, mission statement, values, and institutional goals (Cox & Steiner, 2013b). This information is typically available online and may be useful as preliminary information into the professional climate and culture of the agency. Organizational culture is generally comprised of the collective assumptions, values, norms, and tangible signs (artifacts) of agency members and their behaviors (Catherall, 1995). Organizational climate is perceptually based on employees' subjective appraisal of the conditions of the work environment (Pryce et al., 2007). Before developing strategies for organizational self-care, it is important to understand the impact of agency culture, climate, administrative structure, policies, and procedures on agency providers and the clients they serve (Lee & Miller, 2013), which may be collectively referred to as methods of organizational support. Organizational support includes concrete elements such as the availability of basic resources to practice efficaciously, appropriate and confidential office space, the provision of resources needed for effective practice with consumers, and funding for office materials, supplies, and equipment (Pearlman & Saakvitne, 1995). This may include assessing employee benefits such as adequate health care coverage, sick leave and vacation time, opportunities for continuing education and professional development, and licensure supervision.

One of the most important elements of supportive organizational culture is the existence of a strong supervisory and peer support system. This includes the collective supportive efforts from agency administrators, supervisors, mentors, and colleagues. Research across human service organizations reveals that effective supervision has a significant impact on the intention of many providers to remain committed to the spirit and importance of the work, even when the stresses of the job seem overwhelming (Bennett et al., 2005; Hamama, 2012; Mor Barak et al., 2001). By its nature, social work and other human service jobs are grounded in building healthy relationships through the development of effective communication. Supervisors of direct service providers play a vital role in cultivating professional resilience by providing effective relational guidance, support, education, and practice wisdom during times of stress and professional insecurity (Cahalane & Sites, 2008; O'Donnell & Kirkner, 2009; Peled-Avram, 2015). In addition to mentoring supervisees directly, organization managers often have influence on elements of the organizational climate that may be contributing to the cumulative effects of job stress and professional burnout, such as work or caseload allocations, the use (or misuse) of overtime and on-call time, and allowing job autonomy (Stalker, Mandell, et al., 2007).

Finally, significant evidence suggests that peer support from colleagues is beneficial in promoting professional resilience and well-being (Hamama, 2012; Lizano & Mor Barak, 2012; Michalopoulos & Aparicio, 2012). Informally, collegiality in the form of peer support includes tangible support such as providing a meal for someone's family during a stressful event or providing coverage during sick or personal leave time. Peers also may provide emotional support by offering contributions to professional self-esteem, practice insights, supportive feedback, appropriate humor, and practice wisdom (Moran, 2002; Maslach, 2003b). Formally, the use of organizational peer groups provide valuable opportunities for the normalization of challenging work conditions, a confidential space for discussion of difficult client material, and opportunities for the exchange of professional ideas and strategies for organizational self-care (Cohen, Underwood, & Gottlieb, 2000; Kim, Sherman, & Taylor, 2008). Formal peer support groups are particularly helpful as spaces for processing the emotionally challenging and sometimes shocking components of trauma work for practitioners chronically engaged in practice with trauma populations (Catherall, 1999; Pearlman & Saakvitne, 1995; Pryce et al., 2007).

JASPER: A CASE STUDY IN FAMILY COURT ADMINISTRATION

Jasper is a senior probation officer for the county juvenile court system. He has recently been promoted to the position of senior probation officer and supervisor, and he has been assigned additional administrative duties. Jasper took the position upon retirement of a senior court administrator of over 25 years. Jasper's supervisor informed him that he would be responsible for supervision of all of the probation officers as well as his caseload until a new officer is hired to fill his position. Although Jasper has been involved with the juvenile court system for seven years, he is not familiar with the administrative duties assigned to the court. Due to a backlog of training sessions with the state office of juvenile corrections, he is not scheduled for his first formal training seminar for at least three months. In the meantime, he is managing a caseload of more than 100 juvenile probationers and their families. During his first administrative supervision session he learned that he would be responsible for representing the juvenile court on several countywide task forces and committees with the city and county public school systems and with the departments of Child Welfare, Mental Health, and Intellectual Disability. As the senior probation officer, he is responsible for attending all weekly family court hearings; approving all family court dockets; managing the countywide teen drug court program for first time offenders; supervising the juvenile detention center staff; and conducting intake assessments for a specialized treatment program for juvenile sex offenders.

Jasper was hesitant after learning about the complexity of his new position. His predecessor seemed to manage the affairs of the juvenile court with ease and rarely complained of feeling overwhelmed. As Jasper begins to explore his new job responsibilities, he realizes that the previous director did not keep a daily or weekly calendar of obligations. He is having a difficult time managing his time and feels pulled from meeting to meeting and disconnected from the other senior administrative court officers, most of whom have been serving the court for at least 10 years. During his first supervision session, he reported feeling that his calendar was "out of control."

To manage the combination of his new job duties and his former caseload obligations, Jasper has been working until 8:00 o'clock each evening and full days on Saturdays and Sundays to keep up. He also reports spending his break and lunch time sitting at his computer and eating a quick bite from the vending machine or the fast-food restaurant across the street. He has stopped his morning workout routine to free up more time to work before the court opens at 8:30 each morning. As a result of the long working hours, he has missed his son's last three soccer games. Although his wife is supportive, she worries that he has "taken on too much—too fast" and that his physical health may suffer as a result of the stress of his new job obligations. When he gets home at night, Jasper feels too tired to enjoy time with his son. Because of the overwhelming stress of his new position, Jasper is questioning his ability to perform his new duties adequately and professionally.

DISCUSSION AND CRITICAL THINKING QUESTIONS

1. Take a moment to critically reflect on Jasper's reactions to the sources of organizational stress associated with his new supervisory position. Based on your previous chapter readings, which of the following concepts seems to most appropriately fit this situation: compassion fatigue, secondary traumatic stress, or professional burnout? (Social Work Competency 1: Demonstrate Ethical and Professional Behavior—through the practice of self-reflection and regulation; Competency 4: Engage in Research-Informed Practice and Practice-Informed Research; Competency 9: Evaluate Practice with Organizations.)

2. Critically appraise Jasper's reactions to his new job requirement to collaborate with other community service agency professionals in mental health, child welfare, public education, and disability. Do you feel his overwhelmed feelings are normal? Why or why not? (Social Work Competency 8: Intervene with Organizations and Communities—through the use of interprofessional collaboration appropriate to achieve beneficial outcomes.)

3. Using the ecological systems framework for self-care, develop a holistic plan of self-care for Jasper consisting of recommendations for personal and professional activities that may enhance Jasper's resiliency in his practice. (Social Work Competency 1: Demonstrate Ethical and Professional Behavior—through the practice of self-reflection and regulation; Competency 4: Engage in Practice-Informed Research and Research-Informed Practice; Competency 9: Evaluate Practice with Organizations and Communities—through the application of knowledge of human behavior and the social environment, person-in-environment, and other multidisciplinary theoretical frameworks.)

4. Compare and contrast the potential individual, organizational, and familial consequences and benefits of Jasper's willingness to work long hours during the week and on weekends. How will this practice affect Jasper's personal and professional resilience if he continues to do this long term? (Social Work Competency 1: Demonstrate Ethical and Professional Behavior—through the use of self-reflection and regulation.)

5. Based on the information provided in the case study, conduct a brief assessment of Jasper's organizational climate. In your assessment, describe the strengths and challenges of the organization. Are there areas of organizational improvement that might contribute to Jasper's professional resilience in his new position as a supervisor? (Social Work Competency 7: Assess Organizations—by developing mutually agreed-on intervention goals and objectives based on the critical assessment of strengths, needs, and challenges of clients and constituencies.)

PART 3: STRATEGIES FOR INTERPERSONAL SELF-CARE

THE USE OF SELF-COMPASSION

The choice to self-select the field of social work or another career path in the human services involves a deep commitment and dedication to the inherently challenging process of helping others improve their quality of life. Unfortunately, the call to help others professionally can be consequential if not regulated with proper forms of self-care. Self-care is a holistic process, and self-compassion is an important component of cultivating resilience and well-being through self-care. Earlier chapters describe the potentially deleterious effects of human service work manifested as vicarious or secondary traumatic stress, compassion fatigue, and, ultimately, professional burnout. The wealth of research in this area provides overwhelming validation that the ongoing practice of self-care is essential in sustaining professional resilience. However, for many social workers and other human service professionals, the interpersonal use of self-compassion is problematic simply because it is counterintuitive (O'Halloran & Linton, 2000). Carl Rogers, himself one of the most influential humanistic psychologists of the twentieth century best known for his use and development of the person-centered approach to understanding human relationships in the context of psychotherapy, stated that "I have always been better at caring for and looking after others than I have been at caring for myself. But in these later years, I have made progress" (Rogers, 1995, p. 80). Self-compassion is the interpersonal use of one's empathy skills and resources to foster continued resilience and self-preservation. Self-compassion is comprised of positive thoughts, attitudes, and behaviors, such as being kind rather than self-judging; the use of tolerance and humanity rather than isolation during times of personal challenge and suffering; and the use of mindful awareness of one's own thoughts and feelings when caring for the needs of others (Neff, 2003, 2011).

Developing strategies for maintaining resilience and well-being through interpersonal self-care is a complex and difficult component of this practice. As previously stated, there is little outcome data on the use of an efficacious model or specific set of strategies for building resilience. One speculative reason for this gap in the practice literature is that all people (and human service professionals) are living in their own unique set of life circumstances, which necessitates a unique and individualized plan for self-care. This has made establishing concrete models, strategies, or standards for self-care difficult. This is particularly true for the interpersonal domain of self-care, which requires an even deeper commitment to the practices of self-awareness, self-reflection, self-compassion, and self-correction (Cox & Sterner, 2013b). The overarching goal of developing the interpersonal component of the self-care process is to create balance between caring for the personal and professional needs of others while nurturing the needs of the self (Cerney, 1995; Pearlman & Saakvitne, 1995). Finding resilience and balance through the development of a deeper personal insight has been described as "part of the dramatic process of truly embracing richer self-knowledge and a more honest self-appreciation. The goal is to live in a compassionate way of giving of ourselves to others, rooted in personal resilience and an ethos that values what is truly good" (Wicks, 2010, p. 9).

The use of self-compassion as a component of the interpersonal self-care process also involves the conscious and deliberate regulation of personal empathy resources. One way to define the use of personal empathy is as "the act of perceiving, understanding, experiencing, and responding to the emotional state and ideas of another person" (Barker, 2014, p. 139). There is no universally accepted definition of empathy, but it has been described as a process of both intellectually and emotionally identifying with a client's current state of being (see chapter 3). Empathy is not a finite psychological resource; it needs to be nurtured and replenished through the practice of self-care, self-compassion, and self-regulation (Norcross, 2000). The professional requirement for the chronic use of empathy is a unique component of human service work in comparison to other careers and professions. The use of empathy has been described as being both a benefit and a liability to direct practitioners because it is helpful for the client while often simultaneously opening a line of vulnerability for the service provider (Pearlman & Saakvitne, 1995; Stamm, 1999). The lack of proper self-regulation of empathy resources through interpersonal self-care may contribute to the experience of negative outcomes in the form of compassion fatigue and professional burnout (Wagaman et al., 2015).

The need for empathy self-regulation is even greater for those in practice with trauma populations. Interviewing survivors of rape and sexual assault, domestic violence, and child physical and sexual abuse can erode empathy resources in the absence of empathy self-regulation and the ongoing practice of self-care (Adams et al., 2006; Bride, 2007; Pearlman & Saakvitne, 1995). For practitioners with their own personal history of trauma, chronic exposure to the trauma material of others adds another complicated dimension to the preexisting challenges of trauma work. Studies have suggested that practitioners with a preexisting anxiety disorder, mood disorder, or with their own history of personal trauma (particularly child abuse and neglect) may be at greater risk of experiencing these conditions (Lerias & Byrne 2003; Nelson-Gardell & Harris, 2003; Trippany et al., 2003). For those who experience work-related stress or anxiety compounded by personal trauma history, the self-care process may require relying on the skills and expertise of other professionals through psychotherapy, psychopharmacology, supportive group therapy, or other counseling interventions

(Norcross, 2000). It is estimated that one-third of all mental health professionals seek their own psychotherapy or counseling, which can simultaneously foster personal healing and enhance professional development (Geller, 2011).

FAMILIAL SELF-CARE

Most human service professionals would agree that work is not always completed within the context of an eight-hour day or a 40-hour week. Hospitals, psychiatric facilities, nursing homes, rehabilitation centers, crisis centers, homeless shelters, and residential care facilities operate 24 hours a day, and the professional staff work irregular hours, nights, and weekends and are on-call. For some, this has become routine in today's work environment, in addition to spending time after hours returning work-related emails, text messaging, and interfacing through social media sites. The technological advances in the last ten years have made it more possible than ever before to be fully available and engaged in work during nonworking hours. Technology has made life easier in some ways for human service professionals, but it has made it more difficult to create a healthy work–life balance (Chesley, 2005). When professionals allow work responsibilities to take time away from family and friends, there is potential for adding an additional layer of stress from the guilt and shame that comes from neglecting those who are most important in our lives.

Social workers and other human service professionals understand the value and importance of human relationships in sustaining personal and professional resilience and well-being over time. The stress of human service work, particularly practice with trauma populations, can be pervasive and have a significant influence on one's thoughts and beliefs about the self and others (Pearlman & Saakvitne, 1995). In the absence of positive forms of self-care, the chronic emotional demands of human service work may result in a depletion of empathy resources in providing care for others, leaving an empty reservoir of compassion and empathy for families, friends, and other loved ones. Part of the practice of self-compassion (as self-care) is to preserve one's natural empathy by valuing and protecting time for the experience of joy, laughter, and compassion with family, friends, and other loved ones (McGoldrick, 1997; Giles, 2014). For some families, this may be as simple as establishing "device-free" meal or family time, scheduling family vacations, attending school functions and sporting events, or scheduling time to celebrate special family events, birthdays, and anniversaries.

Finally, ongoing social support from family, pets, and close friends has been shown to buffer the effects of occupational stress, which ultimately contributes to both the process of self-care and to an overall sense of physical and emotional well-being (Killian, 2008; Viswesvaran, Sanchez, & Fisher, 1999). The application of social support can be broadly conceptualized as including direct or received support from family, friends, and others during times of need (Cohen et al., 2000). The benefits of social support systems may be gained either explicitly, when activated during times of stress or crisis, or implicitly, when the beneficial components of social support networks are accessed outside of extreme stress or crisis situations (Ray & Miller, 1994; Kim et al., 2008).

SPIRITUAL SELF-CARE

Like the other components of the holistic approach to self-care, spirituality or having a spiritual life is something that is individually unique. Spirituality has been defined as a "devotion to the immaterial part of humanity and nature, rather than worldly things or possessions and as an orientation to people's religious, moral, and emotional nature" (Barker, 2014, p. 409). Other components of spirituality may include self-perception, adherence to personal values and ethics, belief in the existence and influence of a higher power, and the formation of meaningful relationships with others who are likeminded subscribers to a common belief system (Csiernik & Adams, 2002). Conceptual differences between spirituality and religion are noted in the literature, with religion defined as an organized method of teaching and worship within a faith community (Brelsford & Farris, 2014). For the purposes of this text, spirituality is used to reference both the spiritual and religious aspects of human well-being.

For those exposed to the emotionally challenging aspects of human service work, particularly direct practice involving chronic exposure to forms of trauma and human suffering, significant changes to the moral and spiritual components of the self may result. Pearlman and Saakvitne (1995) describe "spiritual damage, loss of meaning, connection, and hope" as "profoundly destructive" consequences of the vicarious effects of trauma-related care (p. 167). The presence of spirituality has been shown to buffer the effects of workplace stress and contribute to overall well-being as a vital source of resilience and renewal for individuals and families (Brelsford & Farris, 2014; Collins, 2005; Csiernik & Adams, 2002). The practice of spiritual self-care involves developing and maintaining spiritual or religious-based practices as buffers to the effects of personal and professional stress and as sources of self-renewal and overall well-being. Strategies for maintaining the religious component of spiritual self-care include regularly attending church services and activities, participating in religious observations and rituals, and the use of prayer (Falb & Pargament, 2014). Nonreligious-based components of spiritual self-care include engaging in positive forms of self-expression and revitalization such as painting, journaling, inspirational reading, and playing or listening to music (Baldwin, 1990; Gladding, 2011). Healing and self-renewal through conscious relaxation, yoga, and meditation also have been suggested as positively influencing spirituality and well-being (Collins, 2005;

Richards, Campenni, & Muse-Burke, 2010). Finally, recreational activities that involve separation from the work environment, particularly those with a deeper connection to a natural environment such as hiking, swimming, or camping, may be a source of spiritual healing and self-care for some direct practitioners (Falb & Pargament, 2014; Pearlman & Saakvitne, 1995).

KEY TERMS

employee assistance programs	self-regulation
holistic self-care	social support
organizational climate	spirituality
organizational culture	strengths-based practice
planful problem-solving approach	stress buffer
self-awareness	task-centered approach
self-compassion	

CHAPTER SUMMARY

This chapter discusses the benefits of the ongoing practice of self-care to the individual, the organization, and ultimately to the well-being of clients and their families. The cumulative effects of chronic work-related stress have a pervasive effect on the quality of life of many working professionals. For some, the effects of occupational stress lead to forms of maladaptive coping such as the use of alcohol and other substances. For human service professionals, particularly those engaging clients faced with trauma and other forms of human suffering, stress may manifest itself in indirect trauma, compassion fatigue, and ultimately in professional burnout. Developing an active, ongoing plan of individualized self-care strategies and resources is essential in maintaining a healthy and resilient quality of life over time.

The practice of self-care is a holistic process. The research literature is rich with various strategies for developing and maintaining self-care, but there are no proven formulations or models of best practice for how to prepare or construct a self-care plan. The synthesis of the research literature in this area suggests that a combination of strategies at the organizational and the individual level may be the best approach for self-care and for the cultivation of resiliency over time. The organizational process of self-care consists of stress and time management strategies used by the individual in combination with the supportive culture and climate of the organization itself. Personal self-care includes maintaining physical health through diet, exercise, and the use of appropriate health care resources and professionals. Self-care also includes attending to and nurturing interpersonal needs through self-compassion, familial and social support, and spirituality. The worksheet at the end of the book titled Sample Goals and Objectives for a Plan of Self-Care provides a holistic plan of self-care with suggested goals and objectives related to the physical, interpersonal, organizational, spiritual, and recreational aspects of this process.

RECOMMENDED READING

Balch, P. A. (2010). *Prescription for nutritional healing: A practical A-to-Z reference to drug-free remedies using vitamins, minerals, herbs & food supplements* (5th ed.). Garden City Park, NY: Avery.

Cohen, S., Underwood, L. G., & Gottlieb, B. H. (2000). *Social support measurement and intervention: A guide for health and social scientists.* New York, NY: Oxford University Press.

Figley, C. R. (2002). *Treating compassion fatigue.* New York, NY: Brunner-Routledge.

Kottler, J., & Chen, D. D. (2011). *Stress management and prevention: Daily Applications* (2nd ed.). New York, NY: Routeledge.

Leiter, M. P., & Maslach, C. (2005). *Banishing burnout: Six strategies for improving your relationship with work.* San Francisco, CA: Jossey-Bass.

Norcross, J. C., & Guy, J. D. (2007). *Learning it at the office: A guide to psychotherapist self-care.* New York, NY: Guildford Press.

Wicks, R. J. (2010). *Bounce: Living the resilient life.* New York, NY: Oxford University Press.

SUGGESTED INTERNET RESOURCES

American Institute of Stress (AIS): www.stress.org

This nonprofit organization has information on stress reduction, stress in the workplace, effects of stress, and various other stress-related topics. The mission of AIS is to improve the health of the community and the world by setting the standard of excellence for stress management in education, research, clinical care, and the workplace. Diverse and inclusive, the institute educates medical practitioners, scientists, health care professionals, and the public; conducts research; and provides information, training, and techniques to prevent human illness related to stress. This site contains a wealth of resources on the physical, neurological, and emotional effects of stress across various demographic and occupational populations. The Daily Life tab includes a stress and workplace stress self-assessment and a multitude of resources on various approaches to stress management. The Publications and Multi-Media tab includes access to the online magazines *Combat Stress* and *Contentment* at no cost. AIS members receive access to the publication *Health and Stress*. On the multimedia page are helpful embedded videos, YouTube videos, and podcasts on stress management. The Learning Center tab houses online training sessions and video lectures, which are available at no cost.

National Institutes of Health: www.nih.org

Part of the U.S. Department of Health and Human Services, the NIH is the nation's leading medical research agency. This is the premier site in the United States for epidemiological statistics related to health and human disease. The site serves as a master directory for all the affiliate institutes and centers under the NIH umbrella, including the National Cancer Institute, the Institute on Aging, the National Institute of Mental Health, and the National Center for Complimentary and Integrative Health, to name a few. Under the Health Information tab are links to the Health Information line, a Health Services Locater, and a link to Healthcare.gov. The Community Resources tab has links to health care resources including dieting and weight control, smoking cessation, care for seniors, and alcohol abuse. The site also contains a powerful library search engine that sources all the NIH affiliated institutes, centers, journals, and other publication and Internet sources for information, such as the *NIMH Fact Sheet on Stress*, which can be downloaded at no cost.

ReachOut Professionals: http://au.professionals.reachout.com/

This site provides recommendations and advice for youth support workers, health workers, and education professionals on a range of online interventions, tools, and resources to support young people experiencing mental health difficulties and to build young people's well-being and resilience. Content includes understanding key mental health and well-being concepts, referrals for young people to appropriate services or online tools, and how to teach mental health and well-being skills in the classroom and in support work with young people. This is an innovative site geared toward young professionals entering the teaching and human services workforce. It contains resources for personal and professional mental health, including over 300 printable evidence-based fact sheets. There are helpful and user-friendly resources on developing a plan of personal and professional self-care using a holistic perspective. The Apps and Online Tools tab includes a directory of well-being and resiliency apps with descriptions that can be used as part of the self-care process. The Professional Development tab includes resources specifically for teachers and human service workers such as video trainings, self-activities, and a personal strengths assessment.

8

THE ETHICAL OBLIGATION OF PROFESSIONAL SELF-CARE

With James L. Jackson Jr.

It is an ethical imperative. We have an obligation to our clients—as well as to ourselves, our colleagues, and our loved ones—not to be damaged by the work we do.

—SAAKVITNE & PEARLMAN, 1996

CHAPTER GOALS AND OBJECTIVES

---

1. Discuss the ongoing practice of self-care as an ethical obligation of providers and to the clients who are recipients of their services.
2. Critically analyze the complex intersection of morals, values, and professional ethics as they relate to ethical dilemmas associated with poor self-care practice.
3. Identify and describe the ethical imperative of establishing clear professional boundaries with clients as a key element of resilience and well-being for clients and providers.
4. Discuss the ongoing practice of self-care as it relates to the core values and ethical principles of the social work and counseling professions.
5. Propose training and education on the practice of self-care as an ethical obligation for social worker and counselor education programs.
6. Demonstrate pragmatic strategies for incorporating content on self-care practice and ethics in professional training programs through sample assignments, case analyses, and critical thinking exercises.

INTRODUCTION

Self-care is recognized as a critical component of personal and professional functioning for service providers in the helping professions. The literature of numerous professions including counseling, social work, nursing, and psychology reveals an increasing awareness that maintaining self-care is a responsibility that begins when entering a professional training program and extends throughout one's career. Investing time and resources in sustaining ongoing self-care activities supports a variety of functions associated with the helping role, including maintaining personal wellness, promoting professional growth, increasing therapeutic effectiveness, and maintaining appropriate boundaries with clients (Skinner, 2015). In light of the benefits associated with ongoing self-care, providers should consider self-care to be a nonnegotiable aspect of their professional development and quality of life (NASW, 2009).

The professions of counseling and social work further recognize the critical importance of self-care through inclusion of language referencing the personal wellness of the human service professional as a foundation for providing competent services. Ethics codes mandate that professionals immediately seek help when they become aware that wellness has been compromised (American Counseling Association [ACA], 2014; NASW, 2008). For example, both the ACA and NASW codes stipulate that practitioners seek help for personal concerns that interfere with their professional work, specifically identifying self-care as an ongoing ethical responsibility. NASW (2009) describes self-care as:

> an essential underpinning to best practice in the profession of social work. The need for professional self-care has relevance to all social workers in the setting within which they practice. The practice of self-care is critical to the survival and growth of the profession. (p. 268)

Human service professionals who are aware of these ethical obligations for managing personal concerns and who accept personal responsibility for regularly engaging in self-care activities are better positioned to promote wellness—not only for themselves but among their colleagues and clients as well. This chapter examines self-care as an ethical obligation and as an essential practice behavior for human service professionals. Aspects of self-care discussed in relation to professional ethics and practice include the practices of professional awareness, reflection, and self-correction; adherence to appropriate professional boundaries with clients; and the obligations of higher education programs to provide training on the practice of self-care for future social work, counseling, and other human service professionals.

PART 1: UNDERSTANDING MORALS, VALUES, AND ETHICS

The *Social Work Dictionary* defines *ethics* as "a system of moral principles and perceptions about right versus wrong and the resulting philosophy of conduct that is practiced by an individual, group, profession, or culture" (Barker, 2014, p. 146). Social work and counseling are "value-based" professions, a label that suggests the existence of formally developed and articulated ethics codes that guide practice. The standards for professional behavior outlined in the respective codes of ethics are driven by a core set of beliefs (or values) that reflect the spirit of the professions (Chechak, 2015). The NASW *Code of Ethics* is deeply rooted in the unique values of the social work profession: a commitment to serving those who are in need, practice pursuant to issues of social justice, the value of all humans beings, the importance of human relationships, and the ongoing commitment to professional integrity and competence (NASW, 2008). Both values and ethics are influenced by an interpersonal and societal sense of what is right, wrong, and fair to members of society (Dolgoff, Harrington, & Loewenberg, 2012), principles that are intertwined in the ethics and values of the social work profession. Social workers and other human service professionals often are confronted with the complex intersection of morals, values, and professional ethics, which may lead to value conflicts and ethical dilemmas when making important decisions on behalf of the well-being of clients (Reamer, 2015).

KITCHENER'S FIVE MORAL PRINCIPLES

Ethical conduct is "professional behavior that meets an individual or community's practice needs in a positive and moral way, distinguishing right from wrong and adhering to the right" (Barker, 2014, p. 146). Kitchener (1984) identified five moral principles that serve as foundation concepts underpinning codes of ethics: autonomy, justice, beneficence, nonmaleficence, and fidelity. Because codes of ethics are by necessity limited in scope, understanding these moral principles can assist in making ethical decisions when faced with complex dilemmas. The principle of *autonomy* addresses independence and relates to allowing clients to exercise freedom of choice in making their own decisions. Within this principle also lies a responsibility on the part of the professional to assist clients in recognizing the potential impact, both on themselves and on others, of the actions they take. Counselors must act to protect clients who lack the capacity to make competent choices. The second principle, *nonmaleficence*, means "first do no harm"; avoid actions, whether intentional or unintentional, that risk harming clients. *Beneficence* is the third principle, which simply means to "do good." Professionals must act in ways that prevent harm as well as contribute to client welfare. The fourth principle, *justice*, requires treating clients with equity, recognizing that what is equitable for one client might well be inequitable for another. This includes documenting a rationale for any differences in how clients are treated. The fifth and final principle is *fidelity*, which consists of how human service professionals honor their commitments and are loyal to clients. This is essential to the development of trust, which is the foundation of any helping relationship.

Social workers, counselors, and other human service professionals should be attentive to Kitchener's moral principles as well as to their professional values and codes of ethics as part of their commitment to provide ethical services with positive client outcomes, which also contributes to the self-care and well-being of the provider.

SELF-CARE AND THE VALUES OF SOCIAL WORK

NASW defines the primary mission of the social work profession as the obligation to "enhance human well-being and help meet the needs of all people, with particular attention to the needs of those who are vulnerable, oppressed, and living in poverty" (NASW, 2008, p. 1). To fulfill this mission, the NASW *Code of Ethics* goes on to describe social work as a "value-based" profession deeply rooted in the core values of the profession (Chechak, 2015; Dolgoff et al., 2012). The ongoing practice of self-care by social workers and other human service professionals directly influences their practice ability, efficacy, and the quality of service delivery to those in need of resources, services, and other forms of treatment. Self-care is not only beneficial to practitioners but also to the clients they serve, colleagues, social service organizations, and to the preservation of our human service workforce.

The obligation of social workers to use their professional knowledge and practice skills in the service of others is the overarching and first of the six core values of the social work profession. As providers to those who are poor, vulnerable, oppressed, or otherwise underserved in some way, failure to practice adequate self-care activities may diminish workers' abilities to deliver services efficaciously. Beyond this, social workers are obligated to address personal or psychosocial challenges that impair practice ability, performance, ethical judgment, or jeopardize the well-being of clients (Reamer, 2015). Developing a strategic plan of self-care, which may include personal counseling or other treatment services and resources, is one way to address issues of impaired social work practice. Poor or inadequate service delivery contributes to the challenges and presenting problems of an already compromised individual or group of consumers, a state that is counter to the value of social service.

Social work is a profession built on the development of healthy, empowering, and therapeutic relationships between providers and the consumers of their services. The ability to effectively use empathy resources in the context of the helping relationship is essential to the cultivation of positive client outcomes (Gerdes & Segal, 2011). Social workers confronted with the deleterious effects of conditions such as professional burnout and compassion fatigue may find they are unable to access their empathy resources or other humanistic qualities of social work practice. This depleting effect on empathy resources may lead to a sense of apathy, desensitization, or cynicism about clients and their problems that place the very nature and purpose of the helping relationship at risk (Maslach, 2003b). Social workers, counselors, and other human service professionals engaged in trauma-related practice are particularly vulnerable to the indirect effects of trauma work and to inappropriate countertransference relationships with clients (Cunningham, 1999; Hayes et al., 2011). Further, social workers unable to provide services due to professional burnout or any other identified impairment violate the core values of respecting the value, worth, and dignity of consumers and the spirit of enhancing and restoring client well-being through therapeutic human relationships as vehicles for change (NASW, 2009). The ongoing practice of self-care serves to replenish empathy and other essential interpersonal resources used in direct social work practice (Wicks & Maynard, 2014).

Social workers who do not attend to their own self-care needs risk compromising the integrity of the helping relationship with clients, who are already comprised by virtue of their situation. As a function of the core value of integrity, social workers are obligated to act responsively on behalf of the well-being of the clients they serve. Failure to do so compromises the trust that is essential to the empowerment and change process for the consumers of social work services. Furthermore, the value of competence suggests social workers are aware of current trends in the research literature as they apply to the improved quality of service delivery. Professional self-care has been described as an "ethical imperative" for social workers in their efforts to cultivate professional resilience. Social workers affected by professional burnout, compassion fatigue, and the indirect effects of direct practice with clients and their trauma material risk violating the trust of clients due to inability or impairment (Monroe, 1999; Newell & Nelson-Gardell, 2014). The ongoing commitment to self-care serves to benefit both social workers and the clients they serve.

THE CLIENT AND THE SELF: THE ETHICS OF PROFESSIONAL AWARENESS

Just as clients are faced with decisions about engaging in the process of reflection toward personal growth, social workers and counselors are similarly involved in a parallel process of self-reflection (Pompeo & Levitt, 2014). The decision "to reflect—or not reflect" has an impact on the professional growth of practitioners. Counselors and social workers risk stagnation when they are reluctant to receive corrective feedback or avoid discussion of events that affect the helping relationship, which may contribute to the process of professional burnout. By contrast, those who are aware of how they are affected by the process are better positioned to relate to how clients are similarly affected, promoting a deeper level of empathy fundamental to the treatment relationship (Corey & Corey, 2015; Meir & Davis, 2011). It has been suggested that practitioners open to honest appraisal of their behaviors are less likely to engage in unethical behaviors (Corey, Corey, Corey, & Callanan, 2014).

A number of variables influence decisions about engaging in the process of self-reflection. Practitioners positioned to gain the most from self-reflection have a perception of stability in their personal and professional lives, a quality that can be cultivated by the ongoing practice of self-care. Acceptance that growth is an ongoing process throughout one's professional career and realizing that one is never truly a "finished product" also contribute to openness in the process of professional reflection. Comfort with ambiguity and cultivating a nonexpert stance are additional qualities that foster self-awareness. Furthermore, increased empathy associated with the development of self-awareness has the potential to promote enhanced relationships with clients. From this perspective, intentionally seeking opportunities for professional growth and continued vigilance toward maintaining self-awareness contribute to managing personal wellness, improving client outcomes, and maintaining ethical boundaries with clients (Pompeo & Levitt, 2014).

Self-reflection is an important component of professional growth and ethical practice, and a model for understanding how this process works can help practitioners engage in self-reflection. Pompeo and Levitt (2014) present self-reflection as a three-phase process: beginning with self-reflection and stagnation, using the self-awareness process, and achieving self-awareness. In the first phase, self-reflection and stagnation, the professional encounters an event (critical incident) that presents an opportunity for, yet does not guarantee, initiating self-reflection. Many intervening factors influence the initiation of the process, including the amount of support provided in the environment and the practitioner's readiness to engage in self-reflection.

Following the critical incident phase is the self-reflective process, grounded in ethical decision making, personal values, and professional experiences. The ethical decision-making process is particularly useful for providing a context to reflect on ethics codes as well as on personal morality, professional values, and ethical dilemmas (Pompeo & Levitt, 2014). The third and final phase, achieving self-awareness, is characterized by a deeper sense of empathy for clients and an increased flexibility in the perception of clients and their problems. Professionals in this phase may demonstrate behaviors associated with those of master therapists, such as humility, autonomy, awareness of countertransference, and adherence to ethical standards. With increased awareness, therapists may encounter new trigger events with a sense of excitement and opportunity, resulting in a new cycle through the phases of the reflective process.

ATTENDING TO PROFESSIONAL BOUNDARIES IN TRAUMA-RELATED CARE

Self-care is an essential responsibility for practitioners in any setting, but human service workers who regularly work with survivors of trauma face unique demands that place them at increased risk for experiencing work-related stressors (Hernandez, Engstrom, & Gangsei, 2010; Sansbury, Graves, & Scott, 2015; Skovholt & Trotter-Mathison, 2016). A wealth of empirical research has shown that working with clients and their trauma material may evoke responses such as anxiety, shock, feeling overwhelmed, and feelings of destabilization (Jankoski, 2010; Goodyear-Brown, 2009; Skovholt & Trotter-Mathison, 2016). This increased stress on the part of providers of trauma services may strongly influence professional boundaries, resulting in changes in practice efficacy. This is particularly problematic because professional competency and boundary concerns are the first and second most frequently cited reasons for ethics complaints against practitioners (Even & Robinson, 2013; Mattison, 2000).

The stressors associated with providing trauma services can influence the professional boundaries between providers and clients in several ways. For example, professionals providing trauma-related services frequently confront urgent and immediate needs on the part of clients in distress, placing providers in a position of professional responsibility for client well-being that may be accompanied by an overlapping sense of emotional involvement (Brinamen, Taranta, & Johnston, 2012; Smith, Kleijn, & Hutschemaekers, 2007). This additional layer can directly influence therapeutic boundaries when providers experience increased investment through their personal reactions to clients. Clients may express challenging needs through expressions of dependence or dissatisfaction with services, which in the absence of clear boundaries may elicit feelings of being manipulated or provoked. Practice with at-risk clients often involves processing complex psychosocial problems that go beyond standard therapeutic treatment. This may bring an increased sense of responsibility for meeting client needs with additional resources that may not be readily available or that go beyond the scope and practice of the provider or the agency. These reactions on the part of therapists working with clients who have experienced emotional trauma or other forms of human suffering demonstrate the potential impact of client–practitioner interactions on boundaries in the treatment process and underscore the necessity for trauma service providers to attend to their own wellness needs (Smith et al., 2007).

Professionals who are unaware of the potential impact of boundary erosion may be drawn to "help" clients in ways that fall outside the scope of their ethical boundaries; for example, using personal resources (e.g., money or time) to supplement resources made available to clients through standard agency service profiles. This blurring of professional boundaries sends confusing messages to clients who may already be struggling to maintain appropriate interpersonal boundaries. Such actions place the professional's personal "need to be needed" above the therapeutic needs of clients. Clients who are invited to develop unhealthy dependence will lack opportunities to experience personal empowerment and autonomy. The professional's ability to maintain ethical boundaries is critical for maintaining objectivity in assessing the functioning of the system and the limitations of the professional's role in treatment.

CLIENT MISPERCEPTION OF PROFESSIONAL BOUNDARIES

In addition to the perceptions of clients and their presenting problems, variations in the settings in which clients receive services also affect professional boundaries through the nature and frequency of contact with providers. Frequent interpersonal interactions have the potential to lead to a level of familiarity that may erode professional boundaries, leading workers to develop a false sense of responsibility for client well-being that extends beyond the scope of the professional relationship. Further, survivors of trauma, particularly child physical and sexual abuse, often have difficulties with appropriate interpersonal boundaries due to the impact of the traumatic experience. Numerous challenges are associated with providing services to clients residing in treatment settings such as domestic violence shelters, and practitioners may feel pulled between a desire to provide assistance by advocating on behalf of the client and the agency's directive to address the client's nonconformity with agency requirements. Service providers confronted with this type of ethical dilemma may respond to such challenges to professional boundaries by purposefully distancing themselves from clients (Brineman et al., 2012), which may damage the helping relationship and the quality of the services provided. It is the responsibility of the professional to ensure that appropriate client boundaries are established within the context of practice.

CASE STUDY: DOMESTIC VIOLENCE SHELTER

Jane is a counselor in a domestic violence shelter directly involved in addressing clients' physical needs through safety planning and establishing support services to assist clients with stabilization for themselves and their dependent children. As part of her role in the agency, Jane is frequently called upon to provide direct and indirect services promoting client physical, mental, and emotional well-being. Residents in the shelter often prematurely end their treatment, sometimes voluntarily and other times being asked to leave due to noncompliance with regulations or to protect the welfare of other residents.

Jane is currently working with a female client, age 32, who has a history of domestic violence and substance abuse. The client entered the shelter three weeks ago after being evicted from her subsidized housing for not paying her rent on time. The client previously lost her job due to missing work because she lacked reliable transportation. Although she still has custody of her two children, a girl (age 8) and a boy (age 7), she is facing allegations of child neglect and has an ongoing case with Child Protective Services (CPS). The client is generally compliant with the shelter requirements regarding curfew and making applications for employment; however, on three separate occasions, the client has failed to keep her appointments at the shelter for group therapy sessions. She also has failed to bring her children to their therapy appointments in the shelter playroom at scheduled times. As the primary therapist and case manager, Jane seeks to advocate for her client by noting that she appears to struggle with understanding her daily schedule, which involves several appointments in the shelter and in the local community. However, the client's apparent difficulties with structure are perceived by the treatment team as manifestations of resistance and treatment noncompliance. The violations of consumer policy have resulted in punitive measures that may ultimately lead to the client and her children being expelled from the facility. The treatment team has strongly suggested that Jane address the concerns of noncompliance with the client. Upon hearing this, Jane experiences an overwhelming sense of failure and personal responsibility for the family leaving the facility. She worries that if they are evicted from the facility the client's family will be homeless and the children will be removed from her custody. Jane has a large home with a garage apartment and has considered allowing the family to stay there temporarily until they can regain stability.

DISCUSSION AND CRITICAL THINKING QUESTIONS

1. As the primary therapist/case manager to the client and her children, consider how Jane might appropriately and proactively address the client's missed appointments for group counseling and the children's missed appointments for individual play therapy. (Social Work Competencies 6–9: Engage, Assess, and Intervene with Individuals, Families, Groups, Organizations, and Communities.)

2. Compare and contrast Jane's perception of her client's noncompliance with agency policy with the treatment team's recommendations for addressing these challenges with the client's treatment plan. Describe how Jane can empower the client's success in the treatment process. (Social Work Competency 3: Advance Human Rights and Social, Economic, and Environmental Justice; Social Work Competencies 6–9: Engage, Assess,

and Intervene with Individuals, Families, Groups, Organizations, and Communities.)

3. Critically appraise Jane's reaction to the possibility that the client and her children may be expelled from the facility. Describe any potential boundary issues or ethical dilemmas that may confront Jane as she continues to engage this family in the treatment process. (Social Work Competency 1: Demonstrate Ethical and Professional Behavior.)

4. Describe how Jane could use the process of self-reflection and correction to negotiate her personal feelings regarding the outcomes in this case. Describe your own reactions to this case study. What are your recommendations for managing the client's challenges? How would you manage the concerns of the treatment team members? (Social Work Competency 1: Demonstrate Ethical and Professional Behavior; Social Work Competencies 6–9: Engage, Assess, and Intervene with Individuals, Families, Groups, Organizations, and Communities.)

5. Using the ecological systems framework for self-care, assess possible ways Jane could incorporate self-care in her daily practice. Develop a plan of self-care for Jane with recommendations from multiple life domains to enhance her professional resilience. (Social Work Competency 1: Demonstrate Ethical and Professional Behavior—through the practice of self-reflection and regulation.)

6. Critically appraise Jane's thought process on providing a safe and stable home for this family in her garage apartment as an ethical dilemma. Describe how this plan would influence the family's perception of appropriate client boundaries and how it would be considered unethical practice behavior. How does this decision intersect with Jane's personal morality, the professional values of social work, and the NASW *Code of Ethics*? (Social Work Competency 1: Demonstrate Ethical and Professional Behavior—through the practice of self-reflection and regulation.)

THE NARRATIVE OF PERSONAL TRAUMA: COMPROMISE AND RESILIENCE

Direct practice with trauma survivors may present increased challenges to professional boundaries through increased demands for empathy and compassion elicited through the presentation of clients and their trauma material. Clients who have experienced trauma need a safe environment for trauma work to proceed, and establishing and maintaining a trusting and empathic relationship is considered a basic element of any therapeutic work or helping relationship (Corey & Corey, 2015). Avoidance of stimuli associated with the trauma is a common behavior for trauma survivors, as noted in the *Diagnostic and Statistical Manual of Mental Disorders* (American Psychiatric Association, 2013), and many evidence-based models include some form of exposure work as a treatment component to address client concerns associated with avoidance behaviors. For example, exposure work involves the construction and expression of a trauma narrative, which sometimes leads to increases in the client's level of emotional distress (Cohen, Mannarino, Kliethermes, & Murray, 2012; Goodyear-Brown, 2009). Correspondingly, therapists who are empathically attuned to clients are also affected by the narrative (Skovholt & Trotter-Mathison, 2016; Pearlman & Saakvitne, 1995). Because clinicians engaged in trauma work serve as an emotional "container" for clients and their trauma material (Goodyear-Brown, 2009), clinicians must be mindful to maintain self-care to be fully present for clients. Clinicians who are uncomfortable with client stories of trauma because they lack the internal resources to be fully present may unintentionally harm clients by reinforcing client avoidance behaviors (Child Sexual Abuse Task Force, 2008).

Additional challenges are faced by trauma counselors who are themselves survivors of trauma. Therapists with a history of trauma are prone to experiencing distress as a result of countertransference reactions that may develop if therapist memories of past trauma are triggered by clients' therapeutic work (Carbonell & Figley, 1996; McCann & Pearlman, 1990). In addition to the risks of countertransference, therapists with past trauma histories have been shown to be at greater risk of the indirect effects of trauma work, compassion fatigue, and professional burnout. Further, without careful examination and self-reflection on the impact of personal trauma history, clinicians risk allowing personal material to influence the therapeutic relationship (Gelso & Hayes, 2007), potentially leading to the development of nonprofessional boundaries (ACA, 2014). However, when managed appropriately in the therapeutic relationship, countertransference can foster growth in clients and practitioners. Counselors resonate with the powerful emotional expressions and experiences clients bring into the therapeutic encounter; such resonance can promote increased counselor self-knowledge and growth (Richards et al., 2010). Clearly, clinicians can benefit from gaining insight about themselves as well as perspective about their work with clients.

ADDRESSING PERSONAL CHALLENGES: IMPAIRMENT VERSUS EMPOWERMENT

Introductory texts in social work and counseling often recommend that trainees be open to exploring personal biases throughout their career, including seeking personal counseling and therapy when needed (Corey & Corey, 2015). There are a variety of opinions on whether students should be required to enter personal counseling while enrolled in the training program (Reamer, 2015).

A potential benefit to seeking personal counseling is that students who have not previously had counseling gain valuable insight into how the counseling process is perceived from the perspective of clients. Moreover, the added stress of attending graduate school while working full-time is considerable, and counseling can provide support for students. Finally, the content of coursework may bring up personal concerns for students, and attending counseling can assist with processing and integrating personal material.

Programs providing clinical training that do not require students to have personal counseling do not negate the potential benefits of counseling; such a position would be paradoxical indeed! Rather, these programs might provide students with a referral list of vetted providers and highly recommend that students engage in counseling for all the reasons noted, yet they stop short of requiring counseling because of the view that the requirement itself has potential problems. These programs recognize that some students might resent such a requirement. If students have the sense of being "made to" participate, an awareness that the choice is being taken from them (that counseling is being imposed on them) may violate the ethical principle of autonomy. Students who might have eagerly entered into a counseling relationship under their own internal locus of control, may feel resistant to the process because it is an external requirement, complicating or even negating what might have otherwise been a rewarding developmental experience. In this example, the "solution" of requiring counseling for students has become the "problem" in that the resistance is invited by the requirement. Also, the outcome of counseling cannot be guaranteed, and it is possible that some students may have a less than positive experience in therapy. How might this affect their perception of counseling or therapy as a profession? Furthermore, how might this pose an ethical concern in terms of the principles of beneficence and nonmaleficence? The question of who is responsible for paying for the therapy is also a consideration related to access; programs would do well to consider the possibility of a disparity in access to services due to financial, cultural, and other student variables, which raises considerations of program responsibilities of fidelity to students. Concerns regarding documentation of attendance are related to the ethical mandates of confidentiality, compliance, and veracity, and these issues must also be addressed. Finally, if a student refuses to enter personal counseling as a program requirement, what recourse might the program have?

PART 2: TRAINING THE ETHICAL PRACTITIONER

Higher education plays a "critical role in educating students about the practice of professional self-care by integrating such content into existing student standards, polices, foundation and advanced curriculums, field practicum, and assignments and projects" (NASW, 2009, p. 270). Professional training programs have the opportunity to promote student awareness of self-care as a component of practitioner identity development by emphasizing content throughout the curriculum, beginning with an initial orientation to the professional training program and continuing by including specific material on self-care in student handbooks and other program resources (Council for Accreditation of Counseling & Related Educational Programs [CACREP], 2016; NASW, 2009; Newell & Nelson-Gardell, 2014). An explanation of the program's expectations regarding students' professional and ethical obligations might include program expectations regarding personal and professional growth. Personal growth is explicitly acknowledged as an anticipated outcome, so it is reasonable to include information regarding self-care resources and expectations as part of the orientation process. Providing this information as part of an initial program orientation is consistent with "real world" practice, much like the ethical mandate of informed consent in the therapeutic or helping relationship. In addition to student orientations, training programs typically provide information concerning program requirements such as program objectives, expectations of students, policies for academic appeal, student retention, remediation, and dismissal (CACREP, 2016; CSWE, 2015). The accrediting bodies for both social work and counseling refer to these requirements in terms of "gatekeeping" to the profession.

Gatekeeping policies and procedures emphasize the ethical responsibility of professional educators to take actions such as remediation and dismissal when students demonstrate significant deficiencies. This reactive approach might well lead programs to develop policies that focus on interventions that address problems only *after* these have become evident, similar to a disciplinary model. When remedial interventions are warranted, the remediation plan and accompanying documentation often require a substantial investment of time and energy on the part of both students and faculty. A more proactive and potentially effective investment might be made through an increased emphasis on retention strategies that assist students in developing and implementing personal wellness plans (see chapters 6 and 7 for self-care plans). Having structured retention strategies in place supporting student wellness might well reduce the incidence of problems and is consistent with both the ethical principle of beneficence and the helping professions' preference for prevention over remediation.

STRATEGIES FOR CLASSROOM INTEGRATION

Within the larger context of professional training programs, program faculty have opportunities, resources, and infrastructure to promote self-care as an ethical obligation of helping professionals. Integrating self-care content into coursework, classroom activities, field education, and internship experiences communicates to students that self-care is a real expectation, not a topic merely given "lip service." One possible strategy is to set aside class time for students to engage in dyadic, small group, and large group conversations regarding self-care. This approach is of particular relevance in direct practice, skill development, or seminar courses tied to internship or field education experiences. Several potential benefits flow from this. First, situating this activity toward the beginning of class communicates that engaging in self-care is a high priority, similar to the analogy of "put your oxygen mask on first." Second, the class activities that follow are grounded in the context of the self-care discussion, implying that self-care is relevant to the class activities. Third, beginning conversations with students around self-care can promote a sense of valuing their voices and experiences, which contributes to students' perceptions of a classroom culture and climate of trust and support. A simple yet pragmatic strategy for creating a supportive learning environment, inclusive of the practice of self-care, is to intentionally integrate time for self-care in the normative work environment. Informal classroom practices such as activities for students to become acquainted, to interact, to express voice, to build trust, make plans for carpooling, and take time for breaks promote an environment in which students can appropriately hold themselves as well as their peers accountable for addressing their own self-care needs.

Faculty who expect students to engage in self-care but fail to care for themselves are sending an incongruent message, lessening the likelihood that students will themselves follow through with self-care. Modeling self-care as an aspect of professional practice adds credibility and demonstrates the ethical principle of veracity, or truthfulness. Self-care activities that faculty are already practicing such as mindfulness, diaphragmatic breathing, progressive muscle relaxation, and guided imagery exercises (see chapter 10) can be readily demonstrated through guided practice in the classroom (Christopher & Maris, 2010). Students often are enthusiastic about incorporating such activities in their own self-care plans as well as in their therapeutic work with clients.

SAMPLE CLASSROOM ASSIGNMENT: INTRODUCING THE SELF-CARE PROCESS

A practical way of introducing self-care early in course content as an ethical responsibility of the practitioner is to incorporate this material in a "theories and techniques or skills" class. This approach was tested in a 15-week class of approximately 23 students meeting once per week for three hours. The class was part of the required coursework for students in their first semester of graduate study in a professional counselor training program. The first class begins with an overview of self-care as a nonnegotiable component of ethical practice, followed by small group discussion of how students are actively engaged in the practice of self-care or have engaged in self-care in the past. Finally, students explore with each other how they might continue or increase self-care strategies in the coming week in a class discussion group. This becomes an ongoing self-reflection assignment for open student discussion at the beginning of each class session.

In subsequent class meetings over the remainder of the semester, ongoing self-care is explored at the beginning of class through a variety of contexts, including role-plays focusing on developing basic practice skills; small-group discussions for exchanging potential self-care strategies; role-plays applying different theoretical models to self-care such as the solution-focused model and strengths-based practice; and exploring current and past strategies for self-care. Featuring the discussion at the beginning of the class invites students to recognize that self-care is a foundation of professional development and identity. This is an easily overlooked component of professional training programs because client care is often given primary emphasis and practitioner care may be excluded (Newell & Nelson-Gardell, 2014). This emphasis invites students to integrate self-care into professional practice. Professionals practice self-care; it is a nonnegotiable component of professional responsibility.

In addition to raising awareness regarding the importance of self-care, training programs can provide examples of practical models and processes that include strategies students might employ in structuring their own self-care plans. Sansbury, Graves, and Scott (2015) describe a practical self-care process consisting of four steps:

Step 1: *Know thyself.* This step emphasizes the importance of clinicians being aware of their own states of internal arousal. Mindfulness is an important tool in developing skill in arousal awareness, which is a foundational tenet of knowing oneself.

Step 2: *Commit to address the stress.* This step involves the clinician actively managing internal arousal states. The clinician should be monitoring somatic indicators of stress such as breathing, posture, facial expression, and so forth for both the client and the self, particularly when the client is engaged in emotionally challenging work. Recognizing signs of stress can serve as a source of motivation to continue to engage in the process. Preemptively developing a "ready-made" list of self-care strategies will further promote the self-awareness process.

Step 3: *Make a personal plan of action.* Studies support the importance of planning as an aspect of successful behavior change. Sustainable results are best achieved through having an active yet practical plan in place.

Step 4: *Act on the plan*. Developing support systems with peers and colleagues who are accountable can help with following through with the identified plan; discussions of self-care with colleagues provide a context for exploring possible adjustments at the organizational level in support of self-care.

The plan should build on steps 1 and 2 as the awareness facilitates personal insight into the impact of stress as key information for selecting optimal self-care activities. Seeking social support by asking family and friends for feedback can provide useful information for assessing one's personal functioning. Such exploration promotes awareness of potentially overlooked positive aspects of providing trauma service; for example, providers of trauma services often report personal growth and a sense of fulfillment as satisfying aspects of their work (Berger, 2015; Tedeschi & Calhoun, 2004; Linley, 2003).

ETHICAL CHALLENGES: SELF-CARE IN INTERNSHIP AND FIELD EDUCATION EXPERIENCES

Students entering graduate programs face a multitude of challenges, and not all are related directly to mastering the knowledge and skills required of a competent professional (Gilin & Kauffman, 2015). Considerable demands, both academic and personal, are placed on students as they complete the sometimes rigorous requirements of professional training programs. Developmental growth as a professional, course assignments, and field experiences require students to think critically through examination of their personal values and the potential challenge those values may have in conflict with the values of the profession (Mathias, 2015). With such an expectation, professional training programs should engage students in course experiences that include an element of examining personal values. Such an examination involves actively and openly discussing any student feelings of discomfort with clients, their psychosocial problems, or challenges within their agency settings.

Internship and field education experiences often challenge personal worldviews that existed prior to professional acculturation (Wilcoxon, Jackson, & Townsend, 2010). Identification and assessment of personal values as part of the ongoing process of self-awareness has been identified as a key component of supervised practice experiences and the practice of self-care (Pompeo & Levitt, 2014). Clinical and field experiences provide a rich context for exploring personal reactions to the perceived challenges of clients. Direct client experiences and interactions give students the opportunity to explore their thoughts, feelings, and the meaningfulness they derive from the work (Black & Weinreich, 2000). Careful contemplation of the aspects of virtue ethics that connect with personal values helps to facilitate the processes of insight development and self-awareness. Supervisors may encourage this development by modeling transparency through acknowledging the duality of opportunity for both professional challenge and professional growth in working with clients, even those perceived as difficult, in direct practice.

Field education, practicum, and internship experiences are among the most significant developmental experiences for promoting the professional identity of future human service professionals. Several models of supervision describe this culminating portion of training as a period of recycling movement toward an integrated sense of self as a professional helper (Auxier, Hughes, & Kline, 2003; Friedman & Kaslow, 1986; Ronnestad & Skovholt, 1992). With these developmental characteristics identified as significant components of the clinical experience, the importance of integrating self-care strategies for promoting professional wellness is evident (Barnet, Baker, Elman, & Schoener, 2007). Engaging emotional challenges, traumas, and other critical incidents are milestones in the development of one's professional identity. The novelty of initial direct practice experiences increases the emotional intensity for students in training. Those in settings providing trauma services are particularly vulnerable to indirect effects of trauma and compassion fatigue, experiences that can significantly affect and change the drive, perception, spirit, and meaning of the work (Saakvitne & Pearlman, 1996). Actively attending to and engaging the risks associated with trauma-related care is critical to developing insight to personal vulnerabilities, creating a sense of value and meaning for the work, engaging in intentional self-care strategies, and in developing organizational and personal support networks (Hernandez, Engstrom, & Gangsei, 2010).

Self-care carries with it an inherent implication that the responsibility for the care resides with the self. At the same time, the systems of care in which service professionals work also have a significant impact on the self-care of providers. Recognition of the influence of the organizational environment suggests self-care is a multisystemic concern and positions agency and field supervisors to promote self-care at multiple hierarchical levels. Self-care needs may vary in accordance with the populations served and increase for students engaged in their field education experiences. Finally, supervisors should be aware of the increased risk of burnout for interns working in direct practice settings (Lent & Schwartz, 2012) and should provide guidance and practice wisdom to students who take proactive steps toward implementing wellness strategies. For example, an intentional self-care plan for monitoring and maintaining wellness should be incorporated in structured learning plans for field education students (see chapter 9).

SARAH: A CASE STUDY OF SUICIDE ON A COLLEGE CAMPUS

Sarah is an MSW student completing her internship hours through the university office of student support services. In this internship, Sarah has received extensive training on crisis management and has been invited to join the campus crisis intervention team as part of the counseling services offered through her placement. Sarah attends a small public liberal arts college with approximately 5,000 students, and she has to practice her skills of client confidentiality and anonymity daily because she often sees students she knows or recognizes from her classes, student activities, or who live in her residence hall.

Early one morning she and her supervisor are notified by one of the resident hall assistants (RAs) that he is unable to get into a student's (Parker's) dormitory room because it has been barricaded. The RA was completing a wellness check because one of Parker's friends saw a social media post that he described as "somewhat disturbing but not out of the ordinary for Parker." However, despite multiple attempts to make contact, he had not heard from Parker since late yesterday afternoon. Sarah and her supervisor walked over to the residence hall and are greeted by campus security. Sarah learns that Parker has committed suicide. Sarah immediately recognizes Parker; they met in the door her first day of freshman year and have been close for over four years.

Many students were present when the door was opened by the police, and they all became upset when they realized that Parker had committed suicide by hanging. Parker was well known to the office of student affairs and involved in many campus and community activities. In addition to living on campus in the residence hall, Parker was active on campus and well liked by his fellow housing residents, friends, and the faculty. He routinely served as a tutor, assisted with program development for several student organizations, was involved in a campus fraternity, and served as a member of the Student Government Association (SGA).

Through her internship, Sarah realized that Parker was receiving services in the counseling center for intermittent episodes of depression, but she was not aware of any indicated suicidal ideation or intent during his counseling sessions. Sarah purposely avoided talking with him about it to maintain Parker's confidentiality and to minimize any awkwardness for him while receiving treatment. Within seconds her phone begins to vibrate with calls and text messages about the incident. Her supervisor immediately sends her to the lobby to meet with students and to keep unauthorized visitors from entering the hallway until the city police arrive. Sarah immediately becomes overwhelmed and feels unable to manage the crisis without the direct support of her supervisor, who is now occupied trying to contact Parker's parents before they learn about the incident on social media.

DISCUSSION AND CRITICAL THINKING QUESTIONS

1. From the perspective of social work ethics, describe how Sarah can effectively manage her responsibilities as student intern to maintain confidentiality and anonymity as they intersect with her personal relationships with Parker, their mutual friends, and the greater campus community. (Social Work Competency 1: Demonstrate Ethical and Professional Behavior—through the practice of self-reflection and regulation; by attending to professional roles and boundaries; by demonstrating professional demeanor in behavior, appearance and communication; and through the use of technology ethically and appropriately.)

2. Describe how the process of "premediation," in which students engage in self-care as a proactive intervention to reduce the need for remediation, would be beneficial for Sarah in this situation. What internal and external resources would benefit Sarah as she engages in the challenging task of personal and professional development in this situation? (Social Work Competency 1: Demonstrate Ethical and Professional Behavior—through the practice of self-reflection and regulation.)

3. Critically appraise Sarah's reaction to the crisis situation. What type of support will Sarah need from her supervisor to process her own thoughts and feelings in a healthy and productive way? Describe any potential boundary issues or ethical dilemmas that may confront Sarah as she continues to be involved with the effects of the suicide on other students on campus and potentially with Parker's family. (Social Work Competency 1: Demonstrate Ethical and Professional Behavior—by attending to professional roles and boundaries and through the use of supervision and consultation.)

4. Using the model proposed by Sansbury, Graves, and Scott (2015), describe how Sarah could apply the four principles of knowing thyself, committing to address the stress, making a plan of action, and acting on the plan to construct a functional and holistic plan of self-care to guide her through the various stages of crisis and grief (including a memorial service) with her fellow students, her colleagues at student support services, and with Parker's friends and family. (Social Work Competency 1: Demonstrate Ethical and Professional Behavior—through the process of self-reflection and correction; Social Work Competencies 6–9: Engage, Assess, and Intervene with Individuals, Families, Groups, and Organizations, and Communities.)

KEY TERMS

American Counseling Association (ACA)
autonomy
beneficence
code of ethics
competency
Council for Accreditation of Counseling and
Related Educational Programs (CACREP)
Council on Social Work Education (CSWE)
ethical dilemma
ethics

moral
National Association of Social Workers
(NASW)
nonmaleficence
premediation
professional boundary
self-awareness
social justice
value

CHAPTER SUMMARY

This chapter provides an overview of the critical nature of professional self-care as a component of ethical practice. Numerous helping professions recognize the importance of self-care in their curriculum standards and codes of ethics. Faculty teaching in professional training programs including social work, clinical psychology, and counseling are responsible for adequately preparing competent practitioners equipped to face the challenges associated with their new professional roles and identities. This includes the ethical obligation to teach students the importance of the ongoing practice of self-care by integrating content into coursework, assignments, and field education experiences. The practice of self-care is not only beneficial to students but also to the clients they serve, colleagues, social service organizations, and to the preservation of our human service workforce. Self-care is a professional responsibility that begins in one's training program and continues as an ongoing practice behavior through processes such as professional awareness, reflection, and self-correction.

Professional training programs have a duty to promote self-care as an ethical mandate for future social work, counseling, and other human service professionals. The nature of academic study places demands on students to engage in personal and professional growth, and programs should balance academic rigor with supportive systems for optimizing student wellness. Programs that assist students with developing and maintaining personal wellness plans may reduce the later need for remediation plans. Programs can increase the likelihood that students will engage in self-care by providing students with information about existing self-care models. Furthermore, modeling and teaching wellness activities in coursework provides students with interventions that benefit them as well as the clients they will serve. The benefits of self-care contribute to the personal and professional well-being of counselors and social workers, increase therapeutic effectiveness, and promote ethical boundaries with clients.

RECOMMENDED READING

Beckett, C., & Maynard, A. (2012). *Values and ethics of social work: An introduction.* London, England: Sage.

Congress, E. P., Black, P. N., & Strom-Gottfried, K. (2009). *Teaching social work values and ethics: A curriculum resource* (2nd ed.). Alexandra, VA: CSWE Press.

Council for Accreditation of Counseling and Related Educational Programs. (2016). *2016 standards for accreditation.* Alexandria, VA: Author.

Dolgoff, R., Harrington, D., & Lowenberg, F. M. (2012). *Ethical decisions for social work practice* (9th ed.). Belmont, CA: Brooks/Cole Cengage Learning.

Herlihy, B., & Corey, G. (2014). *ACA ethical standards casebook.* New York, NY: Wiley.

National Association of Social Workers. (2008). *Code of ethics of the National Association of Social Workers.* Washington, DC: Author.

National Association of Social Workers. (2009). *Social work speaks. National Association of Social Workers policy statements 2009–2012.* Washington, DC: NASW Press.

Reamer, F. G. (2013). *Social work values and ethics* (4th ed.). New York, NY: Columbia University Press.

van Dernoot Lipsky, L., & Burk, C. (2009). *Trauma stewardship: An everyday guide to caring for self while caring for others.* San Francisco, CA: Berrett-Koehler.

SUGGESTED INTERNET RESOURCES

National Association of Social Workers: www.nasw.org
 NASW is the largest membership organization of professional social workers in the world, with 132,000 members. NASW works to enhance the professional growth and development of its members, to create and maintain professional standards, and to advance sound social policies. The NASW Code of Ethics in both English and Spanish is available at no cost. The site includes links to previous versions of the code, including the original version developed in 1960. In addition to resources related to the ethical practice of social work, the site includes a publication area with links to NASW journals, books, NASW news, and a link to the online *Encyclopedia of Social Work*. There also are links to professional development, conference venues, research, jobs, membership information, and other practice resources.

American Counseling Association: http://www.counseling.org
 This nonprofit educational and professional organization is dedicated to the enhancement of the profession of counseling. ACA is the largest counseling association exclusively representing professional counselors, with 20 chartered divisions that provide leadership, information, and resources unique to principles or specialized areas of counseling. Counselors in agencies and private practice, couples and family counselors, rehabilitation counselors, college counselors, school counselors,

and counselor educators will find a wealth of useful resources on the site, including opportunities for continuing education, advocacy, and connections with state and local counseling associations.

ACA Knowledge Center: http://www.counseling.org/knowledge-center/

Counseling competencies and practice briefs address specific areas of advocacy and treatment focus. Licensure and private practice information is also provided, as well as several ethics resources including a downloadable copy of the 2014 *ACA Code of Ethics*; a free podcast about the code; a comprehensive webinar examining components of the 2014 code; and ethics articles published in *Counseling Today*. An ethical decision-making model is provided along with a link for ACA members seeking free consultation with professional counselors in the ACA Ethics Department.

9

TRAUMA-INFORMED EDUCATION, TRAINING, AND PROFESSIONAL DEVELOPMENT

I would not suggest that we leave objectivity behind, but that we recognize that our personal passions drive our desires to do this work; and our training and good supervision—of our clinical work, or research, or teaching—help us keep our balance and objectivity.

—B. HUDNALL STAMM, 1999, P. XV

CHAPTER GOALS AND OBJECTIVES

1. Demonstrate the need for trauma-informed educational curriculum at the micro and macro level of practice in social work, counseling, and other professional training programs.
2. Discuss the applicability of social work practice skills such as the use of task-centered and problem-solving approaches, a strengths-based perspective, and the appropriately regulated use of empathy in the self-care process.
3. Demonstrate the use of social work practice skills in the process of self-care through the application of competency-based classroom and field education assignments.
4. Critically evaluate the challenges for students and faculty when integrating content on direct practice, trauma, and self-care in social work coursework and educational content.
5. Discuss the importance of training and professional development on psychological debriefing for macro- or community-level trauma practitioners, emergency responders, and other humanitarian relief workers.

INTRODUCTION

Emotional risks should be considered when choosing a career in social work, counseling, or other human service professions. The empirical literature is rich with studies documenting the presence of occupational stress conditions such as vicarious traumatization, secondary traumatic stress, compassion fatigue, and professional burnout in direct practitioners across a variety of practice settings. Human service work, particularly direct practice with trauma populations, has great potential to compromise the emotional well-being of the providers themselves (Figley, 1995; Pearlman & Saakvitne, 1995; Stamm, 1999). The emotional risks involved in direct practice with those who are vulnerable or suffering in some way has been described by some as the underestimated and overlooked "occupational hazard" of social work and other human service professions (Pryce et al., 2007; Rudolph & Stamm, 1999).

The wealth of evidence in the research literature on the emotional effects of human service work on direct practitioners implies the need for a well-developed and comprehensive trauma-informed education curriculum, inclusive of content on personal and professional self-care, as part of the academy's obligation to enhance the professional knowledge and resilience of our human service workforce. Yet there appears to be a disconnect between the evidence suggesting the need for self-care education as it relates to trauma-informed practice and the content of the formal education curriculum (Courtois, 2002; Jaynes, 2014; Knight, 2010). Neophyte professionals are often younger, have less organizational training, fewer years of direct practice experience, and therefore are the most vulnerable to the effects of these conditions (Boyas et al., 2012, 2013; Cyphers, 2001; Hamama, 2012; Lizano & Mor Barak, 2012). As there continues to be compelling evidence that practitioner well-being is a substantial challenge for many human service professionals, the gap between research and practice in this area may be contributing to the problem at the expense of our students, our future workforce, and ultimately the clients served (O'Halloran & O'Halloran, 2001; Harr & Moore, 2011; Jones & Sherr, 2014).

This identified gap in the professional education and training for human service professionals bears particular relevance to students and the role of social work educators who are charged with preparing students to assist clients (whether they are individuals, groups, organizations, or entire communities) with their problems in life. Part of that responsibility includes a professional and ethical obligation to educate students in the practice of self-care (Newell & Nelson-Gardell, 2014; Pearlman & Saakvitne, 1995). Most of the research on the emotionally challenging effects of human service work has been conducted in samples of professionals working in full-time practice positions. If those who are fully engaged in practice—some veterans in their respected fields—are vulnerable to the indirect effects of trauma, compassion fatigue, and professional burnout, then undoubtedly professionally inexperienced students entering field education settings are at even greater risk of experiencing these conditions.

This chapter focuses on the need for trauma-informed professional education and training for human service professionals. The profession of social work arguably provides the largest percentage of providers to the collective human service workforce; therefore, the chapter focuses on improving the education of professional social workers. However, the material is applicable for students and faculty teaching or learning in any micro or macro human service profession. Finally, this chapter presents several programmatic assignments that can be integrated in social work education classes and course content including a developmental assessment, an organizational assessment, assignments for developing a plan of self-care, and a table offering additional social work assignments that may be used as measures of social work competencies and practice behaviors.

PART 1: TEACHING SELF-CARE IN PROFESSIONAL TRAINING PROGRAMS

THE NEED FOR TRAUMA-INFORMED EDUCATION

Many human service professionals find themselves challenged when facing the chronically overwhelming emotional challenges of direct practice, which carries the risk of experiencing vicarious trauma, secondary traumatic stress, compassion fatigue, or ultimately burning out of the profession altogether. Given the frequency with which social workers and other human service professionals interact and provide services for clients affected by micro- and macro-level traumas, the inclusion of trauma-informed curriculum as part of the social work practice skill set is an essential component of social work education at both the graduate and undergraduate levels (Strand et al., 2014). Within the trauma-informed curriculum, there is a further need for education and training on the use of professional self-care to properly address the emotional and psychological risks associated with working as a provider of social work services with vulnerable populations (Black, 2006; Courtois, 2002; Cunningham, 2004).

Some argue that content on the primary and indirect effects of trauma practice has been largely overlooked in the social work educational curriculum (Newell & Nelson-Gardell, 2014). There is overwhelming agreement in the literature recommending that content addressing the challenges of direct practice and self-care should be offered in the context of professional social work education (Black, 2006; Cunningham, 2004; Knight, 2010; Newell & MacNeil, 2010), a position that is also supported by the National Association of Social Workers (2009). The following policy statement clearly charges social work education programs with being responsible for preparing students to practice self-care in the context of their undergraduate and graduate education: "the recognition by social work education programs of their critically important roles in educating social work students about the practice of professional self-care by integrating such content into existing student standards, policies, foundation and advanced curriculums, field practicum, and assignments and projects" (p. 247). Despite this recommendation by NASW, which is echoed consistently in the research literature, there is little explanation of why professional self-care has not become a requirement in the education curriculum and standards for social work practice behavior. The most recent revision to the Educational Policy and Accreditation Standards produced by the Council on Social Work Education under Competency 1, Demonstrate Ethical and Professional Behavior, loosely addresses the issue of self-care by stating: "social workers understand how their personal experiences and affective reactions influence their professional judgment and behavior" (CSWE, 2015). Although practitioner subjective well-being pursuant to the maintenance of social work ethics and professionalism may be implied here, no explicit language addresses trauma-informed practice or "self-care" as a required component of the curriculum. It is an ethical imperative for social work education programs to assume some responsibility in providing students with content in this area in the formal teaching environment where material on topics such as professional burnout, compassion fatigue, and self-care can be infused in social work courses and classroom exercises in a meaningful and practical way (Newell & Nelson-Gardell, 2014; NASW, 2009; Strand et al., 2014).

THE PRACTICE OF SOCIAL WORK AS SELF-CARE

Self-care is defined here as social workers and other human service professionals using skills and strategies to maintain their own personal, familial, emotional, physical, and spiritual needs to actively and consciously promote holistic well-being and professional resilience while attending to the complex emotional needs and demands of their clients (Cox & Sterner, 2013b; Lee & Miller, 2013; Pearlman & Saakvitne, 1995; Stamm, 1999). Studies have shown that many graduates of social work, counseling, and other human service programs are not competent in understanding and engaging the signs and symptoms of problems such as professional burnout and compassion fatigue or in using methods of self-care as a preventive measure (Harr & Moore, 2011; O'Halloran & O'Halloran, 2001; Shackelford, 2006). Although deficits related to this knowledge area are not yet known, such a lack of awareness among social work students increases their vulnerability to the effects of these conditions (Cunningham, 2004; Knight, 2010; Lerias & Byrne, 2003). One speculative answer is that current curriculum requirements on the theory and practice of social work compete for valuable instructional time in many social work course offerings as well as for space in social work textbooks.

Most human service professionals, particularly those trained in social work education programs, garner the professional education, skills, and abilities to practice self-care, but the biggest challenge is simply to make the commitment to embrace self-care as an essential and ongoing practice behavior (see chapter 6). Basic social work skills, knowledge, and abilities easily can be used by the professional to develop an ongoing and effective plan of self-care. For example, understanding human behavior as interfaces with the social environment, the use of a task-centered approach to problem solving, maintaining a strengths-based orientation to practice, and the application of psychosocial and organizational assessment have each been highlighted in previous chapters as being useful in maintaining the self-care process. The appropriate use of empathy, an essential skill in the practice of social work, includes the collective affective, emotional, cognitive, and somatic responses to clients and their situations in an effort to appropriately engage the client in a helping relationship (Decety & Jackson, 2004). It has been suggested that empathy also can be cultivated and developed as a practice skill, which can be helpful as part of the interpersonal processes of self-care (Gerdes et al., 2011). Finally, the holistic framework presented in chapters 6 and 7 for self-care strategies across biological, organizational, interpersonal, spiritual, and recreational domains of the psychosocial self is conceptualized from the theoretical perspective of ecological systems.

INTEGRATING SELF-CARE IN THE EDUCATION CURRICULUM

Chapters 6 and 7 describe in detail the individual, social, and institutional strategies useful in either preventing or intervening with the emotionally challenging aspects of direct practice. However, the research is both subjective and anecdotal; there are few tested models for the treatment of these conditions once they occur. Social work educators should teach students the key features, warning signs, and symptoms associated with the effects of vicarious and secondary trauma, compassion fatigue, and professional burnout as well as self-care strategies and techniques as preventive practice behaviors. Training, resources, and continuing education opportunities for professional social workers in the area of self-care have historically been scarce; however, recently more effort has been placed on training in this area through professional organizations in areas such as child welfare (Collins, 2009), a pattern that should be mirrored preventively in higher education. There are few validated models for integrating material on self-care in course content and classroom experiences; however, it is a topic that is applicable across most micro and macro course offerings in social work education programs. For students, taking responsibility for developing their own self-care activities in the context of coursework will assist as a preventive measure for the future challenges of field education and professional practice.

SAMPLE ASSIGNMENT: DEVELOPMENTAL ASSESSMENT

Social work courses such as direct practice with individuals and families, human behavior and the social environment, and life-span development courses supply multiple contexts for providing education and skills training on individual self-care strategies as preventive measures (Pryce et al., 2007). Material on the use and development of professional self-care is also appropriate for any specialty area course in mental health, public health or hospital social work, or child welfare practice, particularly when integrated with lectures on crisis intervention and crisis management. For example, students may be given an assignment on the psychosocial or developmental assessment of the behavioral influences of child physical or sexual abuse trauma across the life span. As part of the assignment, students may choose to research best practices for providing services to survivors of child-hood trauma at various stages of adult development and develop a plan for appropriate self-care while engaged in this practice. (Social Work Competency 4: Engage in Research-Informed Practice and Practice-Informed Research; Competencies 7 & 8: Assess and Intervene with Individuals, Families, Groups, Organizations, and Communities.) Using a strengths-based perspective as part of the self-care assessment component, students should include potential opportunities for professional growth and resilience as a result of working with survivors of child physical and sexual abuse.

SAMPLE ASSIGNMENT: ORGANIZATIONAL ASSESSMENT

Content on the organizational risk factors associated with professional burnout and com-passion fatigue can be infused in macro social work course offerings. An assignment on the organizational assessment of agency climate and culture on professional behav-ior and provider well-being could be incorporated in coursework on social work practice with communities and organizations and agency planning and management. As part of the assessment, students may be interested in participating in classroom discussions or brief writing assignments on the role of agency directors, supervisors, and program managers in setting the climate and organizational culture for the social service agency. Assignments such as this challenge students to think critically about the effects of indirect trauma practice, professional burnout, and compassion fatigue beyond individual direct practice experiences. To further develop organizational assessment skills, students may include an exploration of what beliefs have been embedded in the agency culture and how this influences the thinking and practice behavior of social work practitioners and other agency employees. (Competency 2: Engage Diversity and Difference in [mezzo] Practice; Social Work Competency 7: Assess Individuals, Families, Groups, Organizations, and Communities.) A thorough organizational assessment should include an analysis of the strengths of organizational mission, culture, and climate in terms of value placed on the ongoing practice, training, and professional development of self-care and well-being. Facilitating students' understanding of organizational climate and culture and the poten-tial risk factors for the experience of compassion fatigue or professional burnout prior to beginning their field education experiences may decrease their vulnerability to these con-ditions as they begin practice.

FIELD EDUCATION AND INTERNSHIP EXPERIENCES

One of the most appropriate places to engage students in coursework and discussion on self-care is in the context of seminar and field education experiences. Risk factors for students to experience emotional distress in response to the experience of their clients increase in field education due to their neophyte status in the social work profession, their underdeveloped abilities to practice professional self-awareness and reflection, and their lack of practice experience (Cunningham, 2004; Knight, 2010). Studies have shown that direct practitioners in social work and other human service professions are at risk of experiencing emotional distress as a result of their work in a variety of roles and service agencies. Social workers engaged in practice that involves chronic exposure to the graphic material and images associated with trauma work are at even greater risk of experiencing the indirect emotional effects of trauma work (Bride, 2007). Practice with hospice patients, incarcerated clients, combat veterans, survivors of domestic violence, sexual assault, and child physical and sexual abuse have all been described as high-risk settings for the experience of indirect trauma effects, compassion fatigue, and professional burnout (Adams et al., 2006; Conrad & Keller-Guenther, 2006; Pearlman & MacIan, 1995; Saimos et al., 2012; Tyson, 2007). These agency settings are common placements for undergraduate and graduate field education students. Therefore, working with students in real time as they are actively engaged in social work practice is ideal for integrating this material in a way that is meaningful, pragmatic, and beneficial to students as beginning practitioners (Cunningham, 2004; O'Halloran & O'Halloran, 2001).

One potential challenge to addressing the issue of self-care is that field professors may find that there is little opportunity or time available to process the individual reactions of social work students to their field education experiences (Moore, Bledsoe, Perry, & Robinson, 2011); others may believe this is best handled within the agency setting with the field advisor. Field professors and agency supervisors alike may be hesitant to engage students, especially those who have any past history of trauma, in conversation regarding their reactions to social work clients and their trauma material; this is despite the evidence in the research literature that past trauma history is a significant risk factor for secondary trauma reactions (Knight, 2010; Nelson-Gardell & Harris, 2003). One study of graduate counseling students found that approximately 50 percent of the participants indicated having their own personal history of trauma (O' Halloran & O'Halloran, 2001). The reality is that past experiences influence current behaviors and decisions, which may be the reason some students choose work in the human service field. Students should pay careful attention to the issue of inappropriate personal self-disclosure, both in the classroom and in field education because this creates potential for an ethical dilemma in "trauma bonding" with fellow classmates or agency clients. However, having a safe and socially supportive space for discussing the emotional impact of clients and their trauma material through the process of self-reflection is a helpful component of professional education and training (Black, 2006; Hall, 2014; McCammon, 1999; McCann & Pearlman, 1992). Alternatively, some students may be hesitant to disclose their emotional reactions to clients and their situations out of fear or stigma that they may be viewed by field professors or supervisors as unprepared, weak, or limited in their ability to practice efficaciously (Newell & MacNeil, 2010). This is particularly true for students interested in possible employment opportunities after their field education or internship.

For faculty, creating a classroom or seminar environment that honors the appropriate space and time for reflection on and discussion of both positive and negative aspects of field education experiences may be a helpful way to integrate this material in a meaningful way (Cox & Sterner, 2013a; Cunningham, 2004; O'Halloran & O'Halloran, 2001). Open discussion of students' reactions to clients and their experiences is an effective way of normalizing these reactions for students and avoiding any stigmas or hesitancy students might have about disclosing these reactions while in their field practice setting (McCammon, 1999). Open discussion also offers opportunity for valuable teaching moments by engaging students actively in the process of self-reflection and correction (Burke & Hohman, 2014). For students who may be in distress due to exposure to course content or through their professional interactions in field education, instructors should have resources and referral sources available to assist students in the process of actively managing their thoughts, feelings, and behaviors (Cunningham, 2004; Black, 2006). Finally, as appropriate supervision, professional guidance, and mentorship have all been shown to buffer the effects of occupational stress and trauma, field instructors should be properly trained and actively engaged in the professional development, self-care, and resilience of field education and internship students (Hass-Cohen & Chandler-Ziegler, 2014; Rajan-Rankin, 2013). Given the nature of our work, most human service professionals would agree that professional mentorship and practice wisdom are invaluable components of undergraduate and graduate social work curriculum and field education (Bogo & Wayne, 2013; Gutierrez, 2012). Take time to complete the worksheet at the end of the book titled Self-Reflection Exercise: Engaging Group Discussion on Trauma.

SELF-CARE AS A MEASURE OF STUDENT COMPETENCE

Providing social work students with education on the topic of self-care and resiliency is consistent with several of the standards established by the Council on Social Work Education in the most recent Educational Policy and Accreditation

Standards (CSWE, 2015). Further, assessment of social work students' knowledge of the experiences of professional burnout, vicarious traumatization, secondary traumatic stress, and compassion fatigue along with the practice of self-care can be used as a measure of several of the core competencies established by the CSWE. For example, under Competency 1, Demonstrate Ethical and Professional Behavior, knowledge of professional self-care and the methods of preventing or intervening with conditions such as professional burnout could be used to measure students' ability to attend to their professional roles and boundaries and to practice both self-reflection and self-correction. Assignments requiring students to review the research and practice literature in the area of self-care for the most appropriate and effective methods of prevention or intervention with professional burnout and compassion fatigue is reflective of the ability to apply critical thinking and to use and translate research evidence to inform and improve practice, policy, and service delivery. This is included in Competency 4, Engage in Research-Informed Practice and Practice-Informed Research. Educational content on preventing the effects of indirect trauma, professional burnout, and compassion fatigue and the importance of developing a preventive plan of self-care is a useful exercise in facilitating students' understanding of the complexity of individual behavioral responses to the professional work environment from a practitioner's perspective rather than solely from the perspective of clients and their experiences with social and

---

SAMPLE FIELD EDUCATION ASSIGNMENT: CONSTRUCTING A SELF-CARE PLAN

One suggestion for a measurable competency-reflective exercise or class assignment is to require students to develop their own self-care plan as a part of their professional development experiences during field education and seminar training. The self-care plan might include activities such as journaling about the various ways self-care behaviors can be applied emotionally, socially, physically, and spiritually (Moore et al., 2011). As a part of the assignment, students may be required to synthesize and integrate knowledge from both the research and practice literature as part of the critical thinking and professional development process of their self-care plan. The final product can be used as a measure of students' ability to apply both their research and critical thinking abilities to inform professional practice and to facilitate the career-long learning process. (Competency 1: Demonstrate Ethical and Professional Behavior; Competency 4: Engage in Practice-Informed Research and Research-Informed Practice.) Professional self-care should be an ongoing practice behavior (CSWE, 2015). This professional development assignment is modeled after the holistic framework for self-care presented in chapters 6 and 7. The worksheet titled Sample Goals and Objectives for a Plan of Self-Care at the end of the book presents a framework that may be used as a handout to assist students in the holistic development of goals and objectives related to their plan of personal self-care. See also the worksheets on Self-Care Process-Setting Organizational Goals and Self-Care Process-Setting Personal Goals.

environmental stressors. This is included in Competencies 7–9: Assess, Intervene, and Evaluate Individuals, Families, Groups, Organizations, and Communities. Finally, actively encouraging students to discuss their reactions to clients and their situations with field supervisors and field professors can be used as a measure of students' ability to demonstrate the use of both supervision and consultation, which is reflected in Competency 1: Demonstrate Ethical and Professional Behavior.

PART 2: TRAINING AND PROFESSIONAL EDUCATION FOR MACRO-LEVEL PRACTITIONERS

This book is primarily focused on individual or micro-level reactions practitioners' experience when chronically exposed to the stress and trauma material of the clients they serve. However, the increase of national and international world events such as mass shootings, terrorist attacks, and natural disasters has necessitated an increase in humanitarian aid at the macro- or community-level of practice (McCammon & Allison, 1995). Macro-level traumas are local, community, national, or international events that involve a collective response of shock and horror, often resulting in large-scale psychological consequences affecting large groups of people. Examples of macro-level events involving mass interpersonal violence or casualty include the terror attacks on the World Trade Center in 2001; mass school shootings such as the one at Sandy Hook Elementary School in Connecticut in 2012; natural disasters such as hurricanes, tornados, or tsunamis resulting in large-scale damage and casualty; or college campus shootings such as the one at Virginia Tech in 2007. Mass trauma in the United States has been fairly uncommon when compared with other countries in the world (Wainrib, 2006). Overwhelming news coverage in 2015 of multiple incidents of community-level interpersonal violence in the United States suggests that the number of incidents has increased, thus requiring more national-level trauma interventions than ever before.

Internationally, thousands of relief workers and first responders are deployed from the United States each year to provide humanitarian aid to survivors of natural disaster, famine, and other forms of mass casualty and human suffering. In the United States and internationally, humanitarian aid in the wake of natural disasters has existed for some time through the efforts of the Red Cross and the Federal Emergency Management Agency (Figley, 2002a; Wee & Myers, 2002). However, media coverage of survivors and first responders after the terrorist attacks on the World Trade Center in 2001 generated deeply felt global empathy and compassion for those who responded to that catastrophic event (Creamer & Liddle, 2005). Macro-level traumatic events necessitate relief efforts from a multitude of service providers including paramedics and ambulance drivers, providers of emergency medical procedures, law enforcement officials, the military, disaster mental health and grief counselors, journalists, and other mass communication specialists (Cremer & Liddle, 2005; Hyman, 2004: Palm et al., 2004). The U.S. military is the largest formally developed group of first responders that can respond during times of international disaster or crisis. After well over a decade of military engagement in Iraq and Afghanistan, many soldiers returned suffering physically and psychologically from the effects of war and combat-related traumas (Friedman, 2006; Galvoski & Lyon, 2004; Newell, 2012).

Military personnel, forensic investigators, paramedics, providers of emergency medicine, and other first responders are exposed to the physical and psychological trauma associated with natural disasters and acts of mass interpersonal violence including the death of children and adults, death of colleagues or combat unit members, personal injury, and body handling (Campbell, 2007; Regehr et al., 2002; Perron & Hiltz, 2006; Tyson, 2007). Given the number of social workers participating in disaster and emergency relief, continued educational training and professional development are needed (Figley, 2002a), but many practitioners are not receiving formal training on intervening with macro-level traumas professional or interpersonally (Hass-Cohen, Veeman, Chandler-Ziegler, & Brimhall, 2014). As discussed in earlier chapters, the effects of trauma treatment in the absence of proper intervention and self-care can be pervasive, affecting not only the providers themselves but also spouses, children, family members, and friends (Balcom, 1996; Bride & Figley, 2009; Dinshtein, Dekel, & Polliack, 2011). Methods of personal and professional self-care are important components of macro-level practice in the form of humanitarian aid, disaster relief work, or any form of community-level crisis intervention.

Professionals may find themselves seeking information on trauma intervention and self-care through professional development and continuing education. There is strong agreement that education, training, and professional development serve as buffers to the indirect effects of trauma in both micro- and macro-level practitioners (Figley, 1995; Pearlman & Saakvitne, 1995; Stamm, 1999). Professional training for macro-level trauma practitioners, emergency responders, and other crisis and disaster relief workers and volunteers typically occurs at the organizational or community level of intervention. Much of the work in this area revolves around the process of "psychological debriefing," which is typically brief and involves creating a space for relief workers to discuss and reflect on their emotional experiences and reactions with the crisis event prior to reintegration to their normative family and occupation life routines

(McCammon & Allison, 1995). Critical Incident Stress Debriefing (CISD) is a group debriefing that occurs within 24 to 72 hours after exposure to the traumatic event. CISD uses several elements for the debriefing process, including psych education, opportunities for ventilation, and mitigation of posttrauma symptoms including resource referrals (Mitchell & Everly, 1996). It has been suggestedthat models such as CISD have been effective in mitigating the primary and secondary effects of trauma, but there are few outcome studies or meta-analyses in the research literature to validate this claim. However, with adequate debriefing and response training, personal, professional, and community resilience may be a positive outcome of community trauma, crisis, and disaster relief work (Berger, Abu-Raiya & Benatov, 2016; Edward, 2005; Paton & Johnston, 2001).

CASE STUDY: SCHOOL SOCIAL WORKER

Keller is a recent college graduate and has secured her first position as social worker in the public school system. Keller is placed in an alternative school program for students who are "emotionally disturbed" and due to their complex behaviors cannot be educated safely in a public school setting. Her students have a wide range of exceptionalities, including specific learning disabilities, emotional disorders, attention disorders, and autism spectrum disorders. In addition to their mental health concerns, most of the children on her caseload have a history of physical abuse, sexual abuse, neglect, or a combination of these conditions. Keller, the special education teacher, and the classroom aides are responsible for serving approximately 14 students each day. Student instruction takes place in a self-contained classroom setting, which often further complicates the task of meeting the academic needs of students with compounding emotional and behavioral challenges. All of the students receiving services on her caseload have an individual education plan (IEP) with annual goals and benchmark objectives that must be followed to maintain compliance with federal and state educational policy. As part of the IEP, Keller must provide several students with individual counseling each week and conduct daily small processing and anger management groups with each of the children in the classroom.

As a social worker, Keller has found that meeting the complex academic and behavioral needs of her students is challenging and sometimes seemingly impossible. Keller often feels overwhelmed when developing her daily intervention schedule, which must coincide with the teacher and alternative school schedules. In addition to her individual and group counseling duties, she is charged with being the student and family advocate during IEP meetings. This often creates tension and issues of role confusion with the classroom teacher and principal when she advocates for additional student services or funding to meet the educational needs of her students. For example, the majority of students on her caseload are required to have the support of a special education teacher or an aide for academics. This chronically presents a time management issue as Keller is often asked to provide classroom behavioral support when additional assistance is needed with one of the students. When Keller approached her administrators with this issue, she was told simply to "figure it out," meaning she should attempt to rearrange student schedules or request additional assistance from the school's existing aides and paraprofessionals. After her last meeting with the school principal, Keller left feeling that neither option resulted in a resolution to her feelings of being overwhelmed, nor her position that the educational needs of her students are not being addressed efficaciously. Keller realizes that IEPs are considered legally binding documents and serve as working contracts with students and their parents, which has presented her with many professional challenges when interacting with the parents of the children in her caseload.

In addition to the stress of successfully serving her students, she is also responsible for a considerable amount of administrative duty, including creation of a new after school program for first-time drug court offenders. As the social worker for this new program, Keller is responsible for conducting alcohol and substance abuse groups with children and their families. She will conduct at least one home visit and one psych-social assessment for each child and the family. The groups meet twice weekly from 6:00 PM to 8:00 PM. Keller is not yet sure how she will integrate these new responsibilities with her current schedule and assigned duties. She finds that she thinks about work and her students even when at home spending time with her husband, family, and friends. She feels obligated to focus all of her extra time and energy on the well-being of her students and the longevity of her new job because she does not want to be perceived as inefficient or incompetent.

DISCUSSION AND CRITICAL THINKING QUESTIONS

1. Describe how an organizational assessment of both agency climate and culture as it relates professional behavior and provider well-being could assist Keller with her systemic integration in her new position in the public school system. (Social Work Competency 2: Engage Diversity and Difference in [mezzo] Practice; Social Work Competency 7: Assess Individuals, Families, Groups, Communities, and Organizations.)

2. As part of the organizational assessment of climate and culture, conduct a critical analysis of the organization's strengths including the value

placed on ongoing practice, training, and professional development related self-care and well-being. How would this assessment data contribute to Keller's knowledge as she develops her own approach to professional self-care and resilience? (Social Work Competencies 7 & 9: Assess and Evaluate Individuals, Families, Groups, Communities, and Organizations—based on the critical assessment of strengths, needs, and challenges, and by applying evaluation findings to improve practice effectiveness at all system levels.)

3. From an interprofessional practice perspective, describe how the roles of the social worker, teacher, classroom aides, administrators, and parents converge in this setting to provide multidisciplinary educational and psychosocial services to children with multiple needs and challenges. (Competency 8: Intervene with Individuals, Families, Groups, Organizations, and Communities—through the use of interprofessional collaboration as appropriate to achieve beneficial practice outcomes.)

4. Take a moment to reflect on this case study and how Keller's situation may be resolved by assessing her own behavior and the climate of the organization. Identify the individual and organizational challenges that may be contributing to Keller's difficulties adjusting to her new position in the school system. Following your assessment, refer to table 9.1 for several competency-based activities for conducting a thorough individual and organizational assessment of this case. (Competency 1: Demonstrate Ethical and Professional Behavior—through the use of self-reflection; Competencies 7 & 9: Assess and Evaluate Individuals, Families, Groups, Communities, and Organizations—based on the critical assessment of strengths, needs, and challenges, and by applying evaluation findings to improve practice effectiveness at all system levels.)

KEY TERMS

crisis management	humanitarian relief work
critical incident	macro-level or community-based trauma
competency-based education	personal self-disclosure
continuing education	practice behavior
Council on Social Work Education (CSWE)	professional development
disaster mental health	psychological debriefing
Educational Policy and Accreditation Standards (EPAS)	trauma bonding
	trauma-informed education and practice
field education	

TABLE 9.1 Competency-Based Activities for Keller Case Study

Social Work Competency	Sample Field Seminar Exercises
Competency 1: Demonstrate ethical and professional behavior.	• Using the case study, engage in a discussion focused on Keller's use of supervision and consultation for assistance. • Discuss or write about the process of personal self-reflection and correction and the application of this practice behavior to this situation. • Using the NASW *Code of Ethics*, write a one-page summary of the ethical dilemmas involved in this case. As part of the assignment, ask students to address how Keller should engage her principal and other supervisors in resolving any identified ethical dilemmas.
Competency 4: Engage in research-informed practice and practice-informed research.	• Develop a literature review assignment requiring students to review at least five scholarly works in the area of professional burnout and compassion fatigue and submit a summary or annotated bibliography of their findings.
Competency 7: Assess individuals, families, groups, communities, and organizations.	• Conduct an assessment of both the organizational and individual factors involved in this case and compare how these factors affect Keller's risk for professional burnout and compassion fatigue.
Competency 9: Evaluate individuals, families, groups, communities, and organizations.	• Initiate a class discussion on Keller's behavior in terms of her professional setting. Is this behavior appropriate for a new social work student with no previous exposure to practice in a child welfare setting? Why or why not?
Competencies 7–9: Assess, intervene, and evaluate individuals, families, groups, organizations, and communities.	• Based on the case study and the literature review assignment, develop a self-care plan for Keller addressing strategies for managing compassion fatigue at both the individual and the organizational level. • After the case study exercise, have students develop their own plan of self-care as part of their field seminar requirements.

CHAPTER SUMMARY

It has been suggested that the best defense against indirect trauma and professional burnout is education, training, and professional development. Considerable evidence in the research literature documents the existence of these conditions in human service work, but there is little indication that the education curriculum offers adequate content for students training in professional programs (Courtois, 2002; Cunningham, 2004; Shackelford, 2006). With the likelihood that students preparing to practice in the human service professions will encounter clients involved with trauma and emotional suffering, it seems logical to expect that this topic be addressed as part of the education and training preparing future human service workers. Beyond trauma-informed education and curriculum, future social workers and other human service professionals also need education on the use of self-care to sustain personal and professional resilience over time.

This chapter discusses the importance of including content in this area in formal education training and curriculum. Self-care can be integrated and infused in existing micro- and macro-level social work course offerings and content. Competency-based classroom assignments in developmental and organizational assessment and in the construction of a formal plan of self-care are provided. Assignments for field education and internship experiences are also included in the chapter. Part 2 presents the importance of training and professional education for macro-level practitioners, emergency responders, and humanitarian aid workers responding to natural disasters, acts of community violence, terror, and mass interpersonal violence. A case study describing the experience of a social worker in a public school system is followed by several measurable competency-based assignments, which concludes the chapter.

RECOMMENDED READINGS

Bean, R. A., Davis, S. D., & Davey, M. P. (2014). *Clinical activities for increasing competence and self-awareness.* Hoboken, NJ: Wiley.

Levers, L. L. (2012). *Trauma counseling: Theories and interventions.* New York, NY: Springer.

Pryce, J. G., Shakleford, K. K., & Pryce, D. H. (2007). *Secondary traumatic stress and the child welfare professional.* Chicago, IL: Lyceum.

Saakvitne, K. W., & Pearlman, L. A. (1996). *Transforming the pain: A workbook on vicarious traumatization for helping professionals who work with traumatized clients.* New York, NY: Norton.

Smith, P. (2008). *Healthy caregiving: A guide to recognizing and managing compassion fatigue.* Compassion Fatigue Awareness Project. Retrieved from www.compassionfatigue.org

Wainrib, B. R. (2006). *Healing crisis and trauma with mind, body, and spirit.* New York, NY: Springer.

SUGGESTED INTERNET RESOURCES

Crisis & Trauma Resource Institute: https://us.ctrinstitute.com/

CTRI is a leading provider of training and consulting services for individuals, schools, communities, and organizations affected by or involved in working with issues of crisis and trauma. CTRI's purpose is to provide exceptional training and resources to better lives. Under the belief that mental health, counseling, and safety resources should be accessible to everyone, CTRI's workshops and resources are geared to a wide range of care and service providers including social service, health care, education, employment, and others. The home page offers three main areas of navigation for responders working in the United States, Canada, and internationally. Under the Our Trainings tab, information on webinars, onsite trainings, and workshops are included and classes are offered in a variety of areas for modest registration and continuing education fees. Available for purchase in the Resources area are printed training manuals on various topics in the fields of crisis intervention and emergency management. The Free Resources tab has information on webinars and trainings that can be completed at no cost as well as training manuals, articles, and handouts that can be downloaded at no cost for in-house training and professional development.

Headington Institute: http://www.headington-institute.org/home

The institute partners with humanitarian relief and development organizations and emergency responders before, during, and after deployment to ensure the well-being of individuals. This international institute provides services to humanitarian workers in the United States, Africa, Asia, the Middle East, the United Kingdom, and other parts of Europe. Resources on the topics of professional resilience, stress and burnout, trauma, and women and other gender populations are open to the public at no cost. The resources include an online training and certification module on vicarious traumatization. Many of the resources can be downloaded and have been translated into several languages. The Resource Index tab is an excellent source for Internet resources including YouTube videos on trauma, coping, and self-care for those involved in human service work.

10

THE USE OF MINDFULNESS PRACTICE AS A FUNCTION OF SELF-CARE

Happiness comes when your work and words are of benefit to yourself and others.

—BUDDHA

CHAPTER GOALS AND OBJECTIVES

1. Conceptualize mindfulness as a contemporary practice grounded in the eastern philosophies and spiritual practices of Buddhism.
2. Review the research literature and describe the human qualities associated with mindfulness practice including awareness, openness, nonjudgment, and self-compassion.
3. Discuss the application of active practices such as deep breathing exercises, meditation, and yoga as components of mindfulness.
4. Discuss the impact of mindfulness practices on personal and professional health and well-being through examination of the theoretical and empirical research.
5. Discuss the use of mindfulness practices as a valuable component of the holistic approach to personal and professional self-care.
6. Provide practical ways for students and educators to integrate mindfulness practices in coursework, training, and professional development for social workers, counselors, and other human service professionals.

INTRODUCTION

Mindfulness has varying definitions, approaches, and applications and is broadly defined as a practice that brings balance, clarity, and meaning during times of physical and emotional stress, illness, and pain. Mindfulness has been described in the literature as a state, a trait, a quality, and a skill comprised of intention, attention, and attitude (Langner & Moldoveanu, 2000; Shapiro,

Carlson, Astin, & Freedman, 2006). Mindfulness practice originated in the eastern philosophies and the spiritual practices of Buddhism. The Sanskrit word *sati* (to remember), from early Buddhist scriptures, describes the importance of both conscious and sensory awareness of what is occurring in the present moment as one appraises and processes the human experience in collective thoughts and memory (Brown, Creswell, & Ryan, 2016). Some Buddhist scholars suggest that sati is the original term for what has been conceptualized as mindfulness in contemporary Western society (Chiesa, 2012). In the Western perspective, mindfulness has been defined as seeking deep meaning through awareness of the body, mind, feelings, and perceptions (Hanh, 2006). Refer to the Recommended Readings at the end of this chapter for other works on the origins of mindfulness practice in Buddhism and its influence on eastern philosophy, religion, and spirituality. In this chapter, mindfulness is defined as the "awareness that emerges through paying attention on purpose, in the present moment, and non-judgmentally to the unfolding of experience moment by moment" (Kabat-Zinn, 2003, p. 145).

The contemporary Western conceptualizations of mindfulness have evolved in recent history through the context of Buddhist psychological theory. Mindfulness practice has been explored through various humanistic and existential schools of psychology, including the emerging field of positive psychology, and has been integrated with other forms of psychology including the cognitive behavioral school in the form of intervention models such as mindfulness-based cognitive therapy (MBCT) and dialectic behavioral therapy (DBT) (Hick & Chan, 2010). Researchers suggest that mindfulness practices such as meditation, awareness, and decentering are effective in improving overall health and well-being (Brown & Ryan, 2003). Models such as mindfulness-based stress reduction (MBSR) have been used extensively in the effective treatment of various physical and emotional health conditions including addiction, anxiety, and depression (Cullen, 2011). Finally, as a function of self-care, mindfulness practices have been suggested as a component of self-care helpful for professionals in social work, counseling, nursing, and other human service professions. This chapter explores the concept of mindfulness and the use of mindfulness practices as a functional component of personal and professional self-care and as a potential mediator to the stress of human service work.

ELEMENTS OF MINDFULNESS PRACTICE

Despite the growing interest in mindfulness techniques and practices over the past three decades, a universally accepted operational definition of the mindfulness construct has not emerged (Bishop et al., 2004). Mindfulness practice has been studied from various perspectives as a function of religious or spiritual beliefs, as personality traits, as a state of being, as an interpersonal practice, and as an intervention (Chiesa, 2012; Miller, 2014). The terms *mindfulness* and *mindfulness practice* have been used to describe various spiritual, psychological, and emotional behaviors applied in an effort to increase personal awareness and to create balance. One of the core components of mindfulness practice is to cultivate one's awareness of the present moment. The process of developing a state of awareness through mindfulness involves the conscious engagement of thoughts, feelings, behaviors, and bodily sensations as they relate to events of the present moment independently occurring outside of and without influence from events of the past (Hick & Chan, 2010; Kabat-Zinn, 2003).

Awareness has been described as the "background or *radar* of consciousness, continually monitoring the inner and outer environment" (Brown & Ryan, 2003). Hence, bringing awareness to one's life experiences is achieved in part through the cognitive process of attention self-regulation in the present moment (Bishop et al., 2004). Attention self-regulation involves the use of deliberate methods of concentration in an effort to be fully present and aware of current life experiences, without focus on previously planned engagements, time management, or task completion (Grabovac, Lau, & Willett, 2011). Awareness practice involves observation of internal and external experiences while simultaneously taking mental note of the phenomenological reactions of the mind and the body (Brown, Ryan, & Creswell, 2007). Another goal of awareness through attention self-regulation is to fully live each experience of the present moment, even those that cause emotional or physical pain and suffering, rather than avoiding or being distracted by anxious thoughts, feelings, or emotions associated with the discomfort of these experiences (Brantley, 2007; Christopher & Maris, 2010). The development of awareness as a component of mindfulness practice should not be confused with the use of "self-awareness" and "self-reflection," which are direct practice terms that describe practitioner awareness of personal reactions to clients and their psychosocial situations (Richards et al., 2010). The practice of mindful awareness is a holistic, interpersonal process inclusive of work with clients as a part of life, but it is not situational or limited to one life experience as suggested by the term "professional self-awareness" (Brown & Ryan, 2003).

A second element of mindfulness practice is the ongoing use of kindness and self-compassion. Self-compassion is derived from Buddhist psychology and is comprised of a combination of positive thoughts, attitudes, and behaviors that include being kind and accepting of oneself rather than being self-judging. Broadly conceptualized, self-compassion involves the use of tolerance and humanity rather than isolation during times of personal challenge and suffering, and the use of mindfulness and awareness rather than self-critical thinking processes, such as internalization and overidentification with interpersonal challenges or failures (Neff, 2011). Part of self-compassion as a mindfulness process is to practice a nonjudgmental attitude toward oneself, the social environment, and others. This process has been referred to as the act of self-kindness. Self-kindness is the opposite of self-judgment, which is often an easier process to conceptualize because people tend to be harder and more demanding on themselves than on others (Gerber, 2009). Self-compassion is different from the commonly used term *self-esteem*, which is often based on performance, judgment, and the comparative analyses of others (Neff, 2011). For practitioners, the act of self-compassion may be described as the use of self-empathy, which is the interpersonal use of one's regulated empathy skills and resources to foster continued resilience and self-preservation. Self-compassion has been associated with the term *loving-kindness*, which involves qualities such as benevolence, forgiveness, and unconditional love, all of which can be used internally as well as externally to show compassionate care to both the self and to others.

Other qualities commonly associated with the practice of mindfulness include having an open and accepting orientation to life experiences. The concept of "openness" describes perceiving things for the first time without contamination from past thoughts, feelings, and experiences. Openness involves attending to the mind with curiosity, even when it wanders during relaxation, and simply taking notice of the drift (Bishop et al., 2009). The use of openness is also associated with the practice of "acceptance." Acceptance, a core component of mindfulness practice, is simply staying in the present moment and remaining open to circumstances that cannot be changed or altered. Acceptance is the opposite of resistance and involves seeing the present moment for what it is rather than what we anticipate or want it to be (Marturano, 2014). The practice of acceptance involves turning into or tolerating resistance and aversion (safely) rather than avoiding the emotional discomfort of painful life experiences. The goal of tolerance and acceptance is to find deeper meaning, value, and ultimately liberation and resilience from the sources of pain and discomfort (Gerber, 2009). Attitudes and qualities such as being nonjudgmental, open, and accepting are important components to practicing and living in a life space influenced by the practice of mindfulness. The qualities or attributes of mindfulness practice should not be considered as forms of passivity; rather, they signal the embrace of an accepting and open nature to what is uncontrollable in the present moment, and a resistance to changing the moment to meet our own needs, thoughts, or expectations (Hick, 2009). Finally, mindfulness is associated with the idea of "letting go" through the practices of openness, awareness, and acceptance by allowing natural change to occur in the absence of thoughts, feelings, and experiences that are no longer relevant or useful in the present moment.

Meditation practice used to seek calmness, clarity, and focus is also associated with the mindfulness perspective. Meditation and conscious relaxation are often described as key components to the cultivation of mindfulness and self-compassion (Gerber, 2009). However, mindfulness is characterized as a holistic state of consciousness with meditation serving as the "scaffolding used to develop the state, or skill, of mindfulness" (Shapiro et al., 2006). Recent research has suggested that when used consistently over time mindfulness meditation practices have positive neurobiological effects such as higher sensory processing, alterations in cognitive reappraisal, and increased focus and attention (Zeidan, 2016). There are two basic forms of meditation. Concentrative meditation involves singular focus on one object, the breath, or a mantra (Sedlmeier et al., 2012). In concentrative meditation, all internal and external stimuli other than the target of focused attention are considered distractions from the meditative state (Smith, 2005). The mindfulness approach is not singularly focused; rather, it is more open to the sensory perception of all internal and external stimuli. Mindfulness meditation involves being open and aware of the events of the present moment and of the body–mind reactions to internal and external stimuli. Meditation can be used to facilitate mindfulness because it enhances conscious efforts to create focus and attention self-regulation, control distraction, foster presence, and promote a balanced mind (Kabat-Zinn, 2003; Coffey, Hartman, & Frederickson, 2010). The Western image of meditation typically involves standard sitting or cushion meditation; however, there are various approaches to the practice of meditation. Meditations may be focused on bodily sensations such as breathing, chanting, or tasting food; on the experience and sensations of a physical activity such as walking, sitting in a chair, or rocking; or on the processes of the mind through visual imagery or observation of distracting thoughts and feelings (Smith, 2005; Marturano, 2014). For detailed information on the various types of meditation, refer to the Recommended Readings listed at the end of this chapter. Regardless of the type of meditation practice employed, the goal for meditation (as it applies to mindfulness practice) is to foster a state of conscious relaxation, peace, and balance of the body and of the mind in an effort to cultivate a state of openness and acceptance of life experiences and of the present moment (Sedlmeier et al., 2012).

Finally, yoga practice is often a component of mindfulness practice. The practice of yoga-form stretching helps to relax the physical body and connect it with the mind (Smith, 2005). Yoga is deeply rooted in Buddhist philosophy and can help to cultivate focus, awareness, and openness when used as a component of mindfulness practice (Khanna & Greeson, 2013). There are various approaches to yoga practice, but yoga generally involves a combination of stretching, posturing, and deep breathing (Khanna & Greeson, 2013). Active practices such as yoga and progressive muscle relaxation have been used in models of mindfulness training, such as MBSR, and have been effective in treating a variety of physical and mental health conditions (Carmody & Baer, 2008; Cullen, 2011; Kabat-Zinn, 2003).

MINDFULNESS PRACTICE AND WELL-BEING

Review of the research literature reveals that the use of mindfulness practices and techniques has grown exponentially in the last two decades as a potential intervention to improve the quality of life and well-being across a variety of biological and psychosocial indicators (Carmody & Baer, 2008; Cullen, 2011). With the increase in the use of mindfulness practice across professional disciplines, a subsequent increase has been noted in the number of clinical trials testing mindfulness techniques as interventions for a multitude of physical and emotional health conditions (Brown et al., 2007). Empirical studies indicate that mindfulness-based techniques such as meditation, the practice of awareness, and letting go have positive health effects on physical conditions such as psoriasis, chronic pain, fibromyalgia, cancer, heart disease, and other general medical and health conditions (Grossman, Niemann, Schmidt, & Walach, 2004; Shapiro, Astin, Bishop, & Cordova, 2005). In terms of mental health, conscious awareness, emotional regulation, decreased rumination, nonattachment, and decentering have shown effectiveness in the overall symptom improvement in depression, anxiety, generalized anxiety disorder, social anxiety disorder, eating disorders, posttraumatic stress disorder, and attention deficit hyperactivity disorder (ADHD) (Coffey et al., 2010; Hick & Chan, 2010; Reber, Boden, Mitragotri, Alvarez, Gross, & Bonn-Miller, 2013).

Mindfulness-based practices have been used in a variety of occupational settings, particularly in the fields of health and human services, as a method of mitigating and reducing the effects of work-related stress (Shapiro et al., 2005). Techniques such as mindfulness-based problem solving, positive coping strategies, and yoga practice have been suggested as being effective in preventing professional burnout, improving relationships with patients and clients, and enhancing overall well-being in nurses and other health care professionals (Asuero, Queralto, Pujol-Ribera, Berenguera, Rodriquez-Blanco, & Epstein, 2014; Bazarko, Cate, Azocar, & Kreitzer, 2013). Techniques involving the use of meditative practices have shown effectiveness in decreasing stress and burnout in social workers, counselors, psychotherapists, and other mental health professionals (Christopher & Maris, 2010; Galantino, Maguire, Szapary, & Farrar, 2005; McGarrigle & Walsh, 2011; Richards et al., 2010; Sedlmeier et al., 2012). Finally, training in the practices of self-compassion and self-awareness have been suggested as being helpful in facilitating professional well-being and in fostering commitment, motivation, and energy to the organization and to the profession itself (Lichtenberg, Hartman, & Bushardt, 2013; Youngson, 2014).

MINDFULNESS PRACTICE AS SELF-CARE

The use of mindfulness practices, such as presence and awareness, can be helpful for students and professionals in developing a healthy balance between their personal and professional lives. In terms of self-care, mindfulness practice is holistic with potential benefits far beyond the development of professional resilience. Mindfulness practices have a positive influence on the physical, emotional, spiritual, and interpersonal quality of life domains (Newsome, Christopher, Dallen, & Christopher, 2006). Given the holistic nature of mindfulness techniques and practices, this approach can easily be integrated in the ecological framework for holistic self-care presented in this book. Due to the emotionally demanding nature of human service work, teaching mindfulness practice in the context of professional education programs may provide students with a useful and practical interpersonal resource for managing their own personal stress and emotional well-being as well as efficaciously meeting the needs of those in their care.

It has been suggested that the ongoing use of mindfulness techniques may enhance positive coping skills, increase professional resilience, and potentially buffer the effects of burnout and compassion fatigue (Christopher & Maris, 2010; Lichtenberg, Hartman, & Bushardt, 2013; McGarrigle & Walsh, 2011). Previous chapters have demonstrated that work-related stress can influence multiple areas of psychosocial functioning. Cultivating the mindfulness practice of attention self-regulation may be useful in the creation of conscious barriers between work-related stressors so they do not negatively influence important time in the present moment. This practice may be particularly useful for professionals in trauma-related practice, which often presents an even more difficult and challenging environment for providers to create separation and maintain balance. The practice of being present in the moment, rather than in the past, has been shown to have a positive overall effect on personal and professional well-being and to be a valuable component of the self-care process (Brown & Ryan, 2003; Richards et al., 2010). Integrating mindfulness practices with cognitive techniques, such as guided imagery, decentering, and self-talk, may be effective in negotiating negative thoughts and belief patterns that often emerge as a result of chronic exposure to human service work (Hick & Chan, 2010; Smith, 2005).

Other elements of mindfulness practice, such as the use of self-compassion and self-appreciation, are valuable components of the self-care process. Self-compassion allows for the acceptance of one's past decisions and mistakes in a nonjudgmental way and for letting go of the negative attachments to these past events (Gerber, 2009; Neff, 2003). Conscious relaxation and meditation, used even in small amounts, has shown effectiveness in decreasing both personal and professional anxiety, depression, rumination, and other forms of psychological distress and can easily be incorporated in daily self-care practice (Coffey et al., 2010; Newsome et al., 2006; Sedlmeier et al., 2012). Finally, active mindfulness practices such as deep breathing, stretching, and yoga may be effective when integrated with the ongoing practice of mindfulness as a component of self-care (Asuero et al., 2014, Smith, 2005; Williams, Richardson, Moore, Gambrel, & Keeling, 2010). Take some time now to practice deep breathing as outlined in the worksheet titled Sample Assignment: Deep Breathing Exercise.

INTEGRATING MINDFULNESS TRAINING IN THE EDUCATION CURRICULUM

Mindfulness practice as a component of self-care may be valuable to students in professional training programs in social work, counseling, and other human service professions. As neophyte social service professionals are at the greatest risk of experiencing the indirect effects of trauma and professional burnout, formal training in mindfulness practice has the potential to buffer the indirect effects of trauma-related practice, compassion fatigue, and professional burnout. Mindfulness approaches may be used in the form of client interventions, as a method of engaging clients, as a component of clinical supervision and mentorship, and as part of the self-care process for providers (Gockel, 2015; Hick, 2009). Integrating course content on mindfulness techniques such as awareness, attention self-regulation, openness, and the use of a nonjudgmental attitude have been shown to positively influence the physical and emotional well-being of social workers, counselors, psychotherapists, teachers, nurses, and other health care and human service professionals (Christopher & Maris, 2010; Roeser et al., 2013; Shapiro et al., 2005; Youngson, 2014).

Mindfulness can be integrated in coursework across the education curriculum. From the perspective of client intervention and treatment, mindfulness practices have been integrated in models such as MBCT, DBT, and acceptance and commitment therapy (ACT). MBCT and DBT combine the mindfulness practices of attention, self-awareness, acceptance (as decentering), and meditation with cognitive approaches to change thoughts, feelings, and behaviors (Hick, 2009). ACT has elements of cognitive behavioral therapy as it operates on the cognitive process by reframing the context from which life experiences are perceived and appraised; it also involves finding a path to spiritual meaning and peacefulness with life (Hayes, 2004). Cognitive treatment approaches and mindfulness have been integrated in treating mental health conditions including depression, stress-related anxiety, PTSD, eating disorders, personality disorders, and addictions (Brown et al., 2016; Hick & Chan, 2010; Khanna & Greeson, 2013; Powers, Zum Vörde Sive Vörding, & Emmelkamp, 2009; Reber et al., 2013).

MBSR has been described as the most widely accepted training model for mindfulness. The effects of MBSR have been studied in the treatment of many physical and mental health conditions and have demonstrated positive outcomes across multiple indicators of health and well-being (Brown & Ryan, 2003; Cullen, 2011; Grossman et al., 2004). MBSR has been used extensively in continuing education and professional development in numerous professional settings (Cullen, 2011; Kabat-Zinn, 2003). MBSR was developed by John Kabat-Zinn (2003) as a method of cultivating mindfulness practice pursuant to a more balanced mind and improved emotional and physical well-being. MBSR is commonly delivered as an 8- to 10-week group training process using the four key elements of movement (stretching and yoga), body scanning, awareness, and sitting meditation (Carmoday & Baer, 2008). Training, education, and professional development on the use of MBSR have shown particular effectiveness in reducing the effects of work-related stress, anxiety, and burnout by increasing positive affect, serenity, empathy, and self-compassion in a variety of health and mental health professionals (Bazarko et al., 2013; Brown et al., 2016; Shapiro, Brown, & Biegel, 2007).

Mindfulness practices such as MBSR can be integrated in the training and professional development content for personal and professional training for students (as future professionals). Mindfulness as part of the self-care process has been shown to improve physical, emotional, and spiritual quality of life in social workers, counselors, and psychotherapists in training (Bonifas & Napoli, 2014; Christopher & Maris, 2010; McGarrigle & Walsh, 2011). Mindfulness practices such as increasing self-compassion and decreasing self-judgment may facilitate improved client outcomes by decreasing student fear and anxiety about engaging clients in assessment or treatment processes. Integrating content on mindfulness practice may be particularly useful for students as a component of field education or seminar courses. For example, mindfulness practices can be included as a component of debriefing with students about their field agencies, the clients they serve, and their personal and professional reactions to clients and their psychosocial problems. Mindfulness practice can facilitate role-play exercises and client simulations, provide opportunities for mutual observation and feedback, demonstrate group process and facilitation, and increase reflective listening skills (Bonifas & Napoli, 2014; Gockel, 2015). Finally, mindfulness practices have been applied to the principles and practices of organizational leadership. Through mindfulness practices such as presence and awareness, qualities such as finding focus, mental clarity, creativity, and compassion for self and others have great potential for fostering meaningful and effective leadership and workplace civility (Leiter, Day, Oore, & Laschinger, 2012; Marturano, 2014). Locate the worksheet titled Sample Assignment: Journaling Mindfully, and take some time now to work through this exercise.

CASE STUDY: GERIATRIC SOCIAL WORKER

Jeannie is the only social worker in a residential facility for the care of elderly patients with comorbid dementia and physical health care needs. The facility has 50 patient beds and is typically wait-listed with new referrals readily coming into the facility. Due to the age-related challenges and the complex intersection of the physical and mental illnesses of the client population, patients typically need a wide array of services. Because the facility provides acute palliative care, it is not uncommon to lose as many as three patients or more each month. As the only social worker in the facility, Jeannie is responsible for multiple aspects of the care and service coordination for patients and their families. In her role as care manager, she coordinates and facilitates services from a multidisciplinary team of doctors, nurses, medical specialists, pharmacists, and dieticians. Jeannie is also responsible for working with families in developing and implementing palliative care plans. As part of her role in coordinating palliative care services, Jeannie completes at least one private session of grief counseling with families immediately after the death of their family member. She also conducts an optional four-week evening group for grieving families.

Jeannie feels called to her work in geriatric social work but has recently found herself feeling overwhelmed with the demands of her position. She has requested additional support for social services, but the facility prioritizes medical and nursing staff hires. She has been told her request is "under review" by the administration. Recently, Jeannie has been experiencing difficulty separating from the stresses of her job, even when she gets home in the evening. As the only social worker in the facility, she is always on call for families experiencing loss or complicated grief. Jeannie does not want to leave her job, but she feels that her preoccupation with her work is negatively affecting her time with her husband and her son. After discussing her challenges with her supervisor, it is suggested that she complete a continuing education course on stress management. Jeannie is realistic and knows that the course will not change the demands of her job. However, she is interested in improving her stress management skills through professional development and continuing education. Jeannie has some interest in the idea of mindfulness practice and is considering taking a course in MBSR, but she fears this may not be applicable to her job and may be a waste of valuable time attending the eight-week training sessions.

DISCUSSION AND CRITICAL THINKING QUESTIONS

1. Take a moment to critically reflect on Jeannie's reactions to the responsibilities of her job. Based on previous chapters, which of the following concepts seems to most appropriately fit this situation: compassion fatigue, secondary traumatic stress, or professional burnout? (Social Work Competency 1: Demonstrate Ethical and Professional Behavior—through the practice of self-reflection and regulation; Competency 4: Engage in Research-Informed Practice and Practice-Informed Research; Competency 9: Evaluate Practice with Organizations.)

2. Using the mindfulness-based practices discussed in this chapter, describe how Jeannie could use mindfulness techniques to address the effects of her work-related stress and anxiety. (Social Work Competency 1: Demonstrate Ethical and Professional Behavior—through the practice of self-reflection and regulation; Competency 4: Engage in Research-Informed Practice and Practice-Informed Research; Competency 9: Evaluate Practice with Organizations and Communities—through the application of knowledge of human behavior and the social environment, person-in-environment, and other multidisciplinary theoretical frameworks in the evaluation of outcomes.)

3. Critically assess Jeannie's challenges managing her multiple roles as the social work care coordinator at her facility, particularly in a multidisciplinary care environment. What mindfulness qualities can Jeannie apply to her position to assist with negotiating her obligations to the patients, the patient's families, the facility, and her colleagues? (Competency 8: Intervene with Individuals, Families, Groups, Organizations, and Communities—through the use of interprofessional collaboration as appropriate to achieve beneficial practice outcomes; Competency 9: Evaluate Practice with Organizations.)

4. Using the ecological systems framework for self-care provided in previous chapters, develop a holistic plan of self-care for Jeannie consisting of recommendations for the integration of mindfulness practices in at least one personal and one professional domain of her psychosocial self. (Social Work Competency 1: Demonstrate Ethical and Professional Behavior—through the practice of self-reflection and regulation; Competency 9: Evaluate Practice with Organizations and Communities—through the application of knowledge of human behavior and the social environment, person-in-environment, and other multidisciplinary theoretical frameworks in the evaluation of outcomes.)

5. As the only social worker in the facility with a variety of roles and professional responsibilities, describe how Jeannie can use mindfulness

practices to be a better leader and to facilitate the process of personal and professional resilience and well-being for herself, her clients, their families, her colleagues, and the facility. (Competency 9: Evaluate Practice with Individuals, Families, Groups, Organizations, and Communities — through the application of knowledge of human behavior and the social environment, person-in-environment, and other multidisciplinary theoretical frameworks in the evaluation of outcomes.)

KEY TERMS

acceptance
acceptance and commitment therapy (ACT)
attention self-regulation
awareness
body scan
conscious relaxation
deep breathing
dialectic behavioral therapy (DBT)
letting go

meditation
mindfulness
mindfulness-based cognitive therapy (MBCT)
mindfulness-based stress reduction (MBSR)
nonjudgment
openness
self-compassion
yoga

CHAPTER SUMMARY

Mindfulness is a practice grounded in the eastern philosophies of Buddhism that has been incorporated into many aspects of contemporary Western society. Mindfulness can be defined as the "awareness that emerges through paying attention on purpose, in the present moment, and non-judgmentally to the unfolding of experience moment by moment" (Kabat-Zinn, 2003, p. 145). The use of mindfulness practices has increased significantly over the past two decades. Some have referred to as a "new wave" in the psychological treatment of a wide variety of mental health conditions (Hayes, 2004) using models such as MBCT, DBT, and ACT. This chapter elaborates on the definition of the mindfulness construct by discussing various interpersonal qualities suggested in the literature as contributing to the practice of mindfulness. Mindfulness practices such as awareness, openness, nonjudgment, and self-compassion have been associated with many indicators of improved physical health, emotional health, and overall well-being. Beyond the interpersonal qualities of mindfulness practice, this approach may include active practices such deep breathing exercises, meditation, muscle relaxation, and yoga. Mindfulness approaches have demonstrated effectiveness as components of the self-care practice for social workers, counselors, psychotherapists, teachers, and other human service and humanitarian aid workers. The holistic nature of mindfulness practice makes this approach particularly applicable to the ecological systems framework for self-care presented in previous chapters. Integrating mindfulness practices, both as a form of client intervention and as a component of self-care, may prove beneficial for providers and for the clients they serve.

RECOMMENDED READINGS

Brown, K. W., Creswell, J. D., & Ryan, R. M. (2016). *The handbook of mindfulness: Theory, research, and practice*. New York, NY: Guilford Press.

Gerber, C. K. (2009). *The mindful path to self-compassion: Freeing yourself from destructive thoughts and emotions*. New York, NY: Guilford Press.

Hanh, T. N. (2006). *Transformation and healing: Sultra on the four establishments of mindfulness*. Berkeley, CA: Parallax Press.

Hick, S. F. (2009). *Mindfulness and social work*. Chicago, IL: Lyceum.

Kabat-Zinn, J. (1994). *Wherever you go, there you are*. New York, NY: Hyperion.

Marturano, J. (2014). *Finding the space to lead: A practical guide to mindful leadership*. New York, NY: Bloomsbury.

Miller, L. D. (2014). *Effortless mindfulness: Genuine mental health through awakened presence*. New York, NY: Routledge.

Smith, J. C. (2005). *Relaxation, meditation, & mindfulness: A mental health practitioner's guide to new and traditional approaches*. New York, NY: Springer.

SUGGESTED INTERNET RESOURCES

Self-Compassion: www.selfcompassion.org
This is an excellent resource developed by Kristina Neff whose research has helped to define and operationalize the construct of self-compassion. Under the About tab you can find definitions of the self-compassion and self-appreciation constructs along with embedded YouTube videos of Kristina Neff explaining her work with this concept and embedded links directly to Neff's articles on the use of self-compassion and self-appreciation. The Research tab includes a comprehensive bibliography on the theoretical and empirical research on self-compassion cataloged by date of publication, area of study, and author. This area also includes a link to the Self-Compassion Scale (SCS), including the short form version, and the Compassion for Others Scale. The bibliography and scales can be downloaded at no cost. Permission to use the Self-Compassion Scale is given directly on the site. Guided meditations and self-compassion exercises on journaling, self-talk, loving-kindness, friendship, and caregiving can be downloaded and used for training and education purposes at no cost. The Resources tab includes a list of suggested readings on self-compassion and a comprehensive Web directory on sources for mindfulness and compassion, clinical applications of self-compassion, educating and parenting, and Buddhist meditation.

Center for Mindfulness: http://www.umassmed.edu/cfm/

The mission of the center is to explore, understand, articulate, and further mindfulness in the lives of individuals, organizations, and communities through clinical care, rigorous scientific research, professional training, and informed public discourse. Hosted through the University of Massachusetts Division of Preventative and Behavioral Medicine in the Department of Medicine, this website is grounded in the empirical and scholarly work associated with mind–body research and publication with particular emphasis on the effectiveness of mindfulness-based stress reduction (MBSR) on physical and emotional health and well-being. The Stress Reduction tab links to useful information on the history of MBSR and includes the Standards of Practice, which can be downloaded. The site has a calendar of MBSR trainings available on a sliding fee scale based on household income. The site also provides a bibliography of MBSR research and publications available at no cost. The Resources tab includes links to videos, webinars, hyperlinks to relevant websites, and other educational resources that can be used for classroom or educational purposes.

Garrison Institute: https://www.garrisoninstitute.org/

The mission of the institute is to demonstrate and disseminate the importance of contemplative practices and spiritually grounded values in building sustainable movements for a healthier, safer, and more compassionate world. Working collaboratively with practitioners in diverse fields, the institute develops and hosts retreats and symposia, produces research and publications, and provides a hub for ongoing learning networks. There is an impressive calendar of training for personal and professional development in the areas of physical and emotional health and well-being for therapists, teachers, humanitarian aid workers, and other human service professionals. The About Us tab includes a detailed history of the Garrison Institute properties and the science and benefits of contemplative practices. The institute offers more than 100 retreats each year in various areas related to contemplative and mindfulness practices including organizational leadership, relationships, environmental and social justice, and education. The Insights and Tools tab includes helpful blogs, videos, and other resources from leading experts on the research, training, and education of mindfulness, resilience, and other contemplative practices available at no cost.

EPILOGUE

FINDING BALANCE IN SOCIAL WORK PRACTICE
Self-Care as Practice Wisdom

The meaning of life is to find your gift. The purpose of life is to give it away.
—PABLO PICASSO

WHAT I HAVE LEARNED FROM THIS WORK

My professional career has provided me with the opportunity and the great privilege of focusing my research on the well-being of social workers and other human service professionals. Above all else, I have learned that social work professionals have a deep commitment to their work that is unparalleled in other professions. We do this work every day simply because it is the right thing to do. The reward for providing services to those who are poor, vulnerable, underserved, or suffering comes in the form of gratitude and joy in knowing the quality of life of our clients improves because of the work we do. I also have learned that social work is not always inconsequential. The spirit for the work can be eroded when practitioners do not create a space of personal equanimity from the pain and suffering of their clients. Practice skills, such as the appropriate use of empathy and compassion, are finite resources that must be nourished or they become depleted over time. This deleterious effect may result in a state of disconnection and cynicism about clients, their situations, and the delivery of services. In my trainings, I refer to the phenomenon of cynicism and dissociation from clients and their needs as the "road to professional burnout," an unfortunate path for the social worker and for the clients entrusted to their care. However, I also have learned that professional burnout is often preventable through professional education and training, a supportive agency culture, and a commitment to the organizational and interpersonal practices of self-care.

AN ETHICAL OBLIGATION TO THE SOCIAL WORK PROFESSION

Preparing students to engage their clients with practice efficacy while also attending to their own needs is an ethical obligation to those who self-select social work and other human service professions. As educators, we have over-looked this important issue in direct practice, which has subsequently affected the well-being of our workforce. To describe this effect, I sometimes use the metaphor of training a fireman to do everything necessary to put out a fire and to save lives, but failing to deliver the lecture on the use of protective outerwear and gear in the process. Our profession has lost far too many earnest social work-ers dedicated to the values, mission, and humanitarian spirit of social work to the indirect effects of chronic engagement with clients and their stories of pain and human suffering. This is particularly true for social workers pursuing careers in child welfare, an area of practice that presents substantial risks for indirect trauma effects and has long had a reputation for professional burnout, partic-ularly for neophyte child welfare workers. This claim has been validated over and over again in the research literature. When child welfare workers vacate their positions as a form of personal and professional self-preservation, our most vulnerable children are abandoned once more. In a recent supervision session with a former child welfare worker, the supervisee disclosed that she had more than 30 active sexual abuse assessment cases at one time. Despite a deep com-mitment to working with survivors of child sexual abuse, she departed from the agency because she felt overwhelmed by the work. She had only been with the agency a few months and had received no official training in trauma-informed assessment. This situation is "a recipe for burnout."

This phenomenon is not exclusive to child welfare workers and has been documented across human service professions. Despite overwhelming evi-dence of the deleterious effects of direct practice in the forms of vicarious traumatization, secondary traumatic stress, compassion fatigue, professional burnout, and myriad other terms and references, few empirical studies validate preventative and intervening approaches for these conditions. The synthesis of the research literature strongly suggests that self-care is the best approach to cultivating professional resilience. My professional life and training experi-ences with hundreds of human service professionals has taught me that self-care is counterintuitive to those who dedicate their lives to helping others.

Making self-care a priority is not an easy thing to do, especially for those who have spouses, children, aging parents, pets, and other dependents beyond the clients on their caseloads. For many, this leads to an unintentional and seemingly perpetual cycle of chronically attending to the needs of others, with little or no dedicated time for replenishment and self-renewal. Self-care is only effective when it is a priority and when it is an ongoing part of daily life. Self-care must become a best practice for all human service professionals, and the logical place to plant this seed for change is in our professional training programs. The practice of self-care should be taught as a learned skill and as a practice behavior that is as essential as knowledge of human behavior and the social environment, cultural competence, assessment, policy, and other mainstays of the social work education curriculum.

Social work education programs have the resources and infrastructure to educate students properly on the practice of self-care. Approaches to the practice of self-care can be intertwined across the social work curriculum in both micro and macro course offerings. As a professor and director of a social work program in rural Alabama, I work with students each semester who witness human cruelty, some for the first time, in their field education experiences. Unfortunately, some students even experience the death of clients while in their placements. Recently, a student experienced the unexpected death of a client in a shelter facility for substance abusing women and their children during the first week of placement. Needless to say, dedicated time was required to ensure that this student did not turn away from our profession forever. Throughout this terrible experience, our faculty (myself included) helped the student process her reactions while providing the necessary support to both her and her field supervisor. Fortunately, the student was resilient and remained in her field placement and was offered a job upon graduation.

Beyond the confines of our programs, we owe students the knowledge and practice wisdom to embrace self-care as a life-long professional obligation. We owe it to the preservation of our human service workforce because the need for trauma-related care continues to grow as is evidenced in the United States by the dramatic increase in acts of mass interpersonal violence, such as school and college campus shootings, in the past 10 years. Organizations need qualified "boots on the ground" to continue to do this work so that valuable time, resources, and funding are not lost due to staff turnover. To begin to address this issue, human service organizations must embrace a culture that supports the ongoing practice of self-care to protect workers and their families and other loved ones and the clients they serve. Compassion fatigue and professional burnout have systemic effects, and the quality of the work suffers when the spirit of the work is diminished. In her seminal work, Laurie Ann Pearlman described change in ideas of reference to the profession and the loss of meaning for the work as hallmark features of vicarious trauma resulting from chronic exposure to trauma material disclosed by clients in the context of treatment. This has recently been described in the literature as a form of moral or spiritual injury, which violates the values that guide many us into the profession of social work.

MY OWN PROCESS OF SELF-CARE

In the *Primer to Positive Psychology*, Christopher Peterson (2006) describes his career in this way: "Like many academics, I spent my young adult years postponing many of the small things that I knew would make me happy (reading novels for pleasure, learning to cook, taking a photography class, and joining a gym). I would do all of these when I had time, when I finished school, when I had a job, when I was awarded tenure, and so on." In my mind, this describes me perfectly. I am sure my wife, family, friends, and most colleagues would agree. In doing the research for this book, I revisited this quote in another book on resilience by Robert Wicks (2010). The irony is that I continue to find myself not doing the non-work-related things I planned to do while on sabbatical (spending more time with my wife and daughter, catching up on movies, enjoying a professional conference where I am not the speaker, improving my meditation practice). It has taken most of my sabbatical time to complete this book. I self-disclose this to validate what so many of my workshop participants have echoed so clearly: finding time for self-care can be difficult with work and family obligations—but it can happen. I have now moved all of those activities to the summer break, and I intend to keep this obligation to myself and to my family.

As a self-proclaimed workaholic writing on how not to become overworked, I have learned that I do not always "practice what I preach" and oftentimes violate my own principles and mandates for the ongoing practice of self-care. Just like everyone else, I regularly have to self-reflect on my growth and professional development in this area and remind myself that self-care is an *ongoing* holistic process. Self-care can be as simple as putting the phone on a shelf for an evening, which in this day and age can be more challenging than it should be. Even small forms of self-care and self-renewal have to be a priority or the temptation to distract myself from valuable time with my family is too great, and that time can never be recovered. Recently, my wife reminded me (again) of how much time is absorbed returning emails that could easily be handled at the start of the next business day. Fortunately, I am old enough to remember that social work practice occurred just fine before we allowed ourselves to be available virtually all the time through our mobile devices.

My students laugh when I describe my early days as a rural child welfare worker with no mobile phone, no GPS, and sometimes very poor directions.

I had to learn to follow directions, to be intuitive, and to read a map. I frequently remind myself that "the work always got done," and I actually went home without the distraction of phone or computer. This seems like an idyllic fantasy now. My students (and my daughter) are growing up without knowing that social workers got the job done efficiently before the advent of the digital age. What this means to me and to the future of this work is that self-care is going to become more and more difficult in the future. The time to address this issue is now; we owe it to our future human service workforce. My hope is that this book will turn a slowly moving wheel in the education of future human service professionals and that we will begin to prepare new workers for the risks of the work so they can charge eagerly into their careers armed with the knowledge, skills, and practice wisdom to be resilient practitioners.

FINDING JOY AND MEANING IN SOCIAL WORK PRACTICE

Self-care is "the key to professional resilience." Cultivating professional resilience is accomplished in part by preserving the personal drive, commitment, and spirit for the work. As I near 20 years of combined experience as a social work practitioner-educator, I reflect on clients who have found meaning despite challenges I can only imagine (child physical and sexual abuse, neglect, combat trauma). This book is dedicated to addressing the challenging aspects of social work practice that are a necessity for social work students entering the profession. However, data now suggests that the process of transferring trauma and emotion is reciprocal. This means that resilience can be fostered through positive client experiences in the same way. Vicarious resilience, posttraumatic growth, and compassion satisfaction are being examined in the research literature and have signaled a welcome paradigm shift in traumatology. I hope to see more work in the future describing the elements of social work that empower resilience. I look forward to the pursuit of this agenda as I pursue research on the well-being of social workers and other human service professionals. From this work comes my own professional resilience. For me, preserving our workforce is much more than a faculty research agenda on the road to tenure and promotion. I consider this to be my life's work and my contribution to the profession that has given so much to me. Social work is a profession "rich and full" of opportunity for success, joy, spiritual meaning, and self-renewal. My final thought and wish for the future of our human service workforce is that each of you finds the lifetime of reward you are seeking in helping others through this work.

Be well,

Jason M. Newell

WORKSHEETS

PERSONAL REFLECTION EXERCISE

RESILIENCE AND SELF-APPRECIATION

1. Take a moment to reflect on the most rewarding parts of your field education setting, internship, or professional career. Briefly list a few of your major accomplishments and achievements (individually or through successful client outcomes).

_____

_____

_____

_____

_____

2. What has been the most successful or the proudest moment of your professional career (or internship experience)? This may be an individual success or a success achieved through positive or successful client outcomes. Briefly describe the situation.

_____

_____

_____

_____

_____

3. Briefly describe the positive aspects or components of your work with those entrusted to your care.

_____

_____

_____

_____

_____

182 PERSONAL REFLECTION EXERCISE

4. Describe the impact of positive experiences and how they have con-
tributed to your job (or internship) stability and to your professional
development.

_____

_____

_____

_____

_____

SELF-REFLECTION EXERCISE

ENGAGING GROUP DISCUSSION ON TRAUMA

1. Briefly describe one experience in your practice or field education in which you felt emotional distress related to your interactions with a client and his or her presenting problems.

_____

_____

_____

_____

_____

2. How did you process your reactions to the situation? Describe your thoughts, feelings, and professional behavior related to the event.

_____

_____

_____

_____

_____

3. Have you discussed your reactions with a fellow student, coworker, professor, mentor, or supervisor?

_____

_____

_____

_____

_____

4. Have you ever felt hesitant to disclose this information? Why or why not?

_____

_____

_____

_____

_____

5. How have reactions to your clients and their experiences informed your professional behavior, your competency, and your developing practice wisdom?

_____

_____

_____

_____

_____

SAMPLE ASSIGNMENT

DEEP BREATHING EXERCISE

This short exercise in deep breathing has been used as part of my training sessions on stress management and the prevention of professional burnout. Deep breathing exercises can be used during times of stress to slow down breathing and heart rate, which often increase due to the effects of stress and anxiety. This exercise can be done at your desk, while walking between meetings, in the car (not while driving), or at home.

Step 1: Find a quiet and comfortable space.

Step 2: Get into a comfortable position (seated with feet on the floor or in a cross-legged position).

Step 3: Place one hand on your chest and one hand on your abdominal area.

Step 4: Breathe deeply, feeling the rise and fall of your abdomen as you inhale and exhale.

Step 5: As you breathe, focus your attention only on the sensations of the breath.

Step 6: Stay aware of the inhale and exhale of the breath as thoughts of the inner and outer environment flow in and out of your mind.

Step 7: Take at least three deep breaths and hold for a count of three, then breathe outward slowly.

Step 8: Continue this practice until your mind reaches a more enhanced state of calmness.

SAMPLE ASSESSMENT OF ORGANIZATIONAL AND INDIVIDUAL CHALLENGES

Organizational Challenges	Individual Challenges
•	•
•	•
•	•
•	•
•	•
•	•
•	•
•	•
•	•
•	•
•	•
•	•
•	•
•	•
•	•
•	•
•	•
•	•
•	•
•	•
•	•
•	•
•	•

SELF-CARE PROCESS: SETTING ORGANIZATIONAL GOALS

List at least three professional goals that would result in a less stressful and more productive work environment. Below each goal list the tasks that would need to be accomplished to turn this goal statement into reality.

Professional Goal (1): _____
Task 1 _____
Task 2 _____
Task 3 _____

Professional Goal (2): _____
Task 1 _____
Task 2 _____
Task 3 _____

Professional Goal (3): _____
Task 1 _____
Task 2 _____
Task 3 _____

EVALUATION QUESTIONS

1. Have these goals been accomplished (yes or no)? If no, what organizational barriers or challenges have prevented you from meeting your professional goals?
2. How can this plan be modified to facilitate meeting your professional goals?
3. Could this plan be shared with administrators for feedback and professional development?

SELF-CARE PROCESS: SETTING PERSONAL GOALS

List at least three personal goals that would result in managing your work-related stress once you leave the classroom or agency setting. Personal goal examples could include spending more time with family and friends, going to a movie once a week, exercising more often, eating healthier foods, or going to a yoga class.

Personal Goal (1): _____
Task 1 _____
Task 2 _____
Task 3 _____

Personal Goal (2): _____
Task 1 _____
Task 2 _____
Task 3 _____

Personal Goal (3):_____
Task 1 _____
Task 2 _____
Task 3 _____

EVALUATION QUESTIONS

1. Have these goals been accomplished (yes or no)? If no, what barriers or challenges have prevented you from meeting your personal goals?
2. How have these goals affected your overall quality of life?
3. Do you feel you manage your work stress better as a result of meeting these goals?

PROFESSIONAL DEVELOPMENT ASSIGNMENT

CONSTRUCT A PLAN OF PERSONAL AND PROFESSIONAL SELF-CARE

One of the goals of this book is to assist you in cultivating your professional identity as you develop the skills required to practice social work. Learning the practice of self-care is an important skill that should become part of your daily activities as a professional social worker. Write a brief, professional development essay (five pages minimum) outlining your personal plan of self-care. Your essay should address the following three topics.

1. One important component of professional social work practice is understanding the process of personal self-reflection and correction. Describe some personal strengths that may enhance your ability to practice self-care, and describe some challenges that could promote stress, burnout, or compassion fatigue.
2. Develop and discuss your own approach to professional self-care as you begin your career in social work practice. Discuss strategies for preventing, managing, and coping with the effects of burnout and compassion fatigue. Your activities may consist of current strategies or proposals for new activities. Your plan can include strategies from multiple areas (health, emotional, social, spiritual, or recreational behaviors).
3. Discuss any barriers to maintaining your own self-care practices. What might challenge your commitment to your self-care plan? How can you address these barriers as they materialize so you maintain your commitment to professional self-care over the long term?

SUGGESTIONS FOR DEVELOPING A COMPREHENSIVE PLAN OF SELF-CARE

Self-care domain	Suggested strategies
Biological	Plan a balanced diet with good nutrition; have an adequate sleep schedule; plan a regular exercise regime; use alcohol in moderation; use health and mental health days to recover from physical or emotional illness including grief work
Interpersonal	Maintain professional boundaries with clients; create a healthy balance between personal and professional obligations; use adaptive rather than maladaptive coping skills; actively engage anxiety associated with clients through techniques such as mindfulness, self-talk, and self-awareness; use psychotherapy, counseling, or support group help (particularly for those with a personal trauma history)
Organizational	Seek organizations with missions consistent with your personal values and career aspirations; participate in education, training, and professional development opportunities throughout your career; participate in active supervision and ongoing mentorship; engage in supportive relationships with professional colleagues; set realistic goals and objectives for the workday or workweek; use coffee and lunch breaks for non-work-related activities; participate in the celebration of client success and fulfillment; maintain a realistic worldview about the impact of client work on the self
Familial	Accept social support from family and close friends; participate in nonstressful family events; engage in "no-technology" dinners and family time; schedule family and couples vacation time; participate in children's activities, school functions, and sports events (if applicable); protect time to celebrate special family events, birthdays, or anniversaries; schedule nonfamily time to catch up with close friends; enjoy caring for and spending time with family pets

SAMPLE GOALS AND OBJECTIVES FOR A PLAN OF SELF-CARE

Physical goals	Objective
1. Maintain a balanced diet	Prepare a healthy lunch each day; avoid eating fast food; avoid processed food from vending machines; make time during the weekend to shop for healthy food options; take time in the evening to prepare a sensible dinner; choose an appropriate healthy lifestyle or weight loss plan; keep an eating and meal journal for the first three weeks to establish a diet pattern
2. Develop and commit to an ongoing exercise and/or weight loss schedule	Set an initial goal to exercise at least three times a week; begin with cardiovascular exercise of at least 30 minutes per session; set an appropriate weight loss goal (if needed) for the first 90 days; add additional cardio or weight time as needed
3. Take time to schedule and maintain personal health visits as needed	Schedule annual physical exam or wellness appointments; schedule primary care and other health-related medical appointments as needed and proactively when possible; avoid waiting until illness is chronic to seek medical care; take sick leave as needed to recover adequately from illness; avoid cancellation of medical appointments for work-related activities unless it is absolutely necessary; schedule massage therapy appointments for muscle aches and relaxation as needed
Interpersonal goals	Objectives
1. Maintain professional boundaries with clients and colleagues	Set realistic goals and expectations for client success; help clients exercise client empowerment versus dependency; avoid overextension of client services or agency time; learn to say "no" to client requests when it does not directly affect the treatment plan or the client's safety and well-being; exercise professional tolerance for office behavior
2. Actively engage stress or work-related anxious thoughts and behaviors	Avoid starting the day with negative thoughts or behaviors; regulate negative thoughts with positive thoughts and affirmations; use deep breathing techniques during times of personal or professional anxiety; use self-talk or other adaptive coping mechanisms as needed

Familial goals	Objectives
1. Schedule and maintain protected time for family events	Establish no-technology meal and leisure time with family members; avoid work-related discussion during protected family time; allow each member of the family unit to participate actively in the family dialogue; attend all children's school or sporting events (avoid all unnecessary cancellations); protect time to celebrate special events such as birthdays and anniversaries
2. Schedule leave time from work for vacations and family events	Use vacation and leave time each year; avoid canceling scheduled leave time; use family time to discuss possible future family events or vacation time; research possible alternatives for vacation time
3. Schedule and maintain protected time with friends	Spend at least two hours each month in nonfamily or work-related time with friends or in peer group activities; avoid discussing work-related stress with friends; avoid engaging the emotional needs of friends beyond a social support relationship

Organizational goals	Objectives
1. Actively participate in regularly scheduled supervision sessions	Spend at least two hours each month with a direct supervisor; use supervision time for professional development; construct targeted questions ahead of supervision sessions
2. Maintain a standard office schedule (as close as possible)	Specify time each day for email and phone call returns; avoid spending time on work-related activities during nonworking hours; control calendar and appointment times; set aside protected time for administrative and clerical duties; use coffee and lunch breaks for non-work-related activities; leave the office at least twice a week for lunch break

Spiritual goals	Objectives
1. Actively participate in at least one ongoing spiritual activity	Attend church services or related activity (if appropriate) at least once a week; practice yoga or meditation for at least 20 minutes three times a week

Recreational goals	Objectives
1. Schedule and maintain at least one activity to enhance personal well-being	Purchase at least one new book and dedicate at least two hours a week to pleasure reading; reserve time on the weekend to catch up on missed television shows or movies; schedule at least one outdoor activity each week (walking, hiking, etc.)

BLANK TEMPLATE FOR A COMPREHENSIVE PLAN OF SELF-CARE

Self-care domain	Suggested strategies
Biological	
Interpersonal	
Organizational	
Familial	
Spiritual	
Recreational	

SAMPLE SELF-CARE PLAN

PERSONAL TABLE

Physical goals	Objectives	Timeline
1.		
2.		
3.		
4.		
5.		
Interpersonal goals	Objectives	Timeline
1.		
2.		
3.		
4.		
5.		
Organizational goals	Objectives	Timeline
1.		
2.		
3.		
4.		
5.		

(*continued*)

PERSONAL TABLE (CONTINUED)

Spiritual goals	Objectives	Timeline
1.		
2.		
3.		
4.		
5.		
Recreational goals	Objectives	Timeline
1.		
2.		
3.		
4.		
5.		

JOURNALING MINDFULLY

1. Chart the amount of daily or weekly time spent in the following mindfulness practices:
   a. meditation
   b. body scan
   c. yoga
   d. other mindfulness practices
2. Journal about a particularly challenging client experience both before and after a mindfulness practice such as meditation. In your entry, compare and contrast your thoughts and mental clarity on the client and the client's situation before and after the practice.
3. Take a moment to describe the practice of mindfulness as it applies to organizational leadership. What qualities should agency leaders, supervisors, and directors have to engage their employees in meaningful and productive relationships?
4. Describe a situation with a client when you used a mindfulness-based practice such as mindfulness-based cognitive therapy (MBCT) or acceptance and commitment therapy (ACT). Was the intervention successful? Why or why not?
5. Describe how you plan to incorporate mindfulness practice in your ongoing plan of holistic self-care. What practices and qualities (awareness, openness, self-compassion, meditation, etc.) are particularly suited for your personality structure? How might maintaining mindfulness practice be both beneficial and challenging as daily practice over time?

BIBLIOGRAPHY OF RECOMMENDED READINGS

American Psychiatric Association. (2013). *Diagnostic and statistical manual of mental disorders* (5th ed.). Washington, DC: Author.

Balch, P. A. (2010). *Prescription for nutritional healing: A practical A-to-Z reference to drug-free remedies using vitamins, minerals, herbs & food supplements* (5th ed.). Garden City Park, NY: Avery.

Bean, R. A., Davis, S. D., & Davey, M. P. (2014). *Clinical activities for increasing competence and self-awareness.* Hoboken, NJ: Wiley.

Beckett, C., & Maynard, A. (2012). *Values and ethics of social work: An introduction.* London, England: Sage.

Berg, B. L., & Lune, H. (2012). *Qualitative research methods for the social sciences.* Boston, MA: Pearson.

Berger, R. (2015). *Stress, trauma, and posttraumatic growth: Social context, environment, and identities.* New York, NY: Routledge.

Breggin, P. R. (1997). *The heart of being helpful: Empathy and the creation of a healing presence.* New York, NY: Springer.

Briere, J., & Scott, C. (2015). *Principles of trauma therapy: A guide to symptoms, evaluation, and treatment* (2nd ed.). Thousand Oaks, CA: Sage.

Brown, K. W., Creswell, J. D., & Ryan, R. M. (2016). *The handbook of mindfulness: Theory, research, and practice.* New York, NY: Guilford Press.

Carlson, E. B. (1997). *Trauma assessments: A clinicians guide.* New York, NY: Guilford Press.

Clow, J. (2012). *The work revolution: Freedom and excellence for all.* Hoboken, NJ: Wiley.

Cohen, S., Underwood, L. G., & Gottlieb, B. H. (2000). *Social support measurement and intervention: A guide for health and social scientists.* New York, NY: Oxford University Press.

Congress, E. P., Black, P. N., & Strom-Gottfried, K. (2009). *Teaching social work values and ethics: A curriculum resource* (2nd ed.). Alexandra, VA: CSWE Press.

Council for Accreditation of Counseling and Related Educational Programs. *2016 standards for accreditation.* Alexandria, VA: Author.

Cox, K., & Sterner, S. (2013). *Self-care in social work: A guide for practitioners, supervisors, and administrators.* Washington, DC: NASW Press.

Dolgoff, R., Harrington, D., & Lowenberg, F. M. (2012). *Ethical decisions for social work practice* (9th ed.). Belmont, CA: Brook/Cole Cengage Learning.

Figley, C. R. (1995). *Compassion fatigue: Coping with secondary traumatic stress disorder in those who treat the traumatized.* Levittown, PA: Brunner/Mazel.

Figley, C. R. (2002). *Treating compassion fatigue.* New York, NY: Brunner-Routledge.

Figley, C. R., & Nash, W. P. (2007). *Combat stress injury: Theory, research, and management.* New York, NY: Taylor & Francis.

Frankl, V. E. (1984). *Man's search for meaning: An introduction to logotherapy* (3rd ed.). New York, NY: A Touchstone Book: Simon & Schuster.

Friedman, M. J., Keane, T., & Resick, P. A. (2007). *Handbook of PTSD: Science and practice.* New York, NY: Guilford Press.

Gerber, C. K. (2009). *The mindful path to self-compassion: Freeing yourself from destructive thoughts and emotions.* New York, NY: Guilford Press.

Hanh, T. N. (2006). *Transformation and healing: Sultra on the four establishments of mindfulness.* Berkeley, CA: Parallax Press.

Hick, S. F. (2009). *Mindfulness and social work.* Chicago, IL: Lyceum Books.

Kabat-Zinn, J. (1994). *Wherever you go, there you are.* New York, NY: Hyperion.

Kent, M., Davis, M. C., & Reich, J. W. (2014). *The resilience handbook: Approaches to stress and trauma.* New York, NY: Routledge.

Kottler, J., & Chen, D. D. (2011). *Stress management and prevention: Daily Applications* (2nd ed.). New York, NY: Routledge.

Leiter, M. P., & Maslach, C. (2005). *Banishing burnout: Six strategies for improving your relationship with work.* San Francisco, CA: Jossey-Bass/ Wiley.

Levers, L. L. (2012). *Trauma counseling: Theories and interventions.* New York, NY: Springer.

Lipsky, L. V. D., & Burke, C. (2009). *Trauma stewardship: An everyday guide to caring for self while caring for others.* San Francisco, CA: Berrett-Koehler.

Marturano, J. (2014). *Finding the space to lead: A practical guide to mindful leadership.* New York, NY: Bloomsbury Press.

Maslach, C. (2003). *Burnout: The cost of caring.* Cambridge, MA: Malor Books.

Maslach, C., & Leiter, M. P. (1997). *The truth about burnout.* San Francisco, CA: Jossey-Bass.

Meichenbaum, D. (2012). *Roadmap to resilience: A guide for military, trauma victims and their families.* Williston, VT: Crown House.

Miller, L. D. (2014). *Effortless mindfulness: Genuine mental health through awakened presence.* New York, NY: Routledge.

Morrissette, P. (2004). *The pain of helping: Psychological injury of helping professionals.* New York, NY: Taylor & Francis.

National Association of Social Workers. (2008). *Code of ethics of the National Association of Social Workers.* Washington, DC: Author.

National Association of Social Workers. (2009). *Social work speaks. National Association of Social Workers policy statements 2009–2012.* Washington, DC: NASW Press.

Norcross, J. C., & Guy, J. D. (2007). *Leaving it at the office: A guide to psychotherapist self-care.* New York, NY: Guilford Press.

Pearlman, L. A., & Saakvitne, K. W. (1995). *Trauma and the therapist: Countertransference and vicarious traumatization in psychotherapy with incest survivors.* New York, NY: Norton.

Pines, A., & Aronson, E. (1988). *Career burnout: Causes and cures.* New York, NY: Free Press.

Pryce, J. G., Shakleford, K. K., & Pryce, D. H. (2007). *Secondary traumatic stress and the child welfare professional.* Chicago, IL: Lyceum Books.

Reamer, F. G. (2013). *Social work values and ethics* (4th ed.). New York, NY: Columbia University Press.

Rothschild, B. (2000). *The body remembers: The psychophysiology of trauma and trauma treatment.* New York, NY: Norton.

Rothschild, B. (2006). *Help for the helper: Self-care strategies for managing burnout and stress.* New York, NY: Norton.

Rubin, A., & Babbie, E. (2010). *Essential research methods for social work* (2nd ed.). Belmont, CA: Brooks/Cole Cengage Learning.

Rubin, A., Weiss, E. L., & Coll, J. E. (2013). *Handbook of military social work.* Hoboken, NJ: Wiley.

Rush, J. A., First, M. B., & Blacker, D. (2008). *Handbook of psychiatric measures* (2nd ed.). Washington, DC: American Psychiatric Association.

Russell, A. C. (2014). *A hands-on manual for social work research.* Chicago, IL: Lyceum Books.

Saakvitne, K. W., & Pearlman, L. A. (1996). *Transforming the pain: A workbook on vicarious traumatization for helping professionals who work with traumatized clients.* New York, NY: Norton.

Skovholt, T. M., & Trotter-Mathison, M. (2011). *The resilient practitioner: Burnout prevention and self-care strategies for counselors, therapists, teachers, and health professionals* (2nd ed.). New York, NY: Routledge.

Smith, J. C. (2005). *Relaxation, meditation, & mindfulness: A mental health practitioner's guide to new and traditional approaches.* New York, NY: Springer.

Smith, P. (2008). *Healthy caregiving: A guide to recognizing and managing compassion fatigue.* Compassion Fatigue Awareness Project. Retrieved from www.compassionfatigue.org

Stamm, B. H. (1999). *Secondary traumatic stress: Self-care issues for clinicians, researchers, and educators.* Baltimore, MD: Sidran Press.

van der Kolk, B. A., McFarlane, A. C., & Weisaeth, L. (1996). *Traumatic stress: The effects of overwhelming experience on the mind, body, and society.* New York, NY: Guilford Press.

Wainrib, B. R. (2006). *Healing crisis and trauma with mind, body, and spirit.* New York, NY: Springer.

Wicks, R. J. (2010). *Bounce: Living the resilient life.* New York, NY: Oxford University Press.

Wicks, R. J., & Maynard, E. A. (2014). *Clinician's guide to self-renewal: Essential advice from the field.* Hoboken, NJ: Wiley.

Young, J. E., Klosko, J. S., & Weishaar, M. E. (2003). *Schema therapy: A practitioner's guide.* New York, NY: Guilford Press.

BIBLIOGRAPHY OF SUGGESTED INTERNET RESOURCES

American Counseling Association: http://www.counseling.org

This nonprofit educational and professional organization is dedicated to the enhancement of the profession of counseling. ACA is the largest counseling association exclusively representing professional counselors, and it includes 20 chartered divisions that provide leadership, information, and resources unique to principles or specialized areas of counseling. Counselors in agencies and private practice, couples and family counselors, rehabilitation counselors, college counselors, school counselors, and counselor educators will find a wealth of useful resources including opportunities for continuing education, advocacy, and connections with state and local counseling associations.

The Knowledge Center: http://www.counseling.org/knowledge-center/

Part of the ACA website, counseling competencies and practice briefs address specific areas of advocacy and treatment focus. Licensure and private practice information is provided as well as several ethics resources including the 2014 *ACA Code of Ethics*, which can be downloaded at no cost, a free podcast about the code, a comprehensive webinar examining components of the 2014 code, and ethics articles published in *Counseling Today*. An ethical decision-making model is provided as well as a link for ACA members to free consultation with professional counselors in the ACA Ethics Department.

American Institute of Stress: www.stress.org

This nonprofit organization provides information on stress reduction, stress in the workplace, effects of stress, and various other stress-related topics. The mission of AIS is to improve the health of the community and the world by setting the standard of excellence for stress management in education, research, clinical care, and the workplace. Diverse and inclusive, the institute educates medical practitioners, scientists, health care professionals, and the public; conducts research; and provides information, training, and techniques to prevent human illness related to stress. This site contains a wealth of resources on the physical, neurological, and emotional effects of stress across various demographic and occupational populations. The Daily Life tab includes a stress and workplace self-assessment and a multitude of resources on various approaches to stress management. The Publications and Multi-Media tab includes access to the online magazines *Combat Stress* and

Contentment at no cost. AIS members receive access to *Health and Stress*. Helpful embedded videos, YouTube videos, and podcasts on stress management are also available. The Learning Center tab houses online training sessions and video lectures available at no cost.

Anxiety and Depression Association of America: http://www.adaa.org

The mission of ADAA is to promote the prevention, treatment, and cure of anxiety and mood disorders, OCD, and PTSD through education, practice, and research by improving the quality of life for children and adults affected with these disorders. The site features include educational resources (including podcasts and webcasts) for consumers and their families, treatment resources, and support information. The site includes excellent professional literature for consumers on understanding the facts about various forms of mental illness, including trauma-related disorders. For professionals, the site has information on the empirically supported treatments and best practices across several professional disciplines.

Compassion Fatigue Awareness Project: www.compassionfatigue.org

This project promotes awareness and understanding of compassion fatigue and its effect on caregivers under the vision and belief that compassion fatigue for those in caregiving roles (including animal caregivers) can be alleviated through education and the practice of authentic self-care. This site is tailored to anyone in a personal or professional caregiving role. Features of the site include recognizing compassion fatigue, steps for the path of wellness, and promotion of compassion satisfaction for caregivers. The Resources tab has information on general caregiving, animal caregiving, family caregiving, and traumatic stress caregiving. The Suggested Readings tab provides a directory of printable resources in compassionate caregiving, which are available at no cost.

Crisis & Trauma Resource Institute: https://us.ctrinstitute.com/

The institute is a leading provider of training and consulting services for individuals, schools, communities, and organizations affected by or involved in working with issues of crisis and trauma. CTRI's purpose is to provide exceptional training and resources to better lives. Under the belief that mental health, counseling, and safety resources should be accessible to everyone, CTRI's workshops and resources are geared to a wide range of care and service providers including social service, health care, education, employment, and other organizations. The home page of the site offers three main areas of navigation for responders working in the United States, Canada, and internationally. The Our Trainings tab provides information on webinars, onsite trainings, and workshops that are offered in a variety of areas for modest registration and continuing education fees. Training manuals on various topics in the fields of crisis intervention and emergency management are available for purchase. Information on webinars and trainings that can be completed at no cost are found under the Free Resources tab, which also lists training manuals, articles, and handouts that can be downloaded at no cost for in-house training and professional development.

Figley Institute: http://www.figleyinstitute.com/indexMain.html

The institute's mission is to alleviate human suffering resulting from traumatic life experiences by providing laypeople and professionals with high-quality traumatologist training. This site is an excellent resource for professional training, certification, and development and has a complete catalog of online training sessions and certification programs (with continuing education credits) in the areas of psychological trauma, disaster trauma, compassion fatigue, and professional self-care. There are links to other public resources related to the field of traumatology. A companion site for additional resources related to the scholarly work of Charles Figley can be accessed at www.charlesfigley.com.

Headington Institute: http://www.headington-institute.org/home

The institute partners with humanitarian relief and development organizations and emergency responders before, during, and after deployment to ensure the well-being of individuals. This international institute provides services to humanitarian workers in the United States, Africa, Asia, the Middle East, the United Kingdom, and other parts of Europe. Features include resources on the topics of professional resilience, stress and burnout, trauma, and women and other gender populations, which are available to the public at no cost. The resources include an online training and certification module on vicarious traumatization. Many of the resources can be downloaded and have been translated into several languages. The Resource Index tab is an excellent source for Internet resources including YouTube videos on trauma, coping, and self-care for those involved in human service work.

Helpguide.org: http://www.helpguide.org/home-pages/work-career.htm

This site is hosted by a nonprofit driven by the mission that people can affect fundamental changes in their emotional and physical health with the aid of appropriate online resources. The main site offers a variety of resources related to the emotional and physical aspects of well-being. The site provides free online materials for mental illness, family development across the life span, stress, and suicide prevention. The Work and Career tab includes resources related to effective workplace communication, finding the right job, and preventing job burnout. The job burnout link, embedded in the Work and Career tab, includes information on the warning signs for professional burnout, the differences between stress and burnout, and several practical strategies for preventing and recovering from the effects of stress and burnout.

International Society for Traumatic Stress Studies: www.istss.org

This is the premier society for the exchange of professional knowledge and expertise in the field of traumatology. Membership is international and open to anyone practicing or interested in trauma work. The site includes a wealth of resources on the assessment, treatment, and research of trauma-related disorders. Features include public resources on trauma-related practice at no cost, including a comprehensive list of scales measuring trauma experiences with psychometric data included, teaching resources, access to a trauma blog, and links to the publication *Stress Points*.

McSilver Institute for Poverty Policy and Research: www.mcsilver.nyu.edu

Housed in the New York University Silver School of Social Work, the institute focuses on issues related to the "interrelatedness of race and poverty and is dedicated to dismantling structural racism and other forms of systemic oppression." The institute's research is guided by a collaborative interprofessional model with a systems framework to assess the root of macro-level social problems such as poverty and racism. The site offers many useful features, educational opportunities, and research resources at no cost to the public. The Research and Centers tab has brief descriptions of funded research studies in several areas including poverty, behavioral health, and public health. The Policy and Publications tab stores annual reports, legislative testimonies, research briefs, and embedded videos on topics such as racism and gender oppression in the workplace. The News and Events tab links to a report titled "Facts Matter! Black Lives Matter! The Trauma of Racism," which is available at no cost.

The Melissa Institute: www.melissainstitute.org

This nonprofit organization in memory of Melissa Aptman, who was murdered in St. Louis, is dedicated to the study and prevention of violence through education, community service, research support, and consultation. The institute's mission is to prevent violence and promote safer communities through education and application of research-based knowledge. An excellent resource for those working with survivors of physical and sexual assault, the Resources tab includes quick links to a variety of helpful resources for treating aggressive and anxious children, bullying, faith and family-based interventions, family violence, and suicide. The Resilience tab includes hyperlinks to useful information on resilience as it relates to military populations, children and adolescents, practice interventions, human development, and political decision making. Most of the documents can be downloaded at no cost.

National Association of Social Workers: www.nasw.org

The largest membership organization of professional social workers in the world, with 132,000 members, NASW works to enhance the professional growth and development of its members, to create and maintain professional standards, and to advance sound social policies. The website includes access to the NASW *Code of Ethics* in both English and Spanish at no cost. The site also has links to previous versions of the codes of ethics, including the original version developed in 1960. Resources are available related to the ethical practice of social work as well as a link to NASW journals, books, NASW news, and the online *Encyclopedia of Social Work*. Information on profession development, conference venues, research, jobs, membership, and other practice resources can also be found here.

National Center for PTSD: www.ptsd.va.gov

Managed by the Department of Veterans Affairs, this site is largely dedicated to the treatment of veterans and military families, with an obvious emphasis on the treatment of combat-related trauma and PTSD. However, the trauma resources provided are applicable to anyone either suffering from or treating the effects of trauma-related disorders. Features of the site include professional resources on the assessment, treatment, and research of trauma-related disorders, including a wealth of online continuing education and training at no cost. Two excellent resources, the *Clinician's Trauma Update* and the *PTSD Research Quarterly*, can be accessed at no cost.

National Child Traumatic Stress Network: http://www.nctsnet.org/

The mission of NCTSN is "to raise the standard of care and improve access to services for traumatized children, their families, and communities throughout the United States." This is an excellent resource on trauma-related disorders and treatment in children and adolescents. The site contains portals with information for parents and families, professionals, military families, and educators. Specific features include an online learning center for professional development in the area of child traumatic stress and a comprehensive review of the measures of childhood trauma complete with psychometric information. Other resources include handouts on the presentation of child traumatic stress disorders and a tool kit for natural disaster or terrorist attack response and recovery.

National Institutes of Health: www.nih.org

Part of the U.S. Department of Health and Human Services, the NIH is the nation's leading medical research agency. This is the premier site for epidemiological statistics related to health and human disease and serves as a master directory for all of the affiliate institutes and centers under the NIH umbrella, including the National Cancer Institute, the Institute on Aging, the National Institute of Mental Health, and the National Center for Complimentary and Integrative Health, to name a few. The Health Information tab has links to the Health Information line, a Health Services Locater, and a link to Healthcare .gov. The Community Resources tab links to health care resources including dieting and weight control, smoking cessation, care for seniors, and alcohol abuse. The site also contains a powerful library search engine that sources all NIH affiliated institutes, centers, journals, and other publication and Internet sources for information, such as the NIMH *Fact Sheet on Stress*, which can be downloaded at no cost.

Professional Burnout: http://maslach.socialpsychology.org/

This site provides information on Christina Maslach and use of the Maslach Burnout Inventory (MBI). An overview of Maslach's career includes a short history of the burnout construct as well as a complete review of her research and publication history. The MBI is available for use by purchase by contacting info@mindgarden.com. A lecture by Dr. Maslach on the burnout process and construct is available at no cost on YouTube at https://www.youtube.com /watch?v=4kLPyV8lBbs.

Professional Quality of Life Scale (ProQOL): www.proqol.org

Developed by Dr. Stamm, this is the most comprehensive source of information on the ProQOL scale. The site includes extensive information on the theoretical development, conceptualization , and psychometric qualities of ProQOL. The site provides a complete bibliography on studies using ProQOL and a recently updated comprehensive bibliography on the secondary aspect of caring, citing 2,000 related materials. Additional materials include handouts, PowerPoint slides, and pocket guides related to compassion fatigue. All of the resources can be downloaded at no cost.

ReachOut Professionals: http://au.professionals.reachout.com/

This site provides recommendations and advice for youth support workers, health workers, and education professionals on a range of online interventions, tools, and resources to support young people experiencing mental health difficulties and to build young people's well-being and resilience. Information is provided to help you to understand key mental health and well-being concepts, to refer young people to appropriate services or online tools, and to teach mental health and well-being skills in the classroom and in support work with young people. Geared toward young professionals entering the teaching and human services workforce, the site contains resources for personal and professional mental health including more than 300 printable evidence-based fact sheets. Resources include how to develop a plan of personal and professional self-care using a holistic perspective, and the Apps and Online Tools tab includes a directory of well-being and resiliency apps that can be used as part of the self-care process. Resources specifically for teachers and human service workers including video trainings, self-activities, and a personal strengths assessment.

Self-Care Starter Kit: https://socialwork.buffalo.edu/resources/self-care-starter-kit.html

This site offers excellent resources for students and professionals as they begin to develop their own self-care plans. The site describes the resources as a "Self-Care Starter Kit." A link introduces beginners to the concept of self-care with embedded hyperlinks to additional resources for the development of a holistic approach to self-care practice. Other links include information on developing individual goals and objectives for a plan of self-care, self-care assessments, exercises, activities, and community resources. The Additional Self-Care Resources tab provides links to inspiration materials, suggested readings, and a comprehensive bibliography. Most of these materials can be downloaded and distributed at no cost.

Sidran Institute: http://www.sidran.org/

This institute is devoted to helping people who have experienced traumatic life events and to promoting greater understanding of early recognition and treatment of trauma-related stress in children; understanding of trauma and its long-term effect on adults; strategies leading to success in self-help recovery for trauma survivors; clinical methods and practices leading to success in aiding trauma victims; and development of public policy initiatives responsive to the needs of adult and child survivors of traumatic events. Features of this site include links to training opportunities in the area of traumatology; a comprehensive Internet resource directory with links for trauma professionals, trauma survivors of all types, and loved ones; a help desk with contact information for those in crisis and searching for services; and a book store with audiovisual resources, books on trauma-related material, and assessment tools, which are for purchase at reasonable cost.

GLOSSARY

ACCEPTANCE: a core component of mindfulness practice; staying in the present moment and remaining open to circumstances that cannot be changed or altered.

ACCEPTANCE AND COMMITMENT THERAPY (ACT): a mindfulness-based approach to treatment with elements of cognitive behavioral therapy; operates on the cognitive process of reframing the context in which life experiences are perceived and appraised and finding a path to spiritual meaning and peacefulness with life.

AMERICAN COUNSELING ASSOCIATION (ACA): "the world's largest association representing professional counselors in various practice settings; the mission of the American Counseling Association is to enhance the quality of life in society by promoting the development of professional counselors, advancing the counseling profession, and using the profession and practice of counseling to promote respect for human dignity and diversity" (www.counseling.org).

ANHEDONIA: often associated with mood and trauma-related disorders; a marked lack of interest in the ability to experience interpersonal feelings of joy or to gain pleasure from meaningful activities.

AROUSAL: a symptom associated with PTSD and other trauma-related disorders; experiencing irritability, aggression, hypervigilance, exaggerated startle response, difficulty with concentration and memory, and insomnia resulting from exposure to a traumatic life event (APA, 2013).

ATTENTION SELF-REGULATION: deliberate methods of concentration used in an effort to be fully present and aware of current life experiences without focus on previously planned engagements, time management, or task completion.

AUTONOMY: a principle of ethical practice relationships that encourages clients to exercise freedom of choice in making decisions; the professional assists clients in recognizing the potential impact of the actions they take, both on themselves and others.

AVOIDANCE: a symptom associated with PTSD and other trauma-related disorders; persistent avoidance of both internal and external trigger stimuli associate with a traumatic life event (APA, 2013).

AVOIDANT COPING STYLE: conflict resolution style characterized by conscious and unconscious reluctance to engage in conflict resolution and planful problem solving to alleviate normative and nonnormative levels of stress in the social environment.

AWARENESS: "a core element of mindfulness practice that emerges through paying attention on purpose, in the present moment, and non-judgmentally to the unfolding of experience moment by moment" (Kabat-Zinn, 2003, p. 145).

BENEFICENCE: a principle of ethical practice that means to "do good" through practice behaviors that prevent harm and contribute to client welfare.

BODY SCAN: a component of mindfulness practice in which one consciously takes notice of the body and all of its physical sensations in the present moment.

CENTRAL NERVOUS SYSTEM: the brain and spinal cord that make up the majority of the human nervous system including the limbic system; the CNS and its corresponding systems relay information throughout the body to regulate emotional and behavioral reactions to both internal and external stimuli.

COGNITIVE APPRAISAL: the brain's processing of internal and external stimuli and the corresponding influence of this appraisal on patterns of thought, beliefs, and other areas of cognitive and behavioral functioning.

COGNITIVE SCHEMATA: interpersonal feelings about the self, including one's general orientation to the world, which may be disrupted as a result of the vicarious or indirect effects of trauma work.

COMPASSION FATIGUE: overall experience of emotional and psychological fatigue human service providers experience due to the chronic use of empathy when treating individuals who are suffering in some way; has been conceptualized and measured as a component of overall professional quality of life and as a syndrome consisting of a combination of the symptoms of secondary traumatic stress and professional burnout.

COMPASSION SATISFACTION: aspects of human service work that provide professional success, reward, and fulfillment, including positive interactions with clients, formation of meaning and supportive relationships with colleagues, personal and spiritual satisfaction of being in a helping profession, and positive professional interactions that occur in human service organizations and as benefits of membership in a helping community.

COMPETENCY: the practitioner's ability to efficaciously apply the ethics principles, values, and standard practice behaviors in treating clients through the methods of practice established for the profession of social work.

COMPETENCY-BASED EDUCATION: obligation of accredited undergraduate and graduate social work programs to provide curriculum with content driven by the core competencies established by the Council on Social Work Education.

CONSTRUCT: a conceptual or theoretical variable in human behavioral research not directly observable but that may describe or indicate other behavioral phenomenon, such as using emotional exhaustion and depersonalization to describe the burnout construct.

CONSTRUCT VALIDITY: accurate measurement of an intended construct by evaluation of the individual items on an instrument to determine if the items represent the construct in its entirety.

CONSTRUCTIVIST SELF-DEVELOPMENT THEORY: theoretical orientation proposed by McCann and Pearlman (1992) to explain vicarious trauma; founded on a "constructivist view of trauma in which the individual's unique history shapes his or her experience of traumatic events and defines the adaptation to trauma" (p. 189).

CONTINUING EDUCATION (CE): additional training or certification hours completed by professionals to remain educated within the current contexts of practice and to remain lifelong learners within their respected disciplines; required for maintenance of social work professional licensure.

CONVERGENT VALIDITY: a method of evaluating the construct validity of an instrument by comparing the scores from one instrument intended to measure a construct to another instrument designed to measure the same construct.

COUNCIL FOR ACCREDITATION OF COUNSELING AND RELATED EDUCATIONAL PROGRAMS (CACREP): "the accrediting body for master's and doctoral degree programs in counseling and its specialties that are offered by colleges and universities in the United States and throughout the world" (www.cacrep.org).

COUNCIL ON SOCIAL WORK EDUCATION (CSWE): "Founded in 1952, this partnership of educational and professional institutions, social welfare agencies, and private citizens is recognized by the Council for Higher Education Accreditation as the sole accrediting agency for social work education in the United States. CSWE pursues this mission in higher education by setting and maintaining national accreditation standards for baccalaureate and master's degree programs in social work, by promoting faculty development, by engaging in international collaborations, and by advocating for social work education and research" (www.cswe.org).

CRITERION VALIDITY: a scale's ability to accurately reflect some external criteria believed to be another indicator of the measure; for example, SAT scores predict college success rates.

COUNTERTRANSFERENCE: the collective unconscious response a therapist has to his or her client, the client's clinical material, transference, and reenactments based on the therapists past life events; the therapist's conscious and unconscious defenses against the presentation of information and material by the client, including reactions such as avoidance, detachment, and over-identification with the client and his or her situation.

CRISIS MANAGEMENT: brief treatment services delivered at either the micro or macro levels of practice to address the acute effects of individual, family, group, or community level crisis events.

CRITICAL INCIDENT: any event outside the usual realm of human experience that is markedly distressing or considered "traumatic," which can result in traumatic stress or, in severe cases, in PTSD; sometimes used synonymously with the definition of trauma; often cited in the practice models of critical incident stress debriefing (CISD) or critical incident stress management (CISM).

CYNICISM: negative, cynical, or excessively detached responses to coworkers, job tasks, or to clients and their situations, commonly found in workers experiencing professional burnout; also referred as a depersonalization effect.

DEEP BREATHING: a relaxation technique associated with mindfulness-based interventions and practices in which the individual uses deep diaphragmatic breathing exercises to calm the mind; often used in combination with yoga and meditation.

DIALECTIC BEHAVIORAL THERAPY (DBT): a method of cognitive behavioral therapy with emphasis on the psychosocial challenges of mental illness; DBT applies mindfulness-based approaches such as acceptance and openness in the cognitive behavioral framework.

DISASTER MENTAL HEALTH: acute micro- or macro-level crisis intervention services delivered during natural or manmade disasters to address the immediate physical and psychological impact of the event and to provide resources for ongoing care of victims.

DISSOCIATION: cluster of symptoms associated with PTSD and other trauma-related disorders, includes the presentation of depersonalization, derealization, and dissociative amnesia, which is the inability to recall important aspects of the trauma experience.

DEPERSONALIZATION: characterized by marked feelings of being outside one's current state of being; more commonly described as an "out of body" experience.

DEREALIZATION: feeling like the world and its surroundings (space and time) are blurred, foggy, or even dreamlike rather than based in reality.

DISCRIMINANT VALIDITY: the degree to which a scale measures the intended construct as opposed to another unintended construct.

DOMAIN: a scale property of instrument items that correspond with specific components or elements of a behavioral construct, which are added together as a measure of the holistic presentation of the construct.

EMOTIONAL EXHAUSTION: feeling that one's emotional resources have become depleted by the chronic needs, demands, and expectations of clients, supervisors, and organizations.

EMPLOYEE ASSISTANCE PROGRAM (EAP): support services offered through the benefits of an employing agency to assist employees with personal or professional challenges that directly affect their ability to function productively at work or at home; services include alcohol and substance abuse treatment, counseling and other mental health services, nutrition, diet, health lifestyle consultations, smoking cessation, and services related to sexual harassment or workplace violence.

EGO RESOURCES: the ability to manage both one's own intrinsic psychological needs and the extrinsic interpersonal needs of others.

ETHICS: "a system of moral principles and perceptions about right versus wrong and the resulting philosophy of conduct that is practiced by an individual, group, profession, or culture" (Barker, 2014, p. 146).

ETHICAL DILEMMA: A situation that places the social worker in a position to make a professional decision (often with multiple options) on behalf of a client or family with a potentially negative outcome for one or more parties.

EDUCATIONAL POLICY AND ACCREDITATION STANDARDS (EPAS): the standards by which the CSWE evaluates the curriculum and course content in social work education programs for the purposes of promoting standardization for social work training programs and for maintaining national accreditation (www.cswe.org).

ECOLOGICAL SYSTEMS THEORY: a fundamental perspective in social work practice suggesting that human behavior evolves as a living organism across the life span based on a combination of biological factors and human (nonbiological) experiences that occur in the social environment.

EMPATHY: the cognitive, emotional, and somatic reactions to people by providers; a developed clinical skill essential to the practitioner to meet the needs of clients and their families.

FACE VALIDITY: a scale or instrument that fulfills the purpose of its intention.

FIELD EDUCATION: social work student placement under the direct supervision of a seasoned social work professional; theoretical content and curriculum is translated, demonstrated, and measured in the areas of competency established by the Council on Social Work Education. CSWE currently requires BSW students to complete 400 hours of field education and MSW students to complete 900 hours of field education.

HOLISTIC: a major principle of ecological and family systems theory suggesting that treatment interventions should encompass the "whole" person rather than focusing on one identified challenge or diagnostic label; treatment interventions should focus on the biological, psychological, psychosocial, familial, cultural, spiritual, and financial aspects of life.

HOLISTIC SELF-CARE: an active and comprehensive approach to the self-care process through the application of an ecological systems framework to target resiliency-based activities from the physical, organizational, interpersonal, familial, and spiritual domains of life.

HOMEOSTASIS: a major premise of the ecological systems theory referring to a human system's drive and collective ability to maintain its fundamental nature, even during times of sudden or intense change; collective systems and all of their interrelated domains naturally adapt and adjust to maintain balance or equilibrium.

HUMANITARIAN RELIEF WORK: national or international development, management, or delivery of emergency aid or relief services typically in areas that have been subjected to macro-level traumas such as the effects of war, famine, natural disaster, disease epidemic, or other environmental challenges.

INDIRECT TRAUMA EXPOSURE: potentially positive and negative psychological effects of human service work for those involved in direct treatment with those who are traumatized, poor, vulnerable, or otherwise suffering in some way.

INTERNAL CONSISTENCY: a scale property that references the reliability of the correlation between individual items to produce an overall or combined score.

INTERRATER RELIABILITY: the amount of consistency between or among observers or raters completing measurement scales.

INTRUSION: a cluster of symptoms associated with PTSD and other trauma-related disorders consisting of intrusive thoughts and memories, nightmares, flashbacks, or marked distress when exposed to internal or external stimuli associated with a traumatic life event.

ITEM ANALYSIS: examining the ratings of individual items on a scale and subsequently evaluating the quality of those items against scores on the instrument as a whole as a measure of the instrument's internal consistency.

LETTING GO: an element of mindfulness that occurs through the practices of openness, awareness, and acceptance; allowing natural change to occur in the absence of thoughts, feelings, and experiences that are no longer relevant or useful in the present moment.

MACRO-LEVEL OR COMMUNITY-BASED TRAUMA: local, community, national, or international events such as mass interpersonal violence or casualty, school or college campus shootings, and natural disasters that involve a collective response of shock and horror often resulting in large-scale psychological consequences that affect large groups of people.

MEDITATION: practice used to facilitate mindfulness by enhancing conscious efforts to create focus and attention self-regulation, control distraction, foster presence, and promote a balanced mind; typically involves standard sitting or cushion meditation; may be focused on bodily sensations such as breathing, chanting, or tasting food; on the experience and sensations of a physical activity such as walking, sitting in a chair, or rocking; or on the processes of the mind through visual imagery or observation of distracting thoughts and feelings.

MINDFULNESS: a practice based in eastern philosophy that brings balance, clarity, and meaning during times of physical and emotional stress, illness, and pain by seeking deep meaning through awareness of the body, mind, feelings, and perceptions; described in the literature as a state, a trait, a quality, and a skill comprised of intention, attention, and attitude.

MINDFULNESS-BASED COGNITIVE THERAPY (MBCT): a brief form of cognitive behavior therapy combined with the mindfulness practices of attention, self-awareness, acceptance (as decentering), and meditation with cognitive approaches to change thoughts, feelings, and behaviors; typically conducted in 8 to 10 sessions.

MINDFULNESS-BASED STRESS REDUCTION (MBSR): a mindfulness-based combination practice of meditation and yoga focused on calming the mind; used for the treatment of a variety of physical and emotional illnesses.

MIRROR IMAGING: a neurobiological combination of cognitive and emotional responses resulting from specific pathways created through neurotransmitters called "mirror neurons" that enable people to act and respond in similar ways, or to "mirror" the behaviors of others; mirror neurons fire based on cues from the social environment such as hearing people speak, posturing, gesturing, and facial expressions.

MORAL: acquired values, feelings, and thoughts that lead to behaviors consistent with standards of what is right and wrong.

NATIONAL ASSOCIATION OF SOCIAL WORKERS (NASW): "the largest membership organization of professional social workers in the world, with 132,000 members. NASW works to enhance the professional growth and development of its members, to create and maintain professional standards, and to advance sound social policies" (www.nasw.org).

OPEN-ENDED QUESTION: a form of interviewing and of data collection that allows participants to give extensive answers to questions rather than selecting a response from predetermined categorical offerings.

OPENNESS: perceiving things for the first time without contamination from past thoughts, feelings, and experiences; attending to the mind with curiosity, even when it wanders during relaxation.

ORGANIZATIONAL CLIMATE: one's thoughts and feelings regarding the quality of the working conditions of an organization; can be based on employees' subjective appraisal of the conditions of the work environment.

ORGANIZATIONAL CULTURE: the collective assumptions, values, norms, and tangible signs (artifacts) of agency members and their behaviors.

PERSONAL ACCOMPLISHMENT: feelings of proficiency rather than inadequacy when clients do not respond to an intervention despite diligent efforts to help them; may also occur in response to bureaucratic constraints and administrative demands that often accompany social service practice, such as dictating client records or completing required administrative documentation.

PERSONAL SELF-DISCLOSURE: purposely sharing personal information, thoughts, feelings, or value systems with a consumer of social work services; disclosures should be relevant and relate to the improved well-being and quality of life of the consumer.

PLANFUL PROBLEM SOLVING: an analytical thought process combined with deliberate problem-focused efforts to manage the effects of stressful working environments or personal problems of life.

POSTTRAUMATIC GROWTH: positive changes in the self, in relationships with others, and in overall outlook and philosophy of life that occur for many individuals when confronted with challenging life situations such as physical and sexual assault, major medical illness, natural disaster, or combat stress.

POSTTRAUMATIC STRESS DISORDER: the consequential, complex, and problematic psychological patterns of behavior that result from the impact of a traumatic incident or event involving either actual or perceived threat to the obvious victim or victims of that incident (APA, 2013).

PRACTICE BEHAVIOR: a professional behavior that is both competent and reflective of the skill set of professional social work practice; also describes the benchmarks for educational curriculum reflected in the core competencies for social work practice established by the CSWE.

PRACTICE WISDOM: "the accumulation of information, assumptions, ideologies, and judgments that are practically useful in fulfilling expectations of the job. Practice wisdom is often equated with "common sense" and may not be validated when subjected to empirical or systematic analysis and may or may not be consistent with prevailing theory" (Barker, 2014, p. 331).

PROFESSIONAL BOUNDARY: direct communication by a provider of services to a consumer with regard to the professional nature of the helping relationship and the role of the provider in this process; the ethical obligation of the provider to recognize the distinction between one's personal life and any professional obligations to the client.

PROFESSIONAL BURNOUT: a cumulative state of physical, emotional, psychological, and spiritual exhaustion resulting from chronic exposure to or practice with populations that are vulnerable or suffering with contributing factors related to the individual, the populations served, and the service organization.

PROFESSIONAL DEVELOPMENT: ongoing engagement in activities of lifelong learning, including continuing education and certification to foster practice skill development, competence, improvement, and proficiency in an area of professional practice.

PROFESSIONAL RESILIENCE: positive and growth-promoting outcomes of human service work with potential to balance out the negative and sometimes deleterious outcomes that can result in professional burnout; the process by which those who provide services to vulnerable or at-risk populations thrive in inherently stressful work conditions.

PROFESSIONAL SELF-ESTEEM: an internal sense of proficiency and competency in one's work environment; in human service work, associated with feelings of efficaciousness in the treatment of consumers and their social problems.

PROJECTIVE IDENTIFICATION: experiencing emotions or feelings similar to those of the client when the client projects these feelings onto the therapist; an antecedent behavior to the countertransference relationship.

PSYCHOLOGICAL DEBRIEFING: creating a space for relief workers to discuss and reflect on their emotional experiences and reactions about the crisis event prior to reintegration in their normative family and occupational routines.

PSYCHOMETRIC PROPERTIES: the results of evaluative data collected to determine how accurately an instrument or scale measures the intended construct; collectively referred to as instrument reliability and validity.

QUALITATIVE ASSESSMENT: a data collection paradigm without standardized scales or measures; used to capture phenomenological data on human behavior as it emerges naturally; qualitative methods include observational data collection, focus groups, semistructured interviews, and open-ended questions.

RACE-BASED TRAUMATIC STRESS: "the cumulative negative impact of racism on the lives of people of color encompassing the emotional psychological, health, economic, and social effects of multi-generational and historical trauma" (www.mcsilver.nyu.edu).

RANGE: the distance between the true upper and lower limit values in a scale distribution; for example, a pain scale ranging from "0 = no pain" to "10 = unbearable pain."

RELIABILITY: the amount of random error in a measurement instrument; determines whether the instrument is consistently useful across populations and over time.

RESILIENCE: the ability to "bounce back" or recover from a challenge in a meaningful and productive way; the overall process of well-being generated through intrapersonal, interpersonal, and social dimensions rather than solely being a function of personality.

ROLE CONFUSION: common misunderstandings and dilemmas associated with the convergence of various duties and functions of human service work, such as being an advocate, a provider of services, a policy maker, and an organizational manager.

SECONDARY TRAUMATIC STRESS: "natural and consequential behaviors and emotions resulting from knowing about a traumatizing event experienced by a significant other (or client) and the stress resulting from helping or wanting to help a traumatized or suffering person" (Figley, 1995, p. 7).

SELF-APPRECIATION: rewarding, celebrating, and acknowledging the value of personal and professional strengths, accomplishments, civility, humanity, efficaciousness, and successfulness as components of the self-reflection process.

SELF-AWARENESS: conscious and deliberate examination and reflection on one's own behaviors and reactions to other personal and professional relationships in the social environment and the corresponding impact and influence of one's behavior on others.

SELF-CARE: skills and strategies used by social workers and other human service professionals to maintain their own personal, familial, emotional, physical, and spiritual needs to actively and consciously promote holistic well-being and professional resilience while attending to the complex emotional needs and demands of their clients.

SELF-COMPASSION: positive thoughts, attitudes, and behaviors, such as being kind rather than self-judging; tolerance and humanity rather than isolation during times of personal challenge and suffering; mindful awareness of one's own thoughts and feelings when caring for the needs of others (Neff, 2003, 2011).

SELF-REFLECTION: thinking critically and insightfully about interpersonal thoughts, feelings, and behaviors that manifest from the complex interactions with clients and their social problems.

SELF-REPORT MEASURE: participants complete questionnaires and scales measuring study variables themselves rather than the data being collected by the researcher through structured or clinical interview.

SOCIAL JUSTICE: a core value of the social work profession reflecting the belief that equality and justice pertain to every aspect of society, not just to administration of the law; envisions a world that affords individuals and groups fair treatment and an impartial share of the benefits of society.

SOCIAL SUPPORT: broadly conceptualized as including direct or received support from family, friends, and other social relationships and the individual subjective perception of the availability of support from others during times of need.

SOMATIC EMPATHY: elicited emotional responses from the human body such as a nonverbal response to a look or gesture; often facilitates identification of outward or behavioral signs of chronic stress or crisis.

SPIRITUALITY: "devotion to the immaterial part of humanity and nature, rather than worldly things or possessions and as an orientation to people's religious, moral, and emotional nature" (Barker, 2014, p. 409); may include self-perception, adherence to personal values and ethics, belief in the existence and influence of a higher power, and the formation of meaningful relationships with others who are like-minded subscribers to a common belief system.

STRENGTHS-BASED PRACTICE: social work practice that focuses interventions on client strengths and social support resources to overcome challenges rather than focusing on client challenges, diagnoses, labels, or other deficiencies as the center of practice interventions.

STRESS: environmental stimuli (stressors) and individual or collective behavioral responses to environmental stimuli; originate from various domains of the biopsychosocial self, including physical health, mental health, family well-being, and spirituality.

STRESS BUFFER: social support resources that reduce the impact of stressful life events on physical and emotional health indicators.

STRUCTURED INTERVIEW: each participant answers a predetermined number of questions that are aggregated for categorical or thematic analysis at a later date.

TASK-CENTERED APPROACH: an acute approach to direct social work practice using a process of mutually identifying challenges and applying specific tasks aimed at resolving social problems on a short-term basis.

TEST-RETEST RELIABILITY: a measure of scale reliability determined by administering a scale to the same participants on at least two separate occasions and comparing the scores for consistency.

TRAUMA: a micro- or macro-level life event that surpasses individual, family, group, or community coping resources and results in acute traumatic stress or, in severe cases, in PTSD; examples include rape, physical or sexual assault, psychosis, captivity, human trafficking, suicide, homicide, mass interpersonal violence, natural disaster, combat exposure, witnessing intense cruelty or harm to other people, severe accidents (automobile or plane), severe neglect or poverty, and sudden loss of job or income.

TRAUMA-BONDING: a group phenomenon in which survivors bond over their mutual experiences with a traumatic event in either a positive or negative way; also describes victims of trauma who become sympathetic in some way to the perpetrator and his or her circumstances.

TRAUMA-INFORMED EDUCATION AND PRACTICE: an approach to social work practice, education, and training that recognizes the widespread impact of trauma-related disorders, the importance of trauma treatment, trauma recovery, resilience, and social policy.

TRAUMA-RELATED DISORDERS: psychological distress or illness directly related to exposure to a micro or macro traumatic life event; includes PTSD, acute stress disorder, adjustment disorders, disinhibited social engagement disorder, and reactive attachment disorder.

TRAUMATIC STRESS: occurs when an individual does not have the preexisting psychological coping resources to process and manage the impact of a traumatic event.

VALIDITY: the degree to which an instrument accurately measures the intended construct.

VALUE: social work and counseling are considered "value-based" professions, a label that suggests the existence of formally developed and articulated ethics codes that guide practice; standards for professional behavior outlined in the respective codes of ethics are driven by a core set of beliefs (or values) that reflect the spirit of the professions.

VICARIOUS RESILIENCE: trauma recovery that fosters resilience and growth not only in the client but in the clinician through witnessing and participating with clients suffering from the effects of crisis, trauma, or other human tragedy who overcome these circumstances and rediscover meaningful aspects of life through the healing process.

VICARIOUS TRAUMA: potential cognitive changes in a therapist's collective frame of reference both intrinsically and extrinsically, such as the therapist's sense of self; worldviews regarding issues such as safety, intimacy and trust; and spirituality as a result of chronic exposure to and treatment of trauma-related disorders.

YOGA: a combination of stretching, posturing, and deep breathing to relax the physical body and connect it to the mind; deeply rooted in Buddhist philosophy, yoga can help to cultivate focus, awareness, and openness when used as a component of mindfulness practice.

REFERENCES

Adams, K. B., Matto, H. C., & Harrington, D. (2001). The Traumatic Stress Institute Belief Scale as a measure of vicarious trauma in a national sample of clinical social workers. *Families in Society: The Journal of Contemporary Human Services, 82*(14), 363–374.

Adams, R. E., Boscarino, J. A., & Figley, C. R. (2006). Compassion fatigue and psychological distress among social workers: A validation study. *American Journal of Orthopsychiatry, 76*(1), 103–108.

Adeyemo, S. O., Omoaregba, J. O., Aroyewun, B. A., Modebe, V. O., James, B. O., Uteh, B. E., & Ezemokwe, C. O. (2015). Experiences of violence, compassion fatigue and compassion satisfaction on the professional quality of life of mental health professionals at a tertiary psychiatric facility in Nigeria. *Journal of Clinical Medicine, 3*(2), 69–73.

American Counseling Association. (2014). ACA code of ethics: As approved by the ACA Governing Council, 2014. Alexandria, VA: Author. https://www.counseling.org /Resources/aca-code-of-ethics.pdf.

American Institute of Stress. (2015). *2014 stress statistics.* Retrieved from http://www .stress.org/daily-life/

American Psychiatric Association. (1980). *Diagnostic and statistical manual of mental disorders* (3rd ed.). Washington, DC: Author.

American Psychiatric Association. (1994). *Diagnostic and statistical manual of mental disorders* (4th ed.). Washington, DC: Author.

American Psychiatric Association. (2013). *Diagnostic and statistical manual of mental disorders* (5th ed.). Washington, DC: Author.

American Psychological Association. (2016). *The road to resilience.* Retrieved from http://www.apa.org/helpcenter/road-resilience.aspx

Anderson, D. G. (2000). Coping strategies and burnout among veteran child protection workers. *Child Abuse and Neglect, 24*(6), 839–848.

Appignanesi, R., & Zarate, O. (1979). *Freud for beginners.* New York, NY: Pantheon.

Asuero, A., Queralto, J., Pujol-Ribera, E., Berenguera, A., Rodriquez-Blanco, T., & Epstein, R. M. (2014). Effectiveness of a mindfulness education program in primary health care professionals: A pragmatic controlled trial. *Journal of Continuing Education in the Health Professions, 34*(1), 4–12.

Auxier, C., Hughes, F. R., & Kline, W. B. (2003). Identity development in counselors -in-training. *Counselor Education & Supervision, 43*(1), 25–38.

Baird, K., & Kracen, A. C. (2006). Vicarious traumatization and secondary traumatic stress: A research synthesis. *Counselling Psychology Quarterly, 19*(2), 181–188.

Balch, P. A. (2010). *Prescription for nutritional healing: A practical A-to-Z reference to drug-free remedies using vitamins, minerals, herbs & food supplements* (5th ed.). Garden City Park, NY: Avery.

Balcom, D. (1996). The interpersonal dynamics and treatment of dual trauma couples. *Journal of Marital and Family Therapy, 22*(4), 431–442.

Baldschum, A. (2014). The six dimensions of child welfare employees' occupational well-being. *Nordic Journal of Working Life Studies, 4*(1), 68–87.

Baldwin, C. (1990). *Life's companion: Journal writing as a spiritual quest.* New York, NY: Bantam.

Barak, M. E. M., Nissly, J. A., & Levin, A. (2001). Antecedents to retention and turn-over among child welfare, social work, and other human service employees: What can we learn from the past research? A review and meta-analysis. *Social Service Review,* 625–661.

Barker, R. L. (2014). *The social work dictionary* (6th ed.). Washington, DC: NASW Press.

Barnet, J. E., Baker, E. K., Elman, N. S., & Schoener, G. R. (2007). In pursuit of wellness: The self-care imperative. *Professional Psychology: Research and Practice, 38*(6), 603–612.

Bazarko, D., Cate, R. A., Azocar, F., & Kreitzer, M. J. (2013). The impact of an inno-vative mindfulness-based stress reduction program on the health and well-being of nurses employed in a corporate setting. *Journal of Workplace and Behavioral Health, 28,* 107–133.

Bean, R. A., Davis, S. D., & Davey, M. P. (2014), *Clinical activities for increasing com-petence and self-awareness.* Hoboken, NJ: Wiley.

Bell, H., Kulkarni, S., & Dalton, L. (2003). Organization prevention of vicarious trauma. *Families in society: The Journal of Contemporary Human Services, 84*(4), 463–470.

Bennett, S. S., Plint, A. A., & Clifford, T. J. (2005). Burnout, psychological morbidity, job satisfaction, and stress: A survey of Canadian hospital based child protection pro-fessionals. *Archives of Disease in Childhood, 90*(11), 1112–1116.

Berger, R. (2015). *Stress, trauma, and posttraumatic growth: Social context, environment, and identities.* New York, NY: Routledge.

Berger, R., Aub-Raiya, H., & Benatov, J. (2016). Reducing primary and secondary trau-matic stress symptoms among educators by training them to deliver a resiliency program (ERASE-Stress) following the Christchurch earthquake in New Zealand. *American Journal of Orthopsychiatry, 86*(2), 236–251.

Birmes, P., Hatton, L., Brunet, A., & Schmitt, L. (2003). Early historical literature for post-traumatic symptomatology. *Stress and Health, 19,* 17–26.

Bishop, S. R., Lau, M., Shapiro, S., Carlson, L., Anderson, N. D., Carmody, J., . . . Devins, G. (2004). Mindfulness: A proposed operation definition. *Clinical Psychology: Science and Practice, 11*(3), 230–241.

Black, S., & Weinreich, P. (2000). An exploration of counseling identity in counselors who deal with trauma. *Traumatology, 6*(3), 25–40.

Black, T. (2006). Teaching trauma without traumatizing principles of trauma treatment in the training of graduate counselors. *Traumatology, 12*(4), 266–271.

Blake, D. D., Weathers, F. W., Nagy, L. M., Kaloupek, D. G., Gusman, F. D., Charney, D. S., & Keane, T. M. (1995). The development of a clinician-administered PTSD scale. *Journal of Traumatic Stress, 8*, 75–90.

Bogo, M., & Wayne, J. (2013). The implicit curriculum in social work education: The culture of human exchange. *Journal of Teaching in Social Work, 33*(1), 2–14.

Bonifas, R. P., & Napoli, M. (2014). Mindfully increasing quality of life: A promising curriculum for MSW students. *Social Work Education, 33*(4), 460–484.

Boyas, J., Wind, L. H., & Kang, S. (2012). Exploring the relationship between employment-based social capital, job stress, burnout, and intent to leave among child protection workers: An age-based path analysis model. *Children & Youth Services Review, 34*(1), 50–62.

Boyas, J. F., Wind, L. H., & Ruiz, E. (2013). Organizational tenure among child welfare workers, burnout, stress, and intent to leave: Does employment-based social capital make a difference? *Children & Youth Services Review, 35*(10), 1657–1669.

Brantley, J. (2007). *Calming your anxious mind: How mindfulness & compassion can free you from anxiety, fear, & panic.* Oakland, CA: New Harbinger.

Brelsford, G. M., & Farris, J. R. (2014). Religion and spirituality: A source of renewal for families. In R. J. Wicks & E. A. Maynard (Eds.), *Clinicians guide to self-renewal* (pp. 355–365). New York, NY: Oxford University Press.

Brend, D. M. (2014). A dialogue between theories: Understanding trauma in helping professionals. *Intervention, 140*, 95–113.

Bressi, S. K., & Vaden, E. R. (2016). Reconsidering self-care. *Clinical Social Work Journal.* Advance online publication. doi: 10.1007/S10615-016-0575-4

Bride, B. E. (2007). Prevalence of secondary traumatic stress among social workers. *Social Work, 52*(1), 63–70.

Bride, B. E., & Figley, C. R. (2009). Secondary trauma and military caregivers. *Smith College Studies in Social Work, 79*, 314–329.

Bride, B. E., Radney, M., & Figley, C. R. (2007). Measuring compassion fatigue. *Clinical Social Work Journal, 35*, 155–163.

Bride, B. E., Robinson, M. M., Yegidis, B., & Figley, C. R. (2004). Development and validation of the Secondary Traumatic Stress Scale. *Research on Social Work Practice, 14*(1), 27–35.

Briere, J., & Scott, C. (2015). *Principles of trauma therapy: A guide to symptoms, evaluation, and treatment* (2nd ed.). Thousand Oaks, CA: Sage.

Brinamen, C. F., Taranta, A. N., & Johnston, K. (2012). Expanding early childhood mental health consultation to new venues: Serving infants and young children in domestic violence and homeless shelters. *Infant Mental Health Journal, 33*(3), 283–293. doi:10.1002/imhj.21338

Brown, K. W., Creswell, J. D., & Ryan, R. M. (2016). *The handbook of mindfulness: Theory, research, and practice.* New York, NY: Guilford Press.

Brown, K. W., & Ryan, R. M. (2003). The benefits of being present: Mindfulness and its role in psychological well-being. *Journal of Personality and Social Psychology, 84*(4), 822–848.

Brown, K. W., Ryan, R. M., & Creswell, J. D. (2007). Mindfulness: Theoretical foundations and evidence for its salutary effects. *Psychological Inquiry, 18*(4), 211–237.

Buccino, G., & Amore, M. (2008). Mirror neurons and the understanding of behavioural symptoms in psychiatric disorders. *Current opinion in psychiatry, 21*(3), 281–285.

Buchanan, M., Anderson, J. O., Uhlemann, M. R., & Horwitz, E. (2006). Secondary traumatic stress: An investigation of Canadian mental health workers. *Traumatology, 12*(4), 272–281.

Burke, P., & Hohman, M. (2014). Encouraging self-reflection in reflective listening and processing. In R. A. Bean, S. D. Davis, & M. P. Davey (Eds.), *Clinical activities for increasing competence and self-awareness* (pp. 33–40). Hoboken, NJ: Wiley.

Cahalane, H., & Sites, E. (2008) The climate of child welfare employee retention. *Child Welfare, 87*(1), 91–114.

Campbell, L. (2007). Utilizing compassion fatigue education in hurricanes Ivan and Katrina. *Clinical Social Work Journal, 35,* 165–171.

Carbonell, J., & Figley, C. J. (1996). When trauma hits home: Personal trauma and the family therapist. *Journal of Marriage and Family Therapy, 22,* 53–58.

Carlson, E. B. (1997). *Trauma assessments: A clinicians guide.* New York, NY: Guilford Press.

Carmody, J., & Baer, R. A. (2008). Relationships between mindfulness practice and levels of mindfulness, medical and psychological symptoms and well-being in a mindfulness-based stress reductions program. *Journal of Behavioral Medicine, 31,* 23–33.

Carter, R. T. (2007). Racism and psychological and emotional injury: Recognizing and assessing race-based traumatic stress. *The Counseling Psychologist, 35*(1), 13–15.

Carter, R. T., & Forsyth, J. M. (2007). The examination of race and culture in psychology journals: The case of forensic psychology. *Professional Psychology Research and Practice, 38,* 133–142.

Carter, R. T., & Forsyth, J. M. (2009). A guide to the forensic assessment of race-based traumatic stress reactions. *Journal of the American Academy of Psychiatry and the Law, 37,* 28–40.

Carter, R. T., Mazzula, S., Victoria, R., Vazquez, R., Hall, S., Smith, S., . . . Williams, B. (2013). Initial development of the Race-Based Traumatic Stress Symptoms Scale: Assessing the emotional impact of racism. *Psychological Trauma: Theory, Research, Practice, and Policy, 5*(1), 1–9.

Catherall, D. (1995). Preventing institutional secondary traumatic stress disorder. In C. R. Figley (Ed.), *Compassion fatigue: Coping with secondary traumatic stress disorder in those who treat the traumatized* (pp. 232–247). Levittown, PA: Brunner/Mazel.

Catherall, D. R. (1999). Coping with secondary traumatic stress: The importance of the therapist's professional peer group. In B. Hudall Stamm (Ed.), *Secondary traumatic stress: Self-care issues for clinicians, researchers, and educators* (pp. 80–92). Lutherville, MD: Sidran Press.

Cerney, M. (1995). Treating the "heroic treaters." In C. R. Figley (Ed.), *Compassion fatigue: Coping with secondary traumatic stress disorder in those who treat the traumatized* (pp. 131–149). Levittown, PA: Brunner/Mazel.

Chechak, D. (2015). Social work as a value-based profession: Value conflicts and implications for practitioners' self-concepts. *Journal of Social Work Values and Ethics, 12*(2), 41–48.

Chesley, N. (2005). Linking technology use, spillover, individual distress, and family satisfaction. *Journal of Marriage and Family, 67,* 1237–1248.

Chiesa, A. (2012). The difficulty of defining mindfulness: Current thought and critical issues. *Mindfulness.* doi: 10.1007/s12671-012-0123-4

Child Sexual Abuse Task Force. (2008). Research & Practice Core, National Child Traumatic Stress Network (2004). How to implement trauma-focused cognitive behavioral therapy. Durham, NC and Los Angeles, CA: National Center for Child Traumatic Stress.

Christopher, J. C., & Maris, J. A. (2010). Integrating mindfulness as self-care into counseling and psychotherapy training. *Counselling and Psychotherapy Research, 10*(2), 114–125.

Cicchetti, D. (2013). Annual research review: Resilient functioning in maltreated children—past, present, and future perspectives. *Journal of Child Psychology and Psychiatry, 54*, 402–422.

Clarkson, P., & Nuttall, J. (2000). Working with countertransference. *Psychodynamic Counseling, 6*(3), 359–379.

Coffey, K. A., Hartman, M., & Frederickson, B. L. (2010). Deconstructing mindfulness and constructing mental health: Understanding mindfulness and its mechanisms of action. *Mindfulness, 1*, 235–253. doi: 10.1007/s12671-010-0033-2

Cohen, J. A., Mannarino, A. P., Kliethermes, M., & Murray, L. A. (2012). Trauma-focused CBT for youth with complex trauma. *Child Abuse & Neglect, 36*(6), 528–541.

Cohen, S., Kamarck, T., & Mermelstein, R. (1983). A global measure of perceived stress. *Journal of Health and Social Behavior, 24*, 385–396.

Cohen, S., Underwood, L. G., & Gottlieb, B. H. (2000). *Social support measurement and intervention: A guide for health and social scientists.* New York, NY: Oxford University Press.

Collins, W. L. (2005). Embracing spirituality as an element of professional self-care. *Social Work & Christianity, 32*(3): 263–274.

Collins, J. (2009). Addressing secondary traumatic stress: Emerging approaches in child welfare. *Children's Voice,* March/April, 10–14.

Collins, S., & Long, A. (2002). Too tired to care? The psychological effects of working with trauma. *Journal of Psychiatric and Mental Health Nursing, 10*, 17–27.

Conrad, D., & Keller-Guenther, Y. (2006). Compassion fatigue, burnout, and compassion satisfaction among Colorado child protection workers. *Child Abuse and Neglect, 30*, 1071–1080.

Corey, M., & Corey, G. (2015). *Becoming a helper* (7th ed.). Boston, MA: Cengage Learning.

Corey, G., Corey, M., Corey, C., & Callanan, P. (2014). *Issues and ethics in the helping professions.* Boston, MA: Cengage Learning.

Council for Accreditation of Counseling and Related Educational Programs. (2016). *2016 standards for accreditation.* Alexandria, VA: Author.

Council on Social Work Education. (2010). *Advanced social work practice in military social work.* Alexandra, VA: Author.

Council on Social Work Education. (2015). *Educational policy and accreditation standards.* Retrieved from www.cswe.org.

Courtois, C. A. (2002). Education in trauma practice: Traumatic stress studies, the need for curricula inclusion. *Journal of Trauma Practice, 1*(1), 33–57.

Cox, K., & Sterner, S. (2013a). Preserving commitment to social work service through the prevention of vicarious trauma. *Journal of Social Work Values and Ethics, 10*(1), 52–56.

Cox, K., & Sterner, S. (2013b). *Self-care in social work: A guide for practitioners, supervisors, and administrators.* Washington, DC: NASW Press.

Craig, C. D., & Sprang, G. (2010). Compassion satisfaction, compassion fatigue, and burnout in a national sample of trauma treatment therapists. *Anxiety, Stress & Coping, 23*(3), 319–339.

Creamer, T. L., & Liddle, B. J. (2005). Secondary traumatic stress among disaster mental health workers responding to September 11 attacks. *Journal of Traumatic Stress, 18*(1), 89–96.

Csiernik, R., & Adams, D. W. (2002). Spirituality, stress, and work. *Employee Assistance Quarterly, 18*(2), 29–37.

Cullen, M. (2011). Mindfulness-based interventions: An emerging phenomenon. *Mindfulness.* Advance online publication. doi: 10.1007/s12671-01100058-1

Cunningham, M. (1999). The impact of sexual abuse treatment on the social work clinician. *Child and Adolescent Social Work Journal, 16*(4), 277–290.

Cunningham, M. (2003). Impact of trauma work on social work clinicians: Empirical findings. *Social Work, 48*(4), 451–459.

Cunningham, M. (2004). Teaching social workers about trauma: Reducing the risks of vicarious traumatization in the classroom. *Journal of Social Work Education, 40*(20), 305–317.

Cyphers, G. (2001). *Child welfare workforce survey: State and county data and findings.* American Public Human Services Association. Retrieved from http://www.aphsa.org/cwwsurvey.pdf

Dalenburg, C. J. (2002). Remembering to wonder: The place of scientific research in clinical trauma practice. *Journal of Trauma Practice, 1*(1), 59–79.

Dane, B. (2000). Child welfare workers: An innovative approach for interacting with secondary trauma. *Journal of Social Work Education, 36*(1), 27–39.

Decety, J., & Jackson, P. L. (2004). The functional architecture of human empathy. *Behavioral and Cognitive Neuroscience Reviews, 3,* 71–100.

Dekel, S., Peleg, T., & Solomon, Z. (2013). The relationship of PTSD to negative cognitions: A 17-year longitudinal study. *Psychiatry: Interpersonal and Biological Processes, 76*(3), 241–255.

DePanfilis, D. (2006). Compassion fatigue, burnout, and compassion satisfaction: Implications for retention of workers. *Child Abuse and Neglect, 30,* 1067–1069.

Dill, K. (2007). Impact of stressors on front-line child welfare supervisors. *Clinical Supervisor, 26*(1/2), 177–193.

Dinshtein, Y., Dekel, R., & Polliack, M. (2011). Secondary traumatization among adult children of PTSD veterans: The role of mother-child relationships. *Journal of Family Social Work, 14,* 109–124.

Dolgoff, R., Harrington, D., & Lowenberg, F. M. (2012). *Ethical decisions for social work practice* (9th ed.). Belmont, CA: Brook/Cole Cengage Learning.

Dorahy, M. J., & van der Hart, O. (2015). DSM-5's posttraumatic stress disorder with dissociative symptoms: Challenges and future directions. *Journal of Trauma & Dissociation, 16*(1), 7–28. doi: 10.1080/15299732.2014.908806

Drake, B. D., & Yadama, G. N. (1995). Confirmatory factor analysis of the Maslach Burnout Inventory. *Social Work Research, 19*(3), 184–194.

Duckworth, A. L., Steen, T. A., & Seligman, M. E. P. (2005). Positive psychology in clinical practice. *Annual Review of Clinical Psychology, 1,* 629–651.

Dunkley, J., & Whelan, T. A. (2006). Vicarious traumatization: Current status and future directions. *British Journal of Guidance and Counseling, 34*(1), 107–116.

Easton, S. D., Coohey, C., Rhodes, A. M., & Moorthy, M. V. (2013). Posttraumatic growth among men with histories of child sexual abuse. *Child Maltreatment, 18*(4), 211–220.

Edward, K. L. (2005). The phenomenon of resilience in crisis care mental health clinicians. *International Journal of Mental Health Nursing, 14,* 142–148.

Engstrom, D., Hernandez, P., & Gangsei, D. (2008). Vicarious resilience: A qualitative investigation into its description. *Traumatology, 14*(3), 13–21.

Even, T. A., & Robinson, C. R. (2013). The impact of CACREP accreditation: A multiway frequency analysis of ethics violations and sanctions. *Journal of Counseling & Development, 91*(1), 26–34.

Falb, M. D., & Pargament, K. J. (2014). Spiritual coping resources for the self-renewal of clients and therapists. In R. J. Wicks & E. A. Maynard (Eds.), *Clinicians guide to self-renewal* (pp. 335–353). New York, NY: Oxford University Press.

Farrell, R. S., & Turpin, G. (2003). Vicarious traumatization: Implications for the mental health of health workers? *Clinical Psychology Review, 23*(3), 449–480.

Figley, C. R. (1995). *Compassion fatigue: Coping with secondary traumatic stress disorder in those who treat the traumatized.* Levittown, PA: Brunner/Mazel.

Figley, C. R. (2002a). Compassion fatigue: Psychotherapists' chronic lack of self-care. *Psychotherapy in Practice, 58*(11), 1433–1411.

Figley, C. R. (2002b). The history of trauma practice: Origins of traumatology and prospects for the future, part 1. *Journal of Trauma Practice, 1*(1), 17–32.

Figley, C. R. (2002c). *Treating compassion fatigue.* New York, NY: Brunner-Routledge.

Figley, C. R., & Nash, W. P. (2007). *Combat stress injury: Theory, research, and management.* New York, NY: Taylor & Francis.

Figley, C. R., & Stamm, B. H. (1996). Psychometric review of compassion fatigue self-test. In B. H. Stamm (Ed.), *Measurement of stress, trauma and adaptation.* Lutherville, MD: Sidran Press.

Font, S. (2012). Burnout in child welfare: The role of employment characteristics and workplace opportunities. *Social Service Review, 86*(4), 636–659.

Frankl, V. E. (1984). *Man's search for meaning: An introduction to logotherapy* (3rd ed.). New York, NY: Simon & Schuster/Touchstone.

Fredrickson, B. L. (2004). The broaden-and-build theory of positive emotions. *Philosophical Translational Royal Society of London B Biological Sciences, 359,* 1367–1377.

Freud, S. (1964). A case of hysteria, three essays on sexuality and other works. In J. Strachey (Ed. & Trans.), *The standard edition of the complete psychological works of Sigmund Freud, Vol. 7. (1901–1905).* London, England: Hogarth Press. (Original work published 1923)

Freudenberger, H. J. (1974). Staff burnout. *Journal of Social Issues, 1,* 159–164.

Friedman, D., & Kaslow, N. J. (1986). The development of professional identity in psychotherapists: Six stages in the supervision process. *The Clinical Supervisor, 4*(1/2), 29–50.

Friedman, M. J. (2006). Posttraumatic stress disorder among military returnees from Afghanistan and Iraq. *American Journal of Psychiatry, 163,* 586–593.

Friedman, M. J., Keane, T., & Resick, P. A. (2007). *Handbook of PTSD: Science and practice.* New York, NY: Guilford Press.

Galantino, M., Maguire, M., Szapary, P. O., & Farrar, J. T. (2005). Association of psychological and physiological measures of stress in health-care professionals during an 8-week mindfulness meditation program: *Stress and Health, 21*(4), 255–261.

Galovski, T., & Lyons, J. A. (2004). Psychological sequelae of combat violence: A review of the impact of PTSD on veteran's family and possible interventions. *Aggression and Violent Behavior, 9,* 477–501.

Geller, J. E. (2011). The psychotherapy of psychotherapists. *Journal of Clinical Psychology: In Session, 68*(7), 759–765.

Gelso, C. J., & Hayes, J. A. (2007). *Countertransference and the inner world of the psychotherapist: Perils and possibilities*. Mahwah, NJ. Erlbaum.

Gerber, C. K. (2009). *The mindful path to self-compassion: Freeing yourself from destructive thoughts and emotions*. New York, NY: Guilford Press.

Gerdes, K. A., & Segal, E. (2011). Importance of empathy for social work practice: Integrating new science. *Social Work, 56*(2), 141–148.

Gerdes, K. A., Segal, E. A., Jackson, K. F., & Mullins, J. L. (2011). Teaching empathy: A framework rooted in social cognitive neuroscience and social justice. *Journal of Social Work Education, 47*(1), 109–131.

Gersons, B. P .R., & Carlier, I. V. E. (1992). Post traumatic stress disorder: The history of a recent concept. *British Journal of Psychiatry, 161*, 742–748.

Giles, C. A. (2014). Self-renewal through natural empathy. In R. J. Wicks & E. A. Maynard (Eds.), *Clinicians guide to self-renewal* (pp. 119–129). New York, NY: Oxford University Press.

Gilin, B., & Kauffman, S. (2015). Strategies for teaching about trauma to graduate social work students. *Journal of Teaching in Social Work, 35*, 378–396. doi: 10.1080/08841233.2015.1065945

Gladding, S. T. (2011). *The creative arts in counseling* (4th ed.). Alexandria, VA: American Counseling Association.

Gockel, A. (2015). Practicing presence: A curriculum for integrating mindfulness training into direct practice instruction. *Journal of Social Work Education, 51*, 682–690.

Goodyear-Brown, P. (2009). *Play therapy with traumatized children: A prescriptive approach*. Hoboken, NJ: Wiley.

Grabovac, A. D., Lau, M. A., & Willett, B. R. (2011). Mechanisms of mindfulness: A Buddhist psychological model. *Mindfulness*. doi:10.1007/s12671-011-0054-5

Graham, J. R., & Shier, M. L. (2014). Profession and workplace expectations of social workers: Implications for social worker subjective well-being. *Journal of Social Work Practice: Psychotherapeutic Approaches in Health, Welfare and the Community, 28*(1), 95–110.

Gray, M. J., Litz, B. T., Hsu, J. L., & Lombardo, T. W. (2004). Psychometric properties of the life events checklist. *Assessment, 11*(4), 330–341.

Greatrex, T. (2002). Projective identification: How does it work? *Neuropsychoanalysis, 4*(2), 187–197.

Grossman, P., Niemann, L., Schmidt, S., & Walach, H. (2004). Mindfulness-based stress reduction and health benefits: A meta-analysis. *Journal of psychosomatic research, 57*(1), 35–43.

Gutierrez, L. (2012). Recognizing and valuing our roles as mentors. *Journal of Social Work Education, 48*(1), 1–4.

Hacker, H. (1957). The meanings and uses of countertransference. *The Psychoanalytic Quarterly, 26*, 303–357.

Hackmann, A., Ehlers, A., Speckens, A., & Clark, D. M. (2004). Characteristics and content of intrusive memories in PTSD and their changes with treatment. *Journal of Traumatic Stress, 17*, 231–240.

Hall, J. C. (2014). Creating a safe learning environment for clinicians through group discussion and supervision. In R. A. Bean, S. D. Davis, & M. P. Davey (Eds.), *Clinical activities for increasing competence and self-awareness* (pp. 97–102). Hoboken, NJ: Wiley.

Hamama, L. (2012). Burnout in social workers treating children as related to demographic characteristics, work environment, and social support. *Social Work Research, 36*(2), 113–125.

Hanh, T. N. (2006). *Transformation and healing: Sultra on the four establishments of mindfulness.* Berkeley, CA: Parallax.

Harr, C., & Moore, B. (2011). Compassion fatigue among social work students in field placements. *Journal of Teaching in Social Work, 31*, 350–363.

Harrison, R. L., & Westwood, M. J. (2009). Preventing vicarious traumatization of mental health therapists: Identifying protective factors. *Psychotherapy, Theory, Research, Practice, Training, 46*(2), 203–219.

Harvey, M. R. (1996). An ecological view of psychological trauma and trauma recovery. *Journal of Traumatic Stress, 9*(1), 9–23.

Hass-Cohen, N., & Chandler-Ziegler, K. A. (2014). Developing supervision skills for resiliency and decreased vicarious trauma. In R. A. Bean, S. D. Davis, & M. P. Davey (Eds.), *Clinical activities for increasing competence and self-awareness* (pp. 111–118). Hoboken, NJ: Wiley.

Hass-Cohen, N., Veeman, T., Chandler-Ziegler, K. A., & Brimhall, A. (2014). Increasing competence for working with international and national disasters. In R. A. Bean, S. D. Davis, & M. P. Davey (Eds.), *Clinical activities for increasing competence and self-awareness* (pp. 103–109). Hoboken, NJ: Wiley.

Hayes, S. C. (2004). Acceptance and commitment therapy, relational frame theory, and the third wave of behavioral and cognitive therapies. *Behavior Therapy, 35*, 639–665.

Hayes, J. A., Gelso, C. J., & Hummel, A. M. (2011). Managing countertransference. *Psychotherapy, 48*(1), 88–97.

Hegney, D. G., Rees, C. S., Eley, R., Osseiran-Moisson, R., & Francis, K. (2015). The contribution of individual psychological resilience in determining the professional quality of life of Australian nurses. *Frontiers in Psychology, 6*, 1–8. doi: 10.3389/fpsyg.2015.01613

Hernández, P., Engstrom, D., & Gangsei, D. (2010). Exploring the impact of trauma on therapists: Vicarious resilience and related concepts in training. *Journal of Systemic Therapies, 29*(1), 67–83.

Hernández, P., Gangsei, D., & Engstrom, D. (2007). Vicarious resilience: A new concept in work with those who survive trauma. *Family Process, 46*(2), 229–241.

Hesse, A. (2002). Secondary trauma: How working with trauma survivors affects therapists. *Clinical Social Work Journal, 30*(3), 293–311.

Hick, S. F. (2009). *Mindfulness and social work.* Chicago, IL: Lyceum.

Hick, S. F., & Chan, L. (2010). Mindfulness-based cognitive therapy for depression: Effectiveness and limitations. *Social Work in Mental Health, 8*, 225–237.

Himle, J. A., Baser, R. E., Taylor, R. J., Campbell, R. D., & Jackson, J. S. (2009). Anxiety disorders among African Americans, blacks of Caribbean descent, and non-Hispanic whites in the United States. *Journal of Anxiety Disorders, 23*, 578–590.

Hughes, D. (2013). Occupational social work: Current perspectives. *Social Work in Mental Health, 11*, 377–380.

Hyman, O. (2004). Perceived social support and secondary traumatic stress symptoms in emergency responders, *Journal of Traumatic Stress, 17*(2), 149–156.

Iliffe, G. (2000). Exploring the counselor's experience of working with perpetrators and survivors of domestic violence. *Journal of Interpersonal Violence, 15*(4), 393–413.

Jankoski, J. (2010) Is vicarious trauma the culprit? A study of child welfare professionals. *Child Welfare, 89*(6), 105–120.

Jaynes, S. (2014). Using principles of practice-based research to teach evidence-based practice in social work. *Journal of Evidence-Based Social Work, 11*, 222–235.

Jenkins, S. R., & Baird, S. (2002). *Secondary traumatic stress and vicarious trauma: A validation sciences/clinical psychiatry* (9th ed.). Philadelphia, PA: Lippincott Williams & Wilkins.

Jones, A. C. (2004). Transference and countertransference. *Perspectives in Psychiatric Care, 40*(1), 13–19.

Jones, J. M., & Sherr, M. E. (2014). The role of relationships in connecting social work research and evidence-based practice. *Journal of Evidence-Based Social Work, 11*, 139–147.

Kabat-Zinn, J. (1994). *Wherever you go, there you are.* New York, NY: Hyperion.

Kabat-Zinn, J. (2003). Mindfulness-based interventions in context: Past present, and future. *Clinical Psychology Science and Practice, 10*, 144–156.

Kapoulistas, M., & Corcoran, T. (2015). Compassion fatigue and resilience: A qualitative analysis of social work practice. *Qualitative Social Work, 14*(1), 86–101.

Kent, M., Davis, M. C., & Reich, J. W. (2014). *The resilience handbook: Approaches to stress and trauma.* New York, NY: Routledge.

Khanna, S., & Greeson, J. M. (2013). A narrative review of yoga and mindfulness as complementary therapies for addiction. *Complementary Therapies in Medicine, 21*(3), 244–252.

Killian, K. D. (2008). Helping till it hurts? A multimethod study of compassion fatigue, burnout, and self-care in clinicians working with trauma survivors. *Traumatology, 14*(2), 32–44.

Kim, H. (2011). Job conditions, unmet expectations, and burnout in public child welfare workers: How different from other social workers? *Children & Youth Services Review, 33*(2), 358–367.

Kim, H. S., Sherman, D. K., & Taylor, S. E. (2008). Culture and social support. *American Psychologist, 63*(6), 518–526.

Kitchener, K. S. (1984). Intuition, critical evaluation and ethical principles: The foundation for ethical decisions in counseling psychology. *Counseling Psychologist, 12*(3), 43–55.

Klein, M. (1946). Notes on some schizoid mechanisms. *The International Journal of Psychoanalysis, 27*, 99–110.

Knight, C. (2010). Indirect trauma in the field practicum: Secondary traumatic stress, vicarious trauma, and compassion fatigue among social work students and their field instructors. *Journal of Baccalaureate Social Work, 15*(1), 31–54.

Kopacz, M. S., Simons, K. V., & Chitaphong, K. (2015). Moral injury: An emerging clinical construct with implications for social work education. *Journal of Religion & Spirituality in Social Work, 34*, 252–264.

Kottler, J., & Chen, D. D. (2011). *Stress management and prevention: Daily applications* (2nd ed.). New York, NY: Routledge.

Krakow, B., Haynes, P. L., Warner, T. D., Santana, D. M., Johnston, L., Hollifield, M., . . . Shafer, L. (2004). Nightmares, insomnia, and sleep-disordered breathing in fire evacuees seeking treatment for posttraumatic sleep disturbance. *Journal of Traumatic Stress, 17*(3), 257–268.

Kubler-Ross, E. (1975). *Death: The final stage of growth.* New York, NY: Simon & Schuster/Touchstone.

Kurzman, P. A. (2013). Employee assistance programs for the new millennium: Emergence of the comprehensive model. *Social Work in Mental Health, 11,* 381–403.

Langer, E. J., & Moldoveanu, M. (2000). The construct of mindfulness. *Journal of Social Issues, 56*(1), 1–9.

Lebron, D., Morrison, L., Ferris, D., Alcantara, A., Cummings, D., Parker, G., & McKay, M. (2015). *Facts matter! Black lives matter! The trauma of racism.* New York, NY: McSilver Institute for Poverty Policy and Research, New York University Silver School of Social Work.

Lee, J., & Miller, S. (2013). A self-care framework for social workers: Building a strong foundation for practice. *Families in Society: The Journal of Contemporary Social Services, 94*(2), 96–103.

Lee, J., Weaver, C., & Hrostowski, S. (2011). Psychological empowerment and child welfare worker outcomes: A path analysis. *Child Youth Care Forum, 40,* 479–497.

Lee, R., & Ashworth, B. E. (1996). A meta-analytic examination of the correlates of three dimensions of burnout. *Journal of Applied Psychology, 81,* 123–133.

Leiter, M. P., Day, A., Oore, D. G., & Laschinger, H. K. S. (2012). Getting better and staying better: Assessing civility, incivility, distress, and job attitudes one year after a civility intervention. *Journal of Occupational Health Psychology, 17*(4), 425–434.

Leiter, M. P., & Maslach, C. (2005). *Banishing burnout: Six strategies for improving your relationship with work.* San Francisco, CA: Jossey-Bass.

Leka, S., Griffiths, A., & Cox, T. (2003). *Work organization and stress: Systematic problem approaches for employers, managers, and trade union representatives.* Institute of Work, Health & Organizations: World Health Organization. doi: http://www.who.int/occupational_health/publications/en/oehstress.pdf

Lent, J., & Schwartz, R. C. (2012). The impact of work setting, demographic characteristics, and personality factors related to burnout among professional counselors. *Journal of Mental Health Counseling, 34*(4), 355–372.

Lerias, D., & Byrne, M. K. (2003). Vicarious traumatization: Symptoms and predictors. *Stress and Health, 19,* 129–138.

Levers, L. L. (2012). *Trauma counseling: Theories and interventions.* New York, NY: Springer.

Lichtenberg, H. P., Hartman, S., & Bushardt, S. C. (2013). Rekindling the flame: Using mindfulness to end nursing burnout. *Nursing Management, 44*(11), 24–29.

Linley, P. A. (2003). Positive adaptation to trauma: Wisdom as both process and outcome. *Journal of Traumatic Stress, 16*(6), 601–610.

Lizano, E. L., Hsiao, H., Mor Barak, M. E., & Casper, L. M. (2014). Support in the workplace: Buffering the deleterious effects of work–family conflict on child welfare workers' well-being and job burnout. *Journal of Social Service Research, 40*(2), 178–188.

Lizano, E., & Mor Barak, M. E. (2012). Workplace demands and resources as antecedents of job burnout among public child welfare workers: A longitudinal study. *Children & Youth Services Review, 34*(9), 1769–1776.

Lloyd, C., King, R., & Chenoweth, L. (2002). Social work, stress and burnout: A review. *Journal of Mental Health, 11*(3), 255–265.

Lustyk, M. K. B., Widman, L., Paschane, A. A., & Olson, K. C. (2004). Physical activity and quality of life: assessing the influence of activity frequency, intensity, volume, and motives. *Behavioral Medicine, 30*(3), 124–132.

Luthar, S. S., Cicchetti, D., & Becker, B. (2000). The construct of resilience: A critical evaluation and guidelines for future work. *Child Development, 71,* 543–562.

Mandell, D., Stalker, C., de Zeeuw Wright, M., Frensch, K., & Harvey, C. (2013). Sinking, swimming and sailing: Experiences of job satisfaction and emotional exhaustion in child welfare employees. *Child & Family Social Work, 18*(4), 383–393.

Marturano, J. (2014). *Finding the space to lead: A practical guide to mindful leadership.* New York, NY: Bloomsbury Press.

Maslach, C. (1998). A multidimensional theory of burnout. In C. L. Cooper (Ed.), *Theories of organizational stress* (pp. 68–85). Oxford, England: Oxford University Press.

Maslach, C. (2001). What have we learned about burnout and health? *Psychology and Health, 16,* 607–611.

Maslach, C. (2003a). *Burnout: The cost of caring.* Cambridge, MA: Malor.

Maslach, C. (2003b). Job burnout: New directions in research and intervention. *Current Directions in Psychological Science, 12,* 189–192.

Maslach, C., & Goldberg, J. (1998). Prevention of burnout: New perspectives. *Applied and Preventive Psychology, 7,* 63–74.

Maslach, C., & Jackson, S. E. (1981). The measurement of experienced burnout. *Journal of Occupational Behavior, 2,* 99–113.

Maslach, C., & Leiter, M. P. (1997). *The truth about burnout.* San Francisco, CA: Jossey-Bass.

Masten, A. S. (2001). Ordinary magic: Resilience processes in development. *American Psychologist, 56,* 227–238.

Masten, A. S. (2014). Global perspectives on resilience in children and youth. *Child development, 85*(1), 6–20.

Masten, A. S., & Coatsworth, J. D. (1998). The development of competence in favorable and unfavorable environments: Lessons from research on successful children. *American Psychologist, 53*(2), 205–220.

Mathias, J. (2015). Thinking like a social worker: Examining the meaning of critical thinking in social work. *Journal of Social Work Education, 51,* 457–474.

Mattison, M. (2000). Ethical decision making: The person in process. *Social Work, 45*(3), 201–212.

Maybery, D. J., & Graham, D. (2001). Hassles and uplifts: Including interpersonal events. *Stress and Health, 17,* 91–104.

McCammon, S.L. (1999). Painful pedagogy: Teaching about trauma in academic and training settings. In B. Hudall Stamm (Ed.), *Secondary Traumatic stress: Self-Care issues for clinicians, researchers, and educators* (pp. 105-120). Lutherville, MD: Sidram Press.

McCammon, S. L., & Allison, E. J. (1995). Debriefing and treating emergency workers. In C. R. Figley (Ed.), *Compassion fatigue: Coping with secondary traumatic stress disorder in those who treat the traumatized* (pp. 115–130). Levittown, PA: Brunner/Mazel.

McCann, L., & Pearlman, L. A. (1990). Vicarious traumatization: A framework for understanding the psychological effects of working with victims. *Journal of Traumatic Stress, 3*(1), 131–147.

McCann, I. L., & Pearlman, L. A. (1992). Constructivist self-development theory: A theoretical framework for assessing and treating traumatized college students. *Journal of American College Health, 40*(4), 189–196.

McCann, L., Sakheim, D. K., & Abrahamson., D. J. (1988). Trauma and victimization: A model of psychological adaptation. *The Counseling Psychologist, 16*(4), 531–594.

McGarrigle, T., & Walsh, C. A. (2011). Mindfulness, self-care, and wellness in social work: Effects of contemplative training. *Journal of Religion & Spirituality in Social Work, 30*(3), 212–233.

McGoldrick, M. (1997). *You can go home again: Reconnecting with your family*. New York, NY: Norton.

Medina, A., & Beyebach, M. (2014). The impact of solution-focused training on professionals' beliefs, practices and burnout of child protection workers in Tenerife Island. *Child Care in Practice, 20*(1), 7–36.

Meier, S. T., & Davis, S. R. (2011). *The elements of counseling* (7th ed.). Belmont, CA: Brooks/Cole.

Merriam-Webster. (2017). *Resilience*. Retrieved from http://www.merriam-webster.com /dictionary/resilience

Michalopoulos, L. M., & Aparicio, E. (2012). Vicarious trauma in social workers: The role of trauma history, social support, and years of experience. *Journal of Aggression, Maltreatment & Trauma, 21*, 646–664.

Miller, G. H. (2009). Commentary: The trauma of insidious racism. *Journal of the Academy of Psychiatric Law, 37*(1), 41–44.

Miller, L. D. (2014). *Effortless mindfulness. Genuine mental health through awakened presence*. New York, NY: Routledge.

Mitchell, J. T., & Everly, G. S. (1996). *Critical incident stress debriefing (CISD): An operations manual for the prevention of traumatic stress among emergency service and disaster workers* (2nd ed.). Ellicott City, MD: Chevron.

Monroe, J. F. (1999). Ethical issues associated with secondary trauma in therapists. In B. Hundall Stamm (Ed.), *Secondary traumatic stress: Self-care issues for clinicians, researchers, and educators* (pp. 230–246). Baltimore, MD: Sidran Press.

Moore, S. E., Bledsoe, L. K., Perry, A. R., & Robinson, M. A. (2011). Social work students and self-care: A model assignment for teaching. *Journal of Social Work Education, 47*(3), 545–553.

Mor Barak, M., Nissly, J., & Levin, A. (2001). Antecedents to retention and turnover among child welfare, social work, and other human service employees: What can we learn from past research? A review and meta-analysis. *Social Service Review, 75*(4), 625–661.

Moran, C. C. (2002). Humor as a moderator of compassion fatigue. In. C. R. Figley (Ed.), *Treating compassion fatigue* (pp. 139–154). New York, NY. Brunner-Routledge.

Morrissette, P. (2004). *The pain of helping: Psychological injury of helping professionals*. New York, NY: Taylor & Francis.

National Association of Social Workers. (1996). *Code of ethics*. Washington, DC: Author.

National Association of Social Workers. (2008). *Code of ethics of the National Association of Social Workers*. Washington, DC: Author.

National Association of Social Workers. (2009). *Social work speaks: National Association of Social Workers policy statements, 2009–2012*. Washington, DC: NASW Press.

National Institute of Diabetes and Digestive and Kidney Disease. (2010). *National health and nutrition examination survey (2009–2010): Overweight and obesity statistics*. Retrieved from http://www.niddk.nih.gov/health-information/health-statistics/Pages/overweight-obesity-statistics.aspx

Neff, K. D. (2003). Self-compassion: An alternative conceptualization of a healthy attitude toward oneself. *Self and Identity, 2*, 85–101.

Neff, K. D. (2011). Self-compassion, self-esteem, and well-being. *Social and Personality Psychology, 5*(1), 1–12. doi: 10.111/j.1751-9004-2010.0030

Nelson, B. S., & Wright, D. W. (1996). Understanding and treating post-traumatic stress disorder symptoms in female partners of veterans with PTSD. *Journal of Marriage and Family Therapy, 22*(4), 455–467.

Nelson-Gardell, D., & Harris, D. (2003). Childhood abuse history, secondary traumatic stress, and child welfare workers. *Child Welfare, 31*(1), 5–26.

Newell, J. M. (2012). Addressing the needs of veterans and military families: A generalist practice approach. *Journal of Baccalaureate Social Work, 17*, 53–68.

Newell, J. M., & MacNeil, G. A. (2010). Professional burnout, vicarious trauma, secondary traumatic stress, and compassion fatigue: A review of theoretical terms, risk factors, and preventive methods for clinicians and researchers. *Best Practices in Mental Health, 6*(2), 56–68.

Newell, J. M., & MacNeil, G. A. (2011). A comparative analysis of burnout and professional quality of life in clinical mental health providers and health care administrators. *Journal of Workplace Behavioral Health, 26*(1), 25–43.

Newell, J. M., & Nelson-Gardell, D. (2014). A competency based approach to teaching professional self-care: An ethical consideration for social work educators. *Journal of Social Work Education, 50*(3), 1–13.

Newell, J. M., Nelson-Gardell, D., & MacNeil, G. (2015). Clinician response to client traumas: A chronological review of constructs and terminology. *Journal of Trauma, Violence, & Abuse, 17*(3), 203–313. doi:10.1177/1524838015584365

Newsome, S., Christopher, J., Dahlen, P., & Christopher, S. (2006).Teaching counselor self-care through mindfulness practices. *Teachers College Record, 108*(9), 1881–1900.

Norcross, J. C. (2000). Psychotherapist self-care: Practitioner-tested, research informed strategies. *Professional Psychology: Research and Practice, 31*(6), 710–713.

O'Donnell, J., & Kirkner, S. L. (2009). A longitudinal study of factors influencing the retention of title IV-E master's of social work graduates in public child welfare. *Journal of Public Child Welfare, 3*(1), 64–86.

O'Halloran, T. M., & Linton, J. M. (2000). Stress on the job: Self-care resources for counselors. *Journal of Mental Health Counseling, 22*(4), 354.

O'Halloran, M. S., & O'Halloran, T. (2001). Secondary traumatic stress in the classroom: Ameliorating stress in graduate students. *Teaching in Psychology, 28*(2), 92–97.

Orr, D. W. (1998). Transference and countertransference: A historical survey. *Essential Papers on Countertransference* (pp. 91–110). New York, NY: New York University Press.

Palm, K. M., Polusny, M. A., & Follette, V. M. (2004). Vicarious traumatization: Potential hazards and interventions for disaster and trauma workers. *Prehospital and Disaster Medicine, 19*(1), 73–78.

Pardeck, J. T. (2015). An ecological approach for social work practice. *The Journal of Sociology and Social Welfare, 15*(2), 133–142.

Paton, D., & Johnston, D. (2001). Disasters and communities: Vulnerability, resilience, and preparedness. *Disaster Prevention and Management, 10*(4), 270–277.

Payne, M. (2002). The politics of systems theory within social work. *Journal of Social Work, 2*(3), 269–292.

Payne, M. (2014). *Modern social work theory* (4th ed.). New York, NY: Pelgrave Macmillian.

Pearlman, L. A. (1998). Trauma and the self: A theoretical and clinical perspective. *Journal of Emotional Abuse, 1*(1), 7–25.

Pearlman, L. A. (1999). Self-care for trauma therapists: Ameliorating vicarious traumatization. In B. Hundall Stamm (Ed.), *Secondary traumatic stress: Self-care issues for clinicians, researchers, and educators* (pp. 51–64). Baltimore, MD: Sidran Press.

Pearlman, L. A., & MacIan, P. S. (1995). Vicarious traumatization: An empirical study of the effects of trauma work on trauma therapists. *Journal of Psychology: Research and Practice, 26*(6), 558–565.

Pearlman, L. A., & Saakvitne, K. W. (1995). *Trauma and the therapist: Countertransference and vicarious traumatization in psychotherapy with incest survivors*. New York, NY: Norton.

Peled-Avram, M. (2015). The role of relational-oriented supervision and personal and work-related factors in the development of vicarious traumatization. *Clinical Social Work Journal*. Advance online publication. doi: 10.1007/S10615-015-0573-Y

Perlman, H. H. (1979). *Relationship: The heart of helping people*. Chicago, IL: University of Chicago Press.

Perron, B. E., & Hiltz, B. S. (2006). Burnout and secondary trauma among forensic interviewers of abused children. *Child and Adolescent Social Work Journal, 23*(2), 216–234.

Peterson, C. (2006). *Primer to positive psychology*. New York, NY: Oxford University Press.

Pines, A., & Aronson, E. (1988). *Career burnout: Causes and cures*. New York, NY: Free Press.

Pole, N., Gone, J. P., & Kulkarni, M. (2008). Posttraumatic stress disorder among ethnoracial minorities in the United States. *Clinical Psychology: Science and Practice, 15*(1), 35–61.

Pompeo, A. M., & Levitt, D. H. (2014). A path of counselor self-awareness. *Counseling & Values, 59*(1), 80–94. doi:10.1002/j.2161-007X.2014.00043.x

Pooler, D. K., Wolfer, T. A., & Freeman, M. L. (2014). Finding joy in social work: Interpersonal resources. *Families in Society: The Journal of Contemporary Social Services, 95*, 1–9.

Powers, M. B., Zum Vörde Sive Vörding, M. G., & Emmelkamp, P. M. G. (2009). Acceptance and commitment therapy: A meta-analytic review. *Psychotherapy and Psychosomatics, 78*, 73–80.

Pryce, J. G., Shakleford, K. K., & Pryce, D. H. (2007). *Secondary traumatic stress and the child welfare professional*. Chicago, IL: Lyceum.

Quinn, T., & Quinn, E. (2011). Trauma and the developmental course of PTSD postdeployment. In D. C. Kelly, S. Howe-Barksdale, & D. Gitelson (Eds.), *Treating young veterans: Promoting resilience through practice and advocacy* (pp. 23–32). New York, NY: Springer.

Radey, M., & Figley, C. R. (2007). The social psychology of compassion. *Clinical Social Work Journal, 35*, 207–214.

Rajan-Rankin, S. (2013). Self-identity, embodiment and the development of emotional resilience. *British Journal of Social Work, 44*(8), 2426–2442.

Ray, E. B., & Miller K. I. (1994). Social support, home/stress, and burnout: Who can help? *Journal of Applied Behavioral Science, 30*(3), 357–393.

Ray, S. L., Wong, C., White, D., & Heaslip, K. (2013). Compassion satisfaction, compassion fatigue, work life conditions, and burnout among frontline mental health care professionals. *Traumatology, 19*(4), 255–267.

Reamer, F. G. (2015). The impaired social work professional. In K. Corcoran & A. R. Roberts (Eds.), *Social workers' desk reference* (3rd ed., pp. 170–176). New York, NY: Oxford University Press.

Reber, C. A. S., Boden, M. T., Mitragotri, N., Alvarez, J., Gross, J. J., & Bonn-Miller, M. O. (2013). A prospective investigation of mindfulness skills and changes in emotion regulation among military veterans in posttraumatic stress disorder treatment. *Mindfulness, 4*, 311–317. doi: 10.1007/s12671-012-01310-4

Regehr, C., Goldberg, G., & Hughes, J. (2002). Exposure to human tragedy, empathy, and trauma in ambulance paramedics. *American Journal of Orthopsychiatry, 72*(4), 505–513.

Richards, K. C., Campenni, C. E., & Muse-Burke, J. L. (2010). Self-care and well-being in mental health professionals: The mediating effects of self-awareness and mindfulness. *Journal of Mental Health Counseling, 32*(3), 247–264.

Rodriquez, P., Holowka, D. W., & Marx, B. P. (2012). Assessment of posttraumatic stress disorder-related functional impairment: A review. *Journal of Rehabilitation Research and Development, 49*, 649–666.

Roeser, R. W., Schonert-Reichl, K. A., Jha, A., Cullen, M., Wallace, L., Wilensky, R., & Harrison, J. (2013). Mindfulness training and reductions in teacher stress and burnout: Results from two randomized, waitlist-control field trials. *Journal of Educational Psychology, 105*(3), 787–804.

Rogers, C. (1995). *On becoming a person: A therapist's view of psychotherapy*. Boston, MA: Houghton Mifflin Harcourt.

Rønnestad, M. H., & Skovholt, T. M. (1992). Themes in therapist and counselor development. *Journal of Counseling & Development, 70*, 505–515.

Rosenburg, E. W., & Hayes, J. A. (2002). Therapist as subject: A review of the empirical countertransference literature. *Journal of Counseling and Development, 80*, 264–270.

Rothschild, B. (2000). *The body remembers: The psychophysiology of trauma and trauma treatment*. New York, NY: Norton.

Rothschild, B., & Rand, M. (2006). *Help for the helper, self-care strategies for managing burnout and stress: The psychophysiology of compassion fatigue and vicarious trauma*. New York, NY: Norton.

Rubin, A., & Babbie, E. (2010). *Essential research methods for social work* (2nd ed.). Belmont, CA: Brooks/Cole Cengage Learning.

Rudolph, J. A., & Stamm, B. H. (1999). Maximizing human capital: Moderating secondary traumatic stress through administrative policy & action. In B. Hudnall Stamm (Ed.), *Secondary traumatic stress: Self-care issues for clinicians, researchers, and educators*. Lutherville, MD: Sidran Press.

Ruggiero, J. A. (2002). "AhHa . . ." Learning: Using cases and case studies to teach sociological insights and skills. *Sociological Practice: A Journal of Clinical and Applied Sociology, 4*(2), 113–128.

Rush, J. A., First, M. B., & Blacker, D. (2008). *Handbook of psychiatric measures* (2nd ed.). Washington, DC: American Psychiatric Association.

Russo, S. J., Murrough, J. W., Han, M-H., Charney, D. S., & Nestler, E. J. (2012). Neurobiology of resilience. *Nature Neuroscience, 15*, 1475–1484.

Rutter, M. (2013). Annual research review: Resilience—clinical implications. *Journal of Child Psychology and Psychiatry, 54*, 474–487.

Ryff, C. D. (2013). Psychological well-being revisited: Advances in the science and practice of eudaimonia. *Psychotherapy and Psychotherapeutics, 83*, 10–28.

Saakvitne, K. W., & Pealrman, L. A. (1996). *Transforming the pain: A workbook on vicarious traumatization for helping professionals who work with traumatized clients.* New York, NY: Norton.

Samios, C., Rodzik, A. K., & Abel, L. M. (2012). Secondary traumatic stress and adjustment in therapists who work with sexual violence survivors: The moderating role of posttraumatic growth. *British Journal of Guidance and Counseling, 40*(4), 341–356.

Sansbury, B. S., Graves, K., & Scott, W. (2015). Managing traumatic stress responses among clinicians: Individual and organizational tools for self-care. *Trauma, 17*(2), 114–122. doi:10.1177/1460408614551978

Schauben, L. J., & Frazier, P. A. (1995). Vicarious trauma: The effects of female counselors working with sexual violence survivors. *Psychology of Women Quarterly, 19*, 49–64.

Schaufeli, W. B., Bakker, A. B., Hoogduin, D., Schaap, C., & Kladler, A. (2001). On the clinical validity of the Maslach Burnout Inventory and the burnout measure. *Psychology and Health, 16*, 565–582.

Schaufeli, W. B., Maslach, C., & Marek, T. (Eds.). (1993). *Professional burnout: Recent developments in theory and research.* Washington, DC: Taylor & Francis.

Schok, M. L., Kleber, R. J., & Lensvelt-Mulders, G. (2010). A model of resilience and meaning after military deployment: Personal resources in making sense of war and peacekeeping experiences. *Aging and Mental Health, 14*(3), 328–338.

Schulte-Ruther, M., Markowitsch, H. J., Shah, N. J., Fink, G. R., & Piefke, M. (2008). Gender differences in brain networks supporting empathy. *NeuroImage, 42*, 393–403.

Seagar, M. (2014). Mind as a dimension & compassion as a relationship issue. *Journal of Compassionate Health Care, 1*(3). doi: 10.1186/s40639-014-0003-y

Sedlmeier, P., Eberth, J., Schwarz, M., Zimmermann, D., Haarig, F., Jaeger, S., & Kunze, S. (2012). The psychological effects of meditation: A meta-analysis. *Psychological Bulletin, 138*(6), 1130–1171.

Shackelford, K. (2006). *Preparation of undergraduate social work students to cope with the effects of indirect trauma.* (Unpublished doctoral dissertation). Department of Social Work, University of Mississippi.

Shapiro, S. L., Astin, J. A., Bishop, S. R., & Cordova, M. (2005). Mindfulness-based stress reduction for health care professionals: results from a randomized trial. *International Journal of Stress Management, 12*(2), 164.

Shapiro, S. L., Brown, K. W., & Biegel, G. M. (2007). Teaching self-care to caregivers: effects of mindfulness-based stress reduction on the mental health of therapists in training. *Training and education in professional psychology, 1*(2), 105.

Shapiro, S. L., Carlson, L. E., Astin, J. A., & Freedman, B. (2006). Mechanisms of mindfulness. *Journal of Clinical Psychology, 62*(3), 373–386.

Shinn, M., Rosario, M., Morch, H., & Chestnut, D. E. (1984). Coping with job stress and burnout in human services. *Journal of Personality and Social Psychology, 46*(4), 863–876.

Simon, V. A., Smith, E., Fava, N., & Feiring, C. (2015). Positive and negative posttraumatic change following childhood sexual abuse are associated with youths' adjustment. *Child Maltreatment, 20*(4), 278–290.

Skinner, J. (2015). Social work practice and professional self-care. In K. Corcoran & A. R. Roberts (Eds.), *Social workers' desk reference* (3rd ed., pp. 130–139). New York, NY: Oxford University Press.

Skovholt, T. M., & Trotter-Mathison, M. (2011). *The resilient practitioner: Burnout prevention and self-care strategies for counselors, therapists, teachers, and health professionals* (2nd ed.). New York, NY: Routledge.

Skovholt, T. M., & Trotter-Mathison, M. (2016). *The resilient practitioner: Burnout and compassion fatigue prevention and self-care strategies for the helping professions* (3rd ed.). New York, NY: Routledge.

Smith, A. (2006). Cognitive empathy and emotional empathy in human behavior and evolution. *The Psychological Record, 56*(1), 3–21.

Smith, A. J., Kleijn, W. C., & Hutschemaekers, G. J. (2007). Therapist reactions in self-experienced difficult situations: An exploration. *Counselling and Psychotherapy Research, 7*(1), 34–41.

Smith, J. C. (2005). *Relaxation, meditation, & mindfulness: A mental health practitioner's guide to new and traditional approaches.* New York, NY: Springer.

Southwick, S. M., Bonanno, G. A., Masten, A. S., Panter-Brick, C., & Yehuda, R. (2014). Resilience definitions, theory, and challenges: Interdisciplinary perspectives. *European Journal of Psychotraumatology.* doi:10.3402/ejpt.v5.25338

Southwick, S. M., Litz, B. T., Charney, D., & Friedman, M. J. (Eds.). (2011). *Resilience and mental health: Challenges across the lifespan.* Cambridge, England: Cambridge Press.

Sprang, G., Clark, J. J., & Whitt-Woosley, A. (2007). Compassion fatigue, compassion satisfaction, and burnout: Factors impacting a professional's quality of life. *Journal of Loss and Trauma: International Perspectives on Stress & Coping, 12*(3), 259–280.

Sprang, G., Craig, C., & Clark, J. (2011). Secondary traumatic stress and burnout in child welfare workers: A comparative analysis of occupational distress across professional groups. *Child Welfare, 90*(6), 149–168.

Stalker, C., Mandell, D., Frensch, K., Harvey, C., & Wright, M. (2007). Child welfare workers who are exhausted yet satisfied with their jobs: How do they do it? *Child and Family Social Work, 12*, 182–191.

Stamm, B. H. (1999). *Secondary traumatic stress: Self-care issues for clinicians, researchers, and educators.* Baltimore, MD: Sidran Press.

Stamm, B. H. (2005). *The ProQOL manual. The Professional Quality of Life Scale: Compassion satisfaction, burnout & compassion fatigue/secondary trauma scales.* Baltimore, MD: Sidran Press.

Stamm, B. H. (2010). *The concise ProQOL manual* (2nd ed.). Pocatello, ID: ProQOL.org.

Stevens, M., & Higgins, D. (2002). The influence of risk and protective factors on burnout experienced by those who work with maltreated children. *Child Abuse Review, 11*, 313–331.

Stix, G. (2011). The neuroscience of true grit. *Scientific American.* Retrieved from http://www.scientificamerican.com/article/the-neuroscience-of-true-grit/

Strand, V. C., Abramovitz, R., Layne, C. M., Robinson, H., & Way, I. (2014). Meeting the need for trauma education in social work: A problem-based learning approach. *Journal of Social Work Education, 50*, 120–135.

Taft, C. T., Creech, S. K., & Kachadourian, L. (2012). Assessment and treatment of posttraumatic anger and aggression: A review. *Journal of Rehabilitation, Research, and Development, 49*(5), 777–788.

Taris, T. W., LeBlanc, P. M., Schaufeli, W. B., & Schreurs, P. J. G. (2005). Are there casual relationships between dimensions of the Maslach Burnout Inventory? A review and two longitudinal tests. *Work and Stress, 19*(3), 238–255.

Tedeschi, R. G., & Calhoun, L. G. (1996). The posttraumatic growth inventory : Measuring the positive legacy of trauma. *Journal of Traumatic Stress, 9*(3), 455–471.

Tedeschi, R. G., & Calhoun, L. G. (2004). Posttraumatic growth: Conceptual foundations and empirical evidence. *Psychological Inquiry, 15*(1), 1–18.

Thomas, J. (2013). Association of personal distress with burnout, compassion fatigue, and compassion satisfaction among clinical social workers. *Journal of Social Service Research, 39*(3), 365–379. doi: 10.1080/01488376.2013.771596

Thomas, R. B., & Wilson, J. (2004). Issues and controversies in the understanding and diagnosis of compassion fatigue, vicarious traumatization, and secondary traumatic stress disorder. *International Journal of Emergency Mental Health, 6*(2), 81–92.

Thorton, P. I. (1992). The relation of coping, appraisals, and burnout in mental health workers. *Journal of Psychology, 126*(3), 261–272.

Ting, L., Jacobson, J. M., Sanders, S., Bride, B. E., & Harrington, D. (2005). The Secondary Traumatic Stress Scale (STSS): Confirmatory factor analyses with a national sample of mental health workers. *Journal of Human Behavior and the Social Environment, 11*(3/4), 177–194.

Trippany, R. L., Wilcoxin, S. A., & Satcher, J. F. (2003). Factors influencing traumatization of therapists of survivors of sexual victimization. *Journal of Trauma Practice, 2*(1), 47–61.

Tyler, T. A. (2012). The limbic model of systemic trauma. *Journal of Social Work Practice, 26*(1), 125–138.

Tyson, J. (2007). Compassion fatigue in the treatment of combat-related trauma during wartime. *Clinical Social Work Journal, 35*, 183–192.

Um, M-Y., & Harrison, D. F. (1998). Role stressors, burnout, mediators, and job satisfaction: A stress-strain-outcome model and empirical test. *Social Work Research, 22*(2), 100–116.

U.S. Department of Veterans Affairs. (2017). *Assessment overview.* Retrieved from http://www.ptsd.va.gov/professional/assessment/overview/index.asp

van der Kolk, B. A., McFarlane, A. C., & Weisaeth, L. (1996). *Traumatic stress: The effects of overwhelming experience on the mind, body, and society.* New York, NY: Guilford Press.

Van der Walt, L., Suliman, S., Martin, L., Lammers, K., & Seedat, S. (2014). Resilience and post-traumatic stress disorder in the acute aftermath of rape: A comparative analysis of adolescents versus adults. *Journal of Child & Adolescent Mental Health, 26*(3), 239–249. doi: 10.2989/17280583.2014.923433

Viswesvaran, C., Sanchez, J. I., & Fisher, J. (1999). The role of social support in the process of work stress: A meta-analysis. *Journal of Vocational Behavior, 54*, 314–334.

Wagaman, M. A., Gieger, J. M., Shockley, C., & Segal, E. A. (2015). The role of empathy in burnout, compassion satisfaction, and secondary traumatic stress among social workers. *Social Work, 60*(3), 201–209.

Wainrib, B. R. (2006). *Healing crisis and trauma with mind, body, and spirit.* New York, NY: Springer.

Waller, M. A. (2001). Resilience in ecosystemic context: Evolution of the concept. *American Journal of Orthopsychiatry, 71*(3), 290–297.

Walsh, F. (2003). Family resilience: A framework for clinical practice. *Family Process, 42,* 1–18.

Walsh, F. (2015). A family resilience framework. In K. Corcoran & A. R. Roberts (Eds.), *Social workers' desk reference* (3rd ed., pp. 427–433). New York, NY: Oxford University Press.

Weathers, F. W., Keane, T. M., & Davidson, J. R. (2001). Clinician-Administered PTSD Scale: A review of the first ten years of research. *Depression and Anxiety, 13,* 132–156.

Wee, D. F., & Myers, D. (2002). Stress responses of mental health workers following disaster: The Oklahoma City bombing. In C. R. Figley (Ed.), *Treating compassion fatigue* (pp. 57–84). New York NY: Brunner-Routledge.

Weiss, D. S., & Marmar, C. R. (1995). The Impact of Event Scale-Revised. In J. P. Wilson & T. M. Keane (Eds.). *Assessing psychological trauma and PTSD: A practitioners handbook.* New York, NY: Guilford Press.

Wicks, R. J. (2008). *The resilient clinician.* New York, NY. Oxford University Press.

Wicks, R. J. (2010). *Bounce: Living the resilient life.* New York, NY: Oxford University Press.

Wicks, R. J., & Maynard, E. A. (2014). *Clinicians guide to self-renewal: Essential advice from the field.* New York, NY: Oxford University Press.

Wilcoxon, A., Jackson, J., & Townsend, K. (2010). Professional acculturation: A conceptual framework for counselor role induction. *Journal of Professional Counseling: Practice, Theory, & Research, 38*(1), 1–15.

Williams, I. D., Richardson, T. A., Moore, D. D., Gambrel, L., & Keeling, M. L. (2010). Perspectives on self-care. *Journal of Creativity in Mental Health, 5*(3), 320–338.

Wilson, J. P., & Lindy, J. D. (1994). Empathic strain and countertransference. In J. P. Wilson & J. D. Lindy (Eds.), *Countertransference in the treatment of PTSD* (pp. 5–30). New York, NY: Guilford Press.

Yamatani, H., Engel, R., & Spjeldnes, S. (2009). Child welfare worker caseload: What's just right? *Social Work, 54*(4), 361–368.

Yehuda, R., Flory, J. D., Southwick, S., & Charney, D. S. (2006). Developing an agenda for translational studies of resilience and vulnerability following trauma exposure. *Annals of the New York Academy of Sciences, 1017,* 379–396.

Young, J. E., Klosko, J. S., & Weishaar, M. E. (2003). *Schema therapy: A practitioner's guide.* New York, NY: Guilford Press.

Youngson, R. (2014). Re-inspiring compassionate caring: The reawakening purpose workshop. *Journal of Compassionate Health Care, 1*(1). doi: 10.1186/s40639-014-00001-0

Zeidan, F. (2016). The neurobiology of mindfulness meditation. In. K. W. Brown, J. D. Creswell, & R. M. Ryan (Eds.), *Handbook of mindfulness: Theory, research, and practice* (pp. 171–189). New York, NY: Guilford Press.

Zimering, R., Munroe, J., & Gulliver, S. B. (2003). Secondary traumatization in mental health care providers. *Psychiatric Times, 20*(4), 20–28.

Zlontnik, J. L., DePanfilis, D., Daining, C., & Lane, M. M. (2005). *Factors influencing retention of child welfare staff: A systematic review of research.* Baltimore, MD: Institute for the Advancement of Social Work Research, University of Maryland School of Social Work Center for Families & Institute for Human Service Policy.

Zosky, D. L. (2010). Wearing your heart on your sleeve: The experience of burnout among child welfare workers who are cognitive versus emotional personality types. *Journal of Public Child Welfare, 4*(2), 117–131. doi:10.1080/15548730903563186

INDEX